ALBANIA

TRAVEL GUIDE 2024 - 2025

Explore the Europe's best kept secrets and the hidden treasures of the Balkans

Wren A. Rove

© 2024 Wren A. Rove
All rights reserved.

No part of this publication may be reproduced, distributed, or transmitted in any form or by any means, including photocopying, recording, or other electronic or mechanical methods, without the prior written permission of the author, except in the case of brief quotations embodied in critical reviews and certain other non-commercial uses permitted by copyright law.

The scanning, uploading, and distribution of this book via the internet or any other means without permission from the author is illegal and punishable by law. Please purchase only authorized editions and do not participate in or encourage piracy of copyrighted materials. Your support of the author's rights is appreciated.

This book is a work of nonfiction. The author has made every effort to ensure that the information provided in this book is accurate and up-to-date as of the date of publication. However, the author assumes no responsibility for errors, omissions, or contrary interpretation of the subject matter. The reader is advised to verify any important details before making travel plans.

TABLE OF CONTENTS

TABLE OF CONTENTS	2
INTRODUCTION	7
HOW TO USE THIS GUIDE	11
WHY YOU SHOULD VISIT ALBANIA	15
THE HISTORY OF ALBANIA	21
CHAPTER 1	27
PRACTICAL INFORMATION FOR TRAVELERS	27
Visa and Entry Requirements	27
Currency and Costs: What to Expect	32
Language and Common Phrases	37
Transportation: Getting Around Albania	42
Best Time to Visit: Weather and Seasons	48
CHAPTER 2	55
TIRANA: THE HEARTBEAT OF MODERN ALBANIA	55
Must-see Sights in Tirana	55
The Colorful Blloku District: A Hub for Nightlife and Cuisine	96
Museums and Galleries to Explore	101
Parks and Outdoor Spaces: A Relaxing Side of the City	143
Where to Stay: Accommodation Options in Tirana	148
CHAPTER 3	156

EXPLORING THE ALBANIAN RIVIERA: SUN, SEA, AND SERENITY 156

    The Beaches Along the Coast 156

    Coastal Villages to Visit 208

    The Llogara Pass: A Scenic Mountain Road 213

    Water Sports and Activities for Adventure Seekers 218

    Best Places to Stay Along the Riviera 223

    Where to Stay: Accommodation Options in Albani Rivera 229

CHAPTER 4 234

THE ENCHANTING ANCIENT CITIES 234

    Gjirokastër: The Stone City of a Thousand Steps 234

    Berat: The City of a Thousand Windows 239

    Archaeological Sites Worth Exploring 244

CHAPTER 5 252

NORTHERN ALBANIA: MAJESTIC MOUNTAINS AND RUGGED LANDSCAPES 252

    The Albanian Alps: Breathtaking Peaks and Valleys 252

    Valbona Valley National Park: Hiking Trails and Nature 254

    Theth: Remote Villages and Waterfalls 255

    Exploring the Accursed Mountains 257

    Local Traditions in the North: Hospitality and Cuisine . 258

CHAPTER 6 262

LAKES AND NATURE RESERVES 262
Lake Ohrid: One of Europe's Oldest Lakes 262
Lake Shkodra: The Largest Lake in the Balkans 263
Karavasta Lagoon: A Paradise for Birdwatchers 264
DivjakëKaravasta National Park: Exploring Untouched Nature 266
CHAPTER 7 268
CUISINE AND DINING IN ALBANIA 268
Traditional Dishes You Must Try 268
Wine and Spirits: A Taste of Albanian Vineyards 270
Best Restaurants in Major Cities 271
Street Food and Local Markets 273
CHAPTER 8 276
CULTURAL FESTIVALS AND EVENTS 276
Tirana International Film Festival 276
Gjirokastër Folk Festival 277
Wine Festivals Across the Country 278
Summer Music Festivals on the Albanian Coast 280
Local Religious Celebrations and Traditions 281
CHAPTER 9 284
ALBANIA'S HIDDEN TREASURES: OFF-THE-BEATEN-PATH 284
Vuno: A Pretty Village Untouched by Time 284

The Forgotten Island of Sazan 285
Syri i Kaltër (The Blue Eye): Albania's Natural Wonder
.... 286
Exploring Remote Monasteries and Churches 287
Remote Hiking Trails for the Adventurous Traveler 289
CHAPTER 10 292
ALBANIA FOR ADVENTURE LOVERS 292
Kayaking and Sailing on the Albanian Coast 292
Paragliding Over the Riviera 293
Caving and Rock Climbing in the North 294
River Rafting in Osum Canyon 296
Diving into the Crystal Waters: Best Scuba Diving Spots
.... 297
CHAPTER 11 300
SHOPPING AND SOUVENIRS 300
Unique Crafts and Handmade Goods to Bring Home ... 300
Traditional Albanian Carpets and Textiles 301
Local Markets: A Taste of Albanian Life 303
Where to Buy Authentic Souvenirs 304
CHAPTER 12 306
DAY TRIPS AND EXCURSIONS 306
From Tirana to Kruja: The Castle and Skanderbeg Museum
.... 306

Day Trip to Durrës: Beaches and Roman Amphitheater 307

Shkodër: The City of Legends and the Rozafa Castle ... 308

A Weekend in Korçë: Culture and Art in Southern Albania
.... 309

Crafting the best itinerary for yourself........................... 310

HOW TO GET THE FREE PLANNER........................... 313

CONCLUSION... 315

INTRODUCTION

This travel guide is designed to offer you an insightful journey into a land that has remained largely overlooked by travelers for decades.

Albania is often referred to as Europe's best kept secret, and for good reason. Tucked away in the heart of the Balkans, this country offers a rich mix of influences from the ancient Illyrians to the Ottomans, all while maintaining its own distinctive identity. Despite its central location, Albania has remained somewhat isolated for much of its recent history, which has contributed to preserving its unspoiled landscapes, unique traditions, and less traveled routes. As a result, many travelers are amazed by the fact that Albania has so much to offer but has stayed under the radar for so long.

If you're picturing a place full of raw natural beauty, Albania exceeds expectations. From the stunning peaks of the Albanian Alps in the north to the sun-soaked beaches along the Adriatic and Ionian coasts, Albania has a landscape that caters to everyone. There's a stretch of coastline known as the Albanian Riviera, which rivals even the most famous Mediterranean destinations, yet remains refreshingly untouched by mass tourism. Picture crystal-clear waters, secluded bays, and dramatic cliffs, all waiting to be explored. Whether you prefer lounging on the beach or seeking out hidden coves by boat, the coastline offers something for everyone.

But Albania isn't just about its beaches and mountains. Its cities tell the story of a country shaped by a long and varied history. Tirana, the capital, is a lively and everchanging city that mixes the old with the new. You'll find traditional markets and historic landmarks sitting side-by-side with colorful modern buildings and trendy cafes. Albania's cities are alive with energy, yet they still offer a sense of tradition and community that's hard to find in more heavily touristed parts of Europe.

As you explore further, you'll discover Gjirokastër and Berat, two ancient cities that have been declared UNESCO World Heritage Sites for their historic Ottomanera architecture. These places are not just relics of the past; they are living cities where people still carryon age-old customs, making them fascinating places to visit for anyone interested in history and culture. Walking through their narrow stone streets is like stepping back in time, yet you'll find yourself welcomed with the warmth and friendliness that Albanians are so famous for.

Speaking of hospitality, it's something that truly sets Albania apart from many other travel destinations. The people of Albania take pride in their culture of hospitality. You will quickly find that they are some of the most welcoming and generous hosts you will ever meet. Whether you're dining at a small family-owned restaurant in the countryside or sharing a conversation with locals in a village, you'll often be invited into their homes and treated like a friend. Albanians are incredibly proud of their country, and they love sharing it with visitors. This makes Albania feel much more personal and enriching as a destination than many of the more commercialized locations around the world.

While this guide will take you through all the top sites and experiences Albania has to offer, it's important to know that Albania is a destination that rewards curiosity and exploration. Some of its greatest treasures are found off the beaten path, where tourism hasn't yet taken hold. You might find yourself stumbling upon a remote mountain village where life seems to have changed little over the centuries or coming across a breathtaking view that you'll have all to yourself. The sense of discovery you'll experience in Albania is unlike anywhere else in Europe.

Additionally, Albania is a place where the past and present often overlap in surprising ways. For instance, Albania was once one of the most isolated countries in the world under its communist regime, and evidence of that era can still be seen today, from the strange pyramid in Tirana to the thousands of concrete bunkers scattered across the countryside. These remnants of the past offer a glimpse into a very different period of Albanian history, but they also contrast sharply with the dynamic and optimistic country Albania is today.

And then there's the food. Albanian cuisine is a reflection of its geography and history, with influences from Greece, Italy, Turkey, and beyond. Expect to be treated to fresh, flavorful dishes everywhere you go. From fresh seafood along the coast to hearty stews in the mountains, the food in Albania is another part of what makes traveling here such a pleasure. Dining in

Albania is not just about the meal itself but also the experience—whether it's a picnic by the beach or a long lunch in a family run taverna.

In this travel guide, we'll be walking you through all of these aspects and more, giving you not only the must-see spots but also tips and insights that will help you get the most out of your trip. Whether you're drawn to Albania's historic sites, its breathtaking natural scenery, or its rich culture, this guide aims to provide you with everything you need to plan your perfect trip.

Albania is a country that has it all but remains largely unspoiled by the crowds that flock to other European hotspots. By the end of this guide, you'll see why Albania is such a rare and special destination, and hopefully, you'll feel inspired to explore everything this incredible country has to offer.

HOW TO USE THIS GUIDE

This guide has been thoughtfully organized to help you plan and enjoy every aspect of your trip, whether you're a first-time visitor or returning to explore more of this beautiful country. To make the most of the information in this book, here's a simple breakdown of how you can navigate and use the guide:

1. Get Inspired

The guide is packed with detailed descriptions of Albania's best destinations, hidden gems, and cultural experiences. Start by browsing through the sections that take your interest—whether it's historical cities, beachside retreats, or rugged mountains. As you read, note down any locations or activities that excite you. Use this information as a foundation to build your ideal itinerary.

2. Personalize Your Itinerary

In the subsequent pages, you'll find a 14page printable itinerary planner to help you craft a travel plan that works for you. This planner is entirely blank, allowing you to customize it based on the places, activities, and experiences that matter most to you. You can access this planner by scanning the QR code provided. Fill it in with your travel dates, must visit locations, and any personal notes to create an itinerary that's tailored to your preferences.

3. Plan Your Days

The guide covers essential travel details, such as transportation options, recommended accommodations, and local dining spots. Refer to these sections when planning the logistics of your trip. Use the practical tips to arrange your travel routes, find the best places to stay, and choose where to eat, so you're fully prepared before you even arrive.

4. Stay Flexible
While this guide offers extensive information on what to do, where to go, and how to experience the best of Albania, it's important to remain flexible during your travels. Sometimes the most memorable moments come from spontaneous decisions and unexpected discoveries. Feel free to adjust your plans as you explore, and don't be afraid to take detours to uncover Albania's hidden treasures.

5. Use the Guide On-the-Go
As you travel, keep the guide handy for quick reference. Whether you're looking for details on a historic site, local markets, or cultural festivals, this book is designed to be a useful tool throughout your journey. If you want to know more about local customs, phrases, or travel tips, the guide has you covered.

6. Maximize Local Experiences
Albania is rich in traditions, festivals, and unique experiences. Be sure to immerse yourself in the local culture, whether it's trying traditional food, attending a festival, or visiting a local market. Use the guide to pinpoint the best times and places for these activities so you don't miss out on any key experiences.

7. Enjoy Stress-free Travel

With the help of this guide, you'll have all the information you need to ensure a smooth, enjoyable trip. From practical advice on entry requirements to detailed descriptions of Albania's top sights, this guide has been crafted to give you peace of mind while you travel.

By following these steps and using the guide to its fullest, you'll be well-prepared to Start on an incredible journey through Albania. Whether you're seeking adventure, relaxation, history, or culture, this book is here to help you make the most of your time in one of Europe's most exciting and beautiful destinations.

WHY YOU SHOULD VISIT ALBANIA

Albania is a country that offers an extraordinary travel experience for those who are looking for something beyond the usual tourist destinations. While many travelers flock to well-known parts of Europe, Albania has remained relatively underexplored. This means it is still full of natural beauty, authentic cultural experiences, and hidden gems waiting to be discovered. If you are wondering why you should visit Albania, the reasons are numerous, and they span from its diverse landscapes and rich history to the hospitality of its people and the affordability of travel.

One of the first things that makes Albania stand out is its incredible mix of landscapes. The country is blessed with mountains, lakes, beaches, and fertile valleys, giving visitors a wide range of places to explore. The Albanian Alps, for example, are a stunning sight for nature lovers and hikers. With rugged peaks, deep valleys, and traditional villages, the region offers plenty of trails for those who enjoy outdoor activities. You can find yourself walking through lush green pastures, climbing steep cliffs, or simply soaking in the beauty of the untouched wilderness around you. Albania's mountains are not just a playground for adventure seekers; they also offer moments of peace and reflection, where you can enjoy the natural world in its purest form.

Albania's coastline is another major draw for visitors. The Albanian Riviera, stretching along the Ionian Sea, boasts some of the most beautiful and least crowded beaches in Europe.

Imagine walking on soft sandy shores, gazing at turquoise waters, and having quiet beaches mostly to yourself—this is the kind of experience that Albania's coast provides. Unlike many other coastal destinations in Europe that have become crowded and overly commercialized, the Albanian Riviera still feels authentic and relaxed. In some places, you'll find small fishing villages where life moves at a slower pace, giving you the chance to enjoy the tranquility and beauty of the sea. Whether you want to swim, sunbathe, or take a boat ride to discover hidden bays, Albania's coast will leave you feeling refreshed and rejuvenated.

In addition to its natural beauty, Albania is a place with a deep and complex history that stretches back thousands of years. Visiting Albania allows you to see traces of ancient civilizations, from the ruins of Greek and Roman settlements to the castles and fortresses that dot the landscape. One of the most fascinating places to visit is Butrint, a UNESCO World Heritage site that offers a glimpse into Albania's ancient past. Walking through Butrint, you can see the remains of temples, theaters, and walls that tell the story of the various civilizations that once ruled this region. Beyond ancient history, Albania's more recent past, including its period under Ottoman rule and its time as an isolated communist state, has also shaped the country in significant ways. This rich historical tapestry is visible in the architecture, the customs, and the stories told by the people who live here.

When you travel through Albania, you'll also be struck by the warmth and hospitality of the Albanian people. Despite the country's challenges throughout history, the locals are known for their generosity and kindness toward visitors. It's common for travelers to be invited into people's homes, offered a meal, or engaged in friendly conversation. Albanians take great pride in welcoming guests, and this hospitality will make your trip feel even more special. It's not just the big cities where you'll find friendly locals; even in the more remote villages, people are eager to share their culture, traditions, and stories with visitors. This sense of community and connection is something that sets Albania apart as a travel destination.

Another compelling reason to visit Albania is the affordability of travel compared to other parts of Europe. Albania offers an excellent value for money, from accommodation to dining and activities. Whether you're staying in a luxury hotel or a budget guesthouse, you'll find that your money goes further here than in more tourist heavy destinations. This makes Albania an attractive option for travelers who want to experience Europe without spending a fortune. The low cost of living means that you can enjoy high-quality food, take part in exciting adventures, and explore all that Albania has to offer without breaking the bank.

Albania is also an ideal destination for those who enjoy discovering lesser-known spots and avoiding crowds. While major cities and tourist sites in Europe are often swarming with visitors, Albania still retains a sense of being off the beaten path. You won't have to contend with long lines at attractions, and you'll often find yourself exploring areas that feel undiscovered by mass tourism. This gives your trip a more intimate and personal feel, as you can engage more deeply with the places you visit and the people you meet. There's something truly magical about discovering a place before it becomes a major tourist destination, and Albania offers that opportunity in abundance.

The diversity of activities available in Albania is another reason why this country should be on your travel list. Whether you're interested in outdoor adventures, cultural experiences, or simply relaxing by the beach, Albania has something for everyone. You can go hiking in the mountains, explore ancient ruins, or enjoy water sports along the coast. For history enthusiasts, there are castles, mosques, and museums to visit, each offering a deeper Knowing of Albania's complex and fascinating past. Food lovers will also be delighted by the diverse and flavorful cuisine, which draws from a mix of Mediterranean, Balkan, and Turkish influences. From fresh seafood to hearty stews, Albanian food is both delicious and satisfying, and dining in Albania is an experience in itself.

Albania's climate is another factor that makes it a great destination year-round. The country enjoys a Mediterranean climate, which means warm, sunny summers and mild winters. This makes it a perfect destination for those looking to escape the cold during the winter months or enjoy a relaxing summer holiday by the sea. The variety of landscapes also means that no matter the season, there's always something to do in Albania, whether it's skiing in the mountains or swimming in the crystal-clear waters of the Ionian Sea.

In addition to all these reasons, visiting Albania allows you to experience a country that is rapidly changing and developing. Albania is undergoing a transformation as it opens up more to the outside world, and there's a sense of optimism and energy in the air. Visiting now allows you to see a country that is both rooted in its traditions and looking toward the future. This blend of old and new makes Albania a truly dynamic place to visit.

THE HISTORY OF ALBANIA

Albania's history is one of the most fascinating and complex stories in Europe. The country's past spans thousands of years, filled with the rise and fall of civilizations, foreign invasions, and significant cultural shifts. Knowing the history of Albania helps to explain the country's unique character, its people, and the diverse cultural influences that have shaped it over the centuries.

The roots of Albania stretch back to ancient times, with the earliest inhabitants believed to be the Illyrians. The Illyrians were a group of tribes who lived in the western Balkans around 1000 BC. They were known for their warrior culture and their skills in metalwork. Over time, the Illyrians developed powerful kingdoms, and their territory extended over much of the western Balkans, including modern-day Albania. The Illyrians had a strong sense of identity, which set the foundation for the Albanian people that would later emerge. However, despite their strength, the Illyrians would eventually face external pressures that would dramatically shape the course of their history.

One of the most significant influences came from the Greeks. Starting in the 7th century BC, Greek colonies began to appear along the coast of Albania, particularly in places like Apollonia and Dyrrachium (modern-day Durrës). These colonies became important centers of trade and culture, and they brought Greek influence into the region. The Illyrians interacted with the Greeks through both conflict and cooperation. While the Greeks introduced new technologies and ideas, the Illyrians managed to maintain their own culture and identity.

In the 2nd century BC, the expanding Roman Empire set its sights on the western Balkans, and this marked the beginning of Roman rule in the region. By 168 BC, the Romans had fully conquered the Illyrians, incorporating their lands into the empire. Albania became part of the Roman province of Illyricum, and later, after the empire was divided, it fell under the rule of the Byzantine Empire. Roman and Byzantine rule left a profound mark on Albania. The construction of roads, cities, and fortifications transformed the landscape, while Roman law and governance influenced local administration. Many ancient Roman structures, such as roads and aqueducts, can still be seen in Albania today.

The Roman period also brought the spread of Christianity to Albania. By the 4th century AD, Christianity had become the dominant religion in the region, and Albania played a significant role in the early Christian church. Several important bishops and religious leaders came from Albania, and early Christian churches were established in cities like Durrës and Butrint. Albania's location on the crossroads of East and West also meant that it was influenced by both the Roman Catholic Church in the West and the Eastern Orthodox Church in the East. This religious diversity is still reflected in the country today, with both Catholic and Orthodox communities.

The collapse of the Western Roman Empire in the 5th century AD and the subsequent invasions by various barbarian tribes threw the Balkans, including Albania, into a period of instability. For several centuries, the region was subject to invasions by Goths, Huns, and Slavs, which led to a fragmentation of political power. The Byzantine Empire managed to retain control over parts of Albania, particularly the coastal areas, but the interior was often left to fend for itself. During this time, Albania became a frontier zone, caught between the ambitions of the Byzantine Empire, the expanding Slavic states, and later, the Bulgarian Empire.

One of the most significant chapters in Albania's history began in the late Middle Ages, when the Ottoman Empire began its expansion into the Balkans. The Ottomans first entered Albania in the 14th century, and by the early 15th century, they had conquered much of the country. Albania became part of the vast Ottoman Empire, and this had profound effects on its people and culture. The Ottomans introduced Islam to Albania, and over the centuries, many Albanians converted to Islam, although there were also significant Christian communities that remained. The Ottoman period also brought changes in governance, architecture, and trade. Many of the mosques, bridges, and other structures built during this time still stand today.

However, the Ottoman rule in Albania was not uncontested. One of the most famous figures in Albanian history is Skanderbeg, a nobleman who led a rebellion against the Ottomans in the 15th century. Skanderbeg, whose real name was Gjergj Kastrioti, became a symbol of Albanian resistance and national pride. He managed to unite various Albanian clans and fought the Ottoman forces for over two decades, successfully defending Albania against several Ottoman invasions. Skanderbeg's resistance was one of the few times in history that the Ottomans faced a prolonged and successful rebellion in the Balkans. Although Albania was eventually reconquered by the Ottomans after Skanderbeg's death, his legacy as a national hero remains deeply ingrained in Albanian identity.

For nearly five centuries, Albania remained under Ottoman rule. During this time, Albania was relatively isolated from the rest of Europe, and its development was shaped by the Ottoman system. Many Albanians served in the Ottoman military, and some even rose to prominent positions within the empire. However, by the 19th century, nationalist movements were spreading across the Balkans, and Albania was no exception. Albanians began to push for greater autonomy and the preservation of their language and culture. The League of Prizren, formed in 1878, was one of the first major movements aimed at defending Albanian territories from being divided by neighboring states and at promoting Albanian national consciousness.

The weakening of the Ottoman Empire in the late 19th and early 20th centuries opened the door for Albania to seek independence. In 1912, following the Balkan Wars and the disintegration of Ottoman control, Albania declared its independence. The country faced immediate challenges, as neighboring states sought to claim Albanian territory, and Albania's borders were contested. Nevertheless, Albania was officially recognized as an independent state by the international community in 1913, though it was left with less territory than many Albanians had hoped for.

The early years of Albania's independence were marked by political instability. The country went through a monarchy, a brief republic, and various governments before falling under the rule of King Zog in the 1920s. King Zog sought to modernize Albania, but his reign was cut short by the outbreak of World War II. In 1939, Albania was invaded by fascist Italy, and later by Nazi Germany. During the war, a communist resistance movement led by Enver Hoxha emerged. After the defeat of the Axis powers, Hoxha and the communists took control of Albania in 1944.

Under Enver Hoxha's rule, Albania became one of the most isolated and repressive communist states in the world. Hoxha broke ties with both the Soviet Union and China, leaving Albania completely isolated from both the East and the West. The regime implemented strict policies of collectivization, suppression of religion, and censorship. Thousands of Albanians were imprisoned or executed for opposing the government, and the country was heavily militarized, with thousands of bunkers built across the landscape to defend against a feared invasion that never came. Hoxha's death in 1985 did not immediately bring change, but by the early 1990s, Albania's communist regime collapsed, and the country began its transition to democracy.

The 1990s were a turbulent time for Albania. The country faced significant economic difficulties, and the collapse of pyramid schemes in 1997 led to widespread protests and near civil war. However, by the early 2000s, Albania began to stabilize, and efforts were made to integrate the country into the wider international community. Albania became a member of NATO in 2009 and has been a candidate for European Union membership since 2014. In recent years, Albania has made significant progress in terms of economic growth, infrastructure development, and tourism, although challenges remain.

Today, Albania is a country that is proud of its past but also looking toward the future. Its history of resilience and adaptation has shaped a nation that is culturally rich, diverse, and full of potential. Albania's story is one of survival, transformation, and hope, making it a place where the past and present come together in fascinating ways. Knowing the history of Albania provides valuable context for anyone interested in exploring this remarkable country.

CHAPTER 1

PRACTICAL INFORMATION FOR TRAVELERS

Visa and Entry Requirements

When planning a trip to Albania, one of the key things travelers need to be aware of is the visa and entry requirements. These rules can vary depending on the country you're coming from, the purpose of your visit, and how long you intend to stay. Knowing these requirements before you go can make your travel experience smoother and help you avoid any unexpected issues at the border.

Albania has made significant efforts in recent years to simplify its visa policies and encourage tourism. As a result, many travelers will find that entering the country is relatively straightforward. Albania has established visa free travel agreements with a number of countries, which means that citizens from these nations can enter Albania without needing to apply for a visa in advance. In most cases, travelers can stay in Albania for up to 90 days within a 180day period. This 90day rule is important to remember, as it is calculated over a rolling sixmonth period, meaning that if you visit Albania multiple times within a short timeframe, the total amount of time you spend in the country cannot exceed 90 days in that period.

For citizens of the European Union (EU), the Schengen Area, the United States, Canada, Australia, and several other countries, visa free entry is allowed for tourism, business, and personal visits. This is a huge benefit for tourists from these regions, as it allows for easy travel to Albania without needing to go through the often time consuming process of applying for a visa. In addition to these countries, Albania also allows visa free travel for citizens of other nations during certain times of the year. For example, citizens of Russia and China can travel to Albania without a visa during the summer months, typically between May and November. This seasonal exemption is part of Albania's strategy to attract more tourists from these countries.

However, not all travelers can enter Albania without a visa. If you are from a country that does not have a visa waiver agreement with Albania, you will need to apply for a visa before you travel. The type of visa you need will depend on the purpose of your visit. The most common type of visa for tourists is the short stay visa, which allows for stays of up to 90 days. This visa is typically issued for purposes such as tourism, business, or family visits. To apply for this visa, you will need to provide several documents, including a valid passport, a completed visa application form, proof of accommodation (such as a hotel reservation), and proof of sufficient funds to support yourself during your stay. You may also need to provide a letter of invitation if you are staying with friends or family in Albania

If you plan to stay in Albania for longer than 90 days, or if you are visiting for purposes other than tourism, such as studying or working, you will need to apply for a longstay visa. This visa is usually issued for stays longer than 90 days and can be extended once you are in the country, depending on your specific situation. Longstay visas require additional documentation, such as proof of enrollment in a school or university for students, or a work contract for those who are moving to Albania for employment.

For all travelers, it's essential to have a passport that is valid for at least three months beyond the date you plan to leave Albania. Some travelers may also be asked to show proof of onward or return travel, meaning you may need to show your airline ticket or another form of transport that proves you have plans to leave the country at the end of your visit. In some cases, border officials may ask to see proof of sufficient funds for your stay, though this is not always required.

In terms of how you enter the country, most travelers will arrive by plane, landing at Tirana International Airport. This is the main entry point for international flights. However, Albania also has several land border crossings with its neighboring countries: Greece, Montenegro, Kosovo, and North Macedonia. If you are traveling by land from one of these countries, the same visa and entry requirements apply. Border crossings are generally straightforward, though you should always have your passport and any necessary documents ready for inspection.

Albania is not part of the Schengen Area, so it operates under its own visa policies. This is important to note for travelers who may be visiting other parts of Europe, as your time in Albania does not count towards the 90day limit for Schengen countries. This can be a great advantage if you are planning a longer trip to Europe and want to spend more time exploring the Balkans without affecting your stay in Schengen countries.

Another thing to consider is Albania's policy regarding travel insurance. While travel insurance is not required to enter the country, it is highly recommended. Travel insurance can protect you in case of unexpected events, such as illness, injury, or travel disruptions. In some cases, particularly for long-term stays or work visas, proof of health insurance may be required, so it's worth checking the specific requirements for your visa category before you travel.

It is also important to note that Albania has agreements with several countries that allow their citizens to enter using only a national identity card rather than a passport. This applies primarily to citizens of neighboring Balkan countries and some EU member states. However, if you are traveling from a country where a passport is required, make sure your passport is up to date and that you have all the necessary documents for your trip.

If you do overstay your visa or the 90day visa free period, you may face fines or restrictions on future visits to Albania. It's always a good idea to keep track of your time in the country and make sure you are complying with the rules. In some cases, travelers may be able to extend their stay by applying for an extension at the local immigration office, but this is not guaranteed, and it's best to plan your trip according to the standard time limits.

For those who need to apply for a visa, the process is typically handled through Albanian embassies or consulates in your home country. In some cases, the application process can be completed online, though you may still need to visit the embassy for an interview or to submit your documents in person. Visa processing times can vary, so it's recommended to apply well in advance of your planned travel date. The application fee for an Albanian visa also varies depending on the type of visa you are applying for and your nationality.

In recent years, Albania has been working to modernize its visa system, and there are ongoing discussions about further simplifying the process for tourists. This is part of the country's broader efforts to attract more visitors and boost its tourism industry. As these changes are implemented, it's always a good idea to check the latest information from official sources, such as the Albanian Ministry of Foreign Affairs or your local Albanian embassy, to ensure you have the most UpToDate details about visa and entry requirements.

Albania has taken significant steps to make it easier for tourists to visit, with many travelers able to enter without a visa for short stays. For those who do need a visa, the process is straightforward, though it's important to ensure you have all the necessary documents and meet the entry requirements. Whether you are visiting Albania for a short holiday or planning a longer stay, Knowing the visa rules will help you have a smooth and enjoyable trip to this beautiful and welcoming country.

Currency and Costs: What to Expect

When you travel to Albania, one of the first things you'll need to familiarize yourself with is the local currency and the overall costs you can expect during your stay. Albania uses the Albanian lek as its official currency, abbreviated as ALL. The currency symbol for the lek is L, and you'll see prices marked with this symbol throughout the country. Knowing the exchange rate, where and how to get your money changed, and what to expect in terms of day-to-day costs are all essential to making your trip as smooth as possible.

The Albanian lek is a relatively stable currency, but its exchange rate against major currencies such as the euro, US dollar, or British pound can fluctuate. It's important to check the exchange rate before your trip to ensure you have a clear idea of how much your money will be worth. Many tourists coming from countries that use the euro will find it easy to calculate prices since the euro is widely accepted in Albania, particularly in tourist areas and larger cities. However, while you might be able to pay in euros in some places, your change will usually be given back in leks. Therefore, it's a good idea to exchange at least some of your money into the local currency upon arrival.

There are several options for exchanging money in Albania. You can exchange your currency at banks, exchange offices, or even some hotels. Banks are considered a reliable option for currency exchange, and they are found in most cities and larger towns. Exchange offices (known as kambimi valutor in Albanian) are also widely available and are often located in areas with heavy tourist traffic. These exchange offices generally offer competitive rates, and in many cases, they may have slightly better rates than the banks. However, it's always a good idea to compare rates before making an exchange to get the best deal. Hotels and other tourist services may also offer currency exchange, but they tend to charge higher fees, so this is often less economical unless it's a matter of convenience.

Another common way to access money in Albania is through ATMs. ATMs are widely available in cities and towns, and they accept most major international debit and credit cards. When using an ATM, you'll typically receive your cash in Albanian leks, and the transaction will be converted based on the current exchange rate. It's worth noting that many ATMs charge a fee for international transactions, so it's a good idea to check with your bank before traveling to find out what fees might apply to your withdrawals. Additionally, some ATMs have a daily withdrawal limit, so it's a good idea to plan accordingly if you anticipate needing a larger amount of cash.

Credit and debit cards are accepted in many places throughout Albania, especially in larger cities, hotels, restaurants, and shops catering to tourists. However, cash is still the most widely used form of payment, particularly in more rural areas or smaller towns where card payment options may be limited. For this reason, it's advisable to carry enough cash with you when traveling outside of major cities, especially if you're planning to visit smaller villages or remote areas. Taxis, local markets, and some smaller restaurants may also only accept cash, so having leks on hand will make your travels easier.

When it comes to costs, Albania is generally regarded as an affordable destination compared to many other European countries. The cost of accommodation, food, transportation, and activities is lower than what you might expect in Western Europe or even neighboring countries like Greece and Italy. This makes Albania an attractive destination for budget conscious travelers or those who want to enjoy a high-quality experience without spending a lot of money.

Accommodation in Albania is relatively inexpensive. For budget travelers, hostels and guesthouses are widely available, especially in cities like Tirana, Berat, and Gjirokastër, with prices often ranging from 10 to 20 euros per night. For midrange travelers, you'll find plenty of three-star hotels and boutique hotels offering comfortable rooms at reasonable rates, usually between 30 to 60 euros per night. Even in high-end hotels, particularly along the Albanian Riviera or in Tirana, prices tend to be much lower than in more established European tourist destinations, with many offering luxurious stays for under 100 euros per night.

When it comes to food, eating out in Albania is also very affordable. A meal at a local restaurant or taverna can cost as little as 5 to 10 euros per person, depending on the type of meal and location. Traditional Albanian cuisine is hearty and often includes grilled meats, fresh vegetables, and seafood, especially in coastal regions. Street food is also popular, with items like byrek (a savory pastry filled with cheese, meat, or vegetables) costing just a few euros. Even in more upscale restaurants, a full meal, including drinks, is unlikely to break the bank, with costs typically around 15 to 30 euros for a more lavish dining experience.

In terms of transportation, Albania offers a variety of options, and the costs are generally low. Buses and furgons (shared minibuses) are the most common means of public transportation between cities and towns, and fares are very affordable. For example, a bus ride between Tirana and Berat, which takes about two hours, costs around 300 to 500 lek (roughly 2 to 4 euros). Taxis are also inexpensive by European standards, though it's a good idea to agree on the fare in advance if the taxi doesn't have a meter. For those who prefer the convenience of a rental car, Albania offers car rental services at reasonable rates, typically starting at around 20 to 30 euros per day. However, be aware that road conditions can vary, especially in rural areas, so driving yourself may not always be the most comfortable option.

Tourist activities and attractions are also reasonably priced. Entrance fees to museums and historical sites are typically low, with most charging between 200 to 500 lek (1 to 4 euros). Popular tourist destinations such as Butrint or Gjirokastër Castle are accessible without significant costs, and guided tours are often available at a fraction of the price you might pay elsewhere in Europe. If you're interested in outdoor activities, such as hiking in the Albanian Alps or kayaking along the Riviera, the costs remain manageable, with many independent guides and small tour operators offering affordable rates.

Shopping in Albania can also be a pleasant experience, especially for those looking to bring home local crafts or handmade goods. Albania is known for its traditional carpets, embroidery, and ceramics, and you can find these items at markets or small shops in cities and towns. Prices are usually fair, but as with many places, bargaining is often part of the shopping experience. It's common for tourists to negotiate prices, especially in markets, so don't be afraid to haggle for a better deal.

In terms of tipping, it's not mandatory in Albania, but it is appreciated, especially in restaurants and for services like taxis or tours. A tip of around 10% of the bill is considered generous, though even rounding up the bill is seen as a polite gesture. For larger groups or more upscale dining experiences, tipping may be more common, but it is not expected in the same way as it might be in other countries.

Albania offers a very affordable travel experience compared to much of Europe, making it an attractive destination for a wide range of travelers. From the moment you exchange your currency to the day-to-day costs of food, accommodation, transportation, and activities, you'll find that Albania allows you to enjoy a high-quality trip without a high price tag. Knowing how the currency works and what costs to expect will help you plan your trip effectively, ensuring that you can fully appreciate all that this beautiful and welcoming country has to offer without worrying about overspending.

Language and Common Phrases

When traveling to Albania, Knowing the language and having a few common phrases at your disposal can greatly enhance your experience. Albania has its own distinct language, **Albanian**, which is spoken by the vast majority of the population. It is one of the oldest languages in Europe and has its own unique linguistic history, separate from the more widely spoken languages like English, French, or Spanish. Albanian belongs to its own branch of the Indo-European language family, which makes it quite different from the languages spoken in neighboring countries. Although it shares some vocabulary with other languages due to historical influences, Albanian remains a language that can be challenging for visitors to pick up at first.

Albanian is known as **Shqip** to the locals, and it has two main dialects: **Gheg** in the north and **Tosk** in the south. The standard Albanian language is based on the Tosk dialect, which is what you'll most commonly hear in the capital, Tirana, and in other major cities. Even though there are regional variations in pronunciation and some vocabulary, the differences between Gheg and Tosk won't affect your ability to communicate with people in Albania as a visitor.

While Albanian is the official language, English is becoming more widely spoken, especially among younger generations and in tourist areas. In major cities, hotels, restaurants, and tourist attractions, you will likely find English-speaking staff who can assist you. However, outside of the more urban or touristic zones, English may not be as commonly spoken, and you could find yourself relying on basic Albanian phrases to communicate with locals. Many older Albanians also speak **Italian**, as Italian television was widely available during the communist era, and the proximity to Italy made it a common second language. You may also find some people, particularly in the south, who speak **Greek**, due to the close ties with Greece. **German** and **French** are also spoken by some, but they are less common than English and Italian.

That said, learning a few key Albanian phrases will go a long way in making your trip smoother and more enjoyable. Albanians are generally very friendly and welcoming, and making an effort to speak their language, even in small amounts, will likely be appreciated and open doors for more positive interactions. It's also a great way to show respect for the local culture, and you may find that even attempting a few phrases leads to warmer receptions and more personalized service.

To help you get started, here are some of the most common Albanian phrases that you can use during your trip:

- **Hello** – "Përshëndetje" (pronounced pershendehtyeh). This is a formal greeting you can use in any situation.

- **Hi** – "Tungjatjeta" (pronounced toongyatyehta). This is a more casual, friendly greeting, similar to saying "hi" in English.
- **Good morning** – "Mirëmëngjes" (pronounced meermehnjess). You can use this in the morning until around noon.
- **Good evening** – "Mirëmbrëma" (pronounced meermbruhma). Use this in the evening when greeting people.
- **Goodbye** – "Mirupafshim" (pronounced meeroopafsheem). This is the most common way to say goodbye.
- **Yes** – "Po" (pronounced poh). Simple and easy to remember.
- **No** – "Jo" (pronounced yo). Another short and straightforward word.
- **Please** – "Ju lutem" (pronounced yoo lootem). This polite phrase can be used in various situations, such as when asking for something.
- **Thank you** – "Faleminderit" (pronounced fahlehmeendehreet). A key phrase to know and use often.
- **Excuse me** – "Më falni" (pronounced muh fahlnee). This is useful when trying to get someone's attention or if you need to apologize for bumping into someone.
- **I'm sorry** – "Më vjen keq" (pronounced muh vyehn kech). This phrase can be used for a more sincere apology.

- **How much does this cost?** – "Sa kushton?" (pronounced sah kooshton). Useful for shopping and bargaining in markets.
- **Where is...?** – "Ku është...?" (pronounced koo esht). For example, you can ask "Ku është banjo?" to find out where the bathroom is.
- **Do you speak English?** – "A flisni anglisht?" (pronounced ah fleesnee ahngleesht). This is a helpful phrase if you're not sure whether someone can speak English.
- **I don't understand** – "Nuk kuptoj" (pronounced nook kooptoy). Use this when you need help Knowing something.
- **Help!** – "Ndihmë!" (pronounced ndeem). An important phrase to know, just in case of an emergency.

Knowing how to greet people is an important part of traveling in Albania, as Albanians tend to place a high value on politeness and respect. It's common to greet people when entering a shop, café, or even passing by someone in a small village. A simple "Përshëndetje" or "Mirëmëngjes" will go a long way in making a positive impression. Additionally, when leaving, it's considered polite to say "Mirupafshim" or even just "Faleminderit" to show appreciation.

While these basic phrases will certainly help you get by, body language and gestures can also play a significant role in communication. Albanians are known for being expressive, and hand gestures often accompany spoken words. For example, when saying "no," Albanians may raise their eyebrows, whereas a nod is used for "yes." In fact, this can be a bit confusing for travelers at first, as the eyebrow raise might be mistaken for agreement if you're not aware of this cultural difference.

When traveling in less touristy areas where English is not widely spoken, knowing how to ask for basic services, such as food, directions, or transportation, in Albanian can be especially useful. The phrase "Sa kushton?" will help you when you're shopping, while "Ku është?" will assist in finding places like bus stops or landmarks. If you're taking a taxi, you might want to ask for the price in advance, and using "Sa kushton për të shkuar në…" (How much to go to…) can be very handy.

Additionally, in restaurants or when buying food, it's good to know the words for common items. For example, "ujë" means water, "bukë" means bread, "mish" means meat, and "peshk" means fish. If you have dietary preferences or restrictions, learning how to say "vegetarian" (vegetarian) or "without meat" (pa mish) can also be helpful. Similarly, if you want something sweet, you might look for "ëmbëlsirë," which means dessert.

Another useful phrase is "Më ndihmoni, ju lutem" (Help me, please), in case you find yourself needing assistance. Albanians are generally very helpful, and if they see that you're trying to speak their language, they'll often go out of their way to assist you.

When traveling in Albania, it's important to remember that while learning a few words and phrases can be very helpful, Albanians are also very patient with visitors who don't speak their language fluently. Many people will appreciate your efforts, even if your pronunciation isn't perfect. Don't be afraid to make mistakes; it's all part of the learning process. You'll likely find that people are eager to help you, and your willingness to engage with the local language will often be met with smiles and encouragement.

Having a few basic Albanian phrases at your disposal will make your travels in Albania more enjoyable and engaging. Whether you're exploring the bustling streets of Tirana, relaxing along the coast, or visiting rural villages, being able to communicate even a little bit in the local language will enrich your experience and help you connect more deeply with the culture. Albania is a country where hospitality is highly valued, and by showing interest in the language, you'll be contributing to that warm, welcoming atmosphere that makes the country such a special place to visit.

Transportation: Getting Around Albania

Traveling around Albania offers a unique and varied experience, but it requires a Knowing of the different modes of transportation available and how to make the most of them. Whether you're navigating the bustling capital city of Tirana, heading to the serene Albanian Riviera, or exploring remote mountain villages, knowing your options will make your trip more enjoyable and stress-free. Albania's transport network has improved significantly in recent years, but there are still some important factors to consider, especially when traveling outside the main urban areas.

The first thing to know is that Albania does not have a well-developed train network like many other European countries. This means that trains are not a practical option for most travelers, and they are only available for very limited routes. As a result, most tourists rely on buses, minibuses, taxis, and rental cars to get around the country. Each of these options has its own benefits and challenges, depending on your specific travel needs, the regions you're visiting, and your budget.

One of the most common ways to travel between cities and towns in Albania is by bus. The country has a fairly extensive bus network that connects major cities, towns, and even some smaller villages. The buses are affordable and generally reliable, though they can be somewhat crowded, especially during peak travel times. The buses range from larger coach style vehicles, which are more comfortable for longer journeys, to smaller minibuses known as furgons. Furgons are a more flexible and faster alternative to larger buses, especially for shorter trips or routes that are not served by the main bus lines.

In Tirana and other large cities, you'll find central bus terminals where buses depart for destinations across the country. In Tirana, the main bus terminal is located near Sheshi Shqiponja, commonly referred to as Eagle Square. From here, you can catch buses to popular tourist destinations like Durrës, Berat, Gjirokastër, Saranda, and more. Bus tickets are generally inexpensive, with prices varying depending on the distance of your journey. For example, a bus ride from Tirana to the coastal city of Durrës, which is about an hour away, costs only a few euros. For longer trips, such as Tirana to Saranda, a coastal town in the south, you can expect to pay around 10 to 15 euros. It's a good idea to bring cash, as most buses do not accept card payments.

Furgons, or minibuses, are another popular way to get around, especially for shorter trips or when traveling to more remote locations that may not be easily accessible by the larger buses. Furgons do not operate on fixed schedules, which can make them more flexible, but also a bit unpredictable. They typically leave when they are full, so depending on the time of day and how busy the route is, you may have to wait a bit before departing. Despite this, furgons are often faster than regular buses because they stop less frequently and can navigate narrow, winding roads more easily. Furgons are widely used for routes between towns and cities, and you'll often find them in city centers or near main bus terminals. It's also worth noting that while furgons may not offer the same level of comfort as larger buses, they are a great way to experience local life and interact with Albanians, as they are commonly used by locals.

For travelers who want more independence or plan to explore off-the-beaten-path destinations, renting a car is a good option. Renting a car in Albania gives you the freedom to travel at your own pace and discover areas that are not easily accessible by public transportation. Car rental services are available in Tirana, as well as in other major cities and near airports. Rental prices are relatively affordable compared to other European countries, with daily rates starting at around 20 to 30 euros for a basic vehicle. It's important to note that while Albania has made significant improvements to its road infrastructure in recent years, driving conditions can still be challenging in some areas, especially in more rural regions. Roads in the countryside can be narrow, winding, and poorly maintained, with occasional potholes and steep inclines. Additionally, Albanian drivers tend to be assertive, and traffic rules are not always strictly followed, so caution is advised, particularly in busy urban areas or on mountain roads.

If you choose to rent a car, make sure you have a valid driver's license. Albania recognizes international driving permits, and if you're coming from the European Union or other countries with agreements in place, your regular driver's license may suffice. It's also a good idea to check with your car rental company about insurance coverage and road assistance, as it's better to be prepared in case of any issues while on the road. While driving in Albania can be an adventure, it's also an opportunity to enjoy some of the country's most scenic routes, especially along the coast. The drive along the Llogara Pass, which connects the coastal towns of Vlorë and Himara, is one of the most breathtaking routes in the Balkans, offering stunning views of the Ionian Sea.

If you prefer not to drive yourself but still want the convenience of private transportation, taxis are widely available throughout Albania. In cities like Tirana, taxis can be easily hailed on the street or found at designated taxi stands. Taxi fares are generally affordable, but it's important to agree on the price before starting your journey, as most taxis do not use meters. This is especially important for longer trips, such as airport transfers or travel between cities. For shorter trips within the city, you can expect to pay only a few euros, but for longer distances, the cost can vary depending on the distance and the negotiating skills of both the driver and the passenger. For tourists who are unfamiliar with local prices, asking at your hotel for an estimate of the correct fare before taking a taxi can help ensure you are not overcharged.

Albania does not have an extensive train network, and the existing rail services are limited and not particularly useful for tourists. The train system is outdated, and routes are often slow and infrequent. There are a few routes that connect major cities like Tirana, Durrës, and Shkodër, but these services are primarily used by locals and are not recommended for tourists who are looking for efficient and comfortable transportation. For most travelers, buses, furgons, and rental cars will be much more practical and convenient.

Another option for getting around Albania, particularly for those visiting the coast or traveling between Albania and its neighboring countries, is by ferry. Albania has several ferry connections to Italy, with regular services from the port cities of Durrës and Vlorë to Italian cities such as Bari and Brindisi. These ferries are a good option for those combining Albania with a trip to Italy or for those who prefer to avoid flying. Additionally, there are local ferries that operate along the Albanian coast, particularly during the summer months. These ferries are useful for travelers wanting to explore the Albanian Riviera or reach some of the more secluded beaches and coastal towns that are difficult to access by road.

For those arriving by plane, Tirana International Airport, also known as Nënë Tereza Airport, is the main international gateway to Albania. Located about 17 kilometers northwest of Tirana, the airport is wellconnected to the city by taxi and shuttle services. Taxis from the airport to the city center take about 20 to 30 minutes, depending on traffic, and cost around 15 to 20 euros. There are also regular bus services that run between the airport and Tirana's city center, offering a more budget friendly option for travelers. Once in Tirana, you can use a combination of walking, taxis, and local buses to explore the city. Tirana's public bus system is inexpensive, though it can be crowded at peak times.

Getting around Albania as a tourist requires a bit of planning, but there are several options available to suit different preferences and budgets. Buses and furgons are the most widely used and costeffective means of travel for most tourists, while rental cars offer the freedom to explore at your own pace. Taxis provide a convenient option for shorter trips, especially in urban areas, and ferries are a great way to connect Albania with its neighboring countries or explore the coast. While Albania's transportation network may not be as developed as some other European countries, the improving infrastructure and diverse transport options make it easier than ever to navigate this beautiful and diverse country.

Best Time to Visit: Weather and Seasons

The best time to visit Albania depends largely on what kind of experience you are looking for, as the country offers a variety of activities and landscapes, all of which change with the seasons. Albania's climate is diverse, ranging from the Mediterranean influence along the coast to more continental and mountainous conditions in the interior.

Albania experiences four distinct seasons: spring, summer, autumn, and winter, each offering something unique for visitors. The climate along the coast tends to be warm and sunny, typical of the Mediterranean, while the inland and mountainous areas experience more variation, with cooler winters and hotter summers. Knowing what to expect during each season will help you make the most of your trip, as different regions of Albania can offer dramatically different experiences at various times of the year.

For many travelers, the ideal time to visit Albania is during the spring months of April, May, and early June. Spring is a wonderful time to explore the country because the weather is mild and pleasant, with temperatures generally ranging between 15°C and 25°C. The landscape is lush and green, especially in the countryside, as the spring rains bring the flowers and vegetation to life. This is an excellent time for outdoor activities like hiking, exploring archaeological sites, and wandering through Albania's cities and towns. The tourist crowds are not as large as they are in the peak summer months, which means you can enjoy popular destinations like Tirana, Berat, and Gjirokastër without feeling overwhelmed by other visitors. The coastal areas along the Albanian Riviera also begin to warm up in late spring, making it a great time for beach lovers who prefer a quieter, more peaceful atmosphere before the summer season kicks in.

If your primary goal is to enjoy the beautiful beaches and crystal-clear waters along Albania's coastline, then the summer months of July and August are the most popular time to visit. Summer is the peak tourist season in Albania, especially along the Albanian Riviera, where destinations like Ksamil, Dhërmi, and Himara attract both locals and international tourists. The weather during this time is hot and dry, with temperatures often reaching 30°C to 35°C or higher, particularly in July and August. These months are perfect for swimming, sunbathing, and water sports, as the sea temperature is ideal for cooling off in the heat. The coastline can get quite busy during the peak summer months, so it's important to book accommodation in advance if you plan to visit during this period. Additionally, many summer festivals and cultural events take place across Albania in July and August, offering tourists a chance to experience the country's lively music, dance, and food scenes.

For travelers who prefer to avoid the intense heat and larger crowds, early summer (late June) and late summer (early September) offer a great alternative. The weather is still warm enough to enjoy the beaches, but the temperatures are slightly cooler, and there are fewer tourists compared to July and August. This can make your trip feel more relaxed and enjoyable, especially if you want to explore more remote areas of the coast or visit historical sites without the summer rush.

Autumn is another fantastic time to visit Albania, particularly for those interested in culture, history, and outdoor activities. The months of September, October, and early November bring cooler temperatures, ranging from 15°C to 25°C, which are ideal for sightseeing and exploring Albania's many cultural and natural attractions. The coastal areas remain pleasant and warm in early autumn, so you can still enjoy time at the beach, while the inland areas and mountains become perfect for hiking and nature walks. Autumn is also harvest season in Albania, which means you'll have the chance to experience the country's agricultural traditions and enjoy fresh, locally produced food and wine. The vineyards in regions like Berat and Shkodra are particularly beautiful in the autumn, and you may be able to participate in grape harvesting or visit local wineries.

Autumn is also a great time to explore Albania's historical and archaeological sites, such as Butrint, Apollonia, and Rozafa Castle, as the cooler weather makes it easier to walk around and fully appreciate these ancient places. Many of these sites are located in areas that can get quite hot in the summer, so visiting in autumn allows for a more comfortable and enjoyable experience. Additionally, the tourist crowds thin out after September, giving you more space to explore at your own pace.

Winter in Albania, particularly in the mountainous regions, offers a completely different experience. If you enjoy winter sports or are looking to see a side of Albania that fewer tourists experience, the winter months of December, January, and February may be the best time for you to visit. In the north of Albania, particularly in the Albanian Alps and areas like Valbona and Theth, snow covers the mountains, creating a winter wonderland perfect for skiing, snowshoeing, and other outdoor activities. These regions are incredibly scenic during the winter months, with pretty snowcovered landscapes that are ideal for photography and peaceful hikes.

While the coastal areas remain relatively mild during the winter, with temperatures hovering around 10°C to 15°C, the mountains and interior regions experience much colder conditions, with temperatures often dropping below freezing. In Tirana and other inland cities, winter can bring cool, rainy weather, though snow is rare in the lower elevations. Winter is the offseason for tourism, so if you visit during this time, you'll find that many tourist attractions and services operate on a reduced schedule, and some hotels or restaurants in coastal areas may close for the season. However, this also means that if you're looking for a quiet, more solitary experience, winter is the time when you can explore Albania without the tourist crowds.

One thing to consider if you plan to visit Albania in the winter is the state of the roads, particularly if you're traveling to rural or mountainous areas. Snow and ice can make some roads difficult to navigate, especially in the more remote northern regions. If you're planning to rent a car and explore the mountains during winter, it's essential to make sure your vehicle is equipped with snow chains and that you are prepared for winter driving conditions.

Albania's shoulder seasons, spring and autumn, are often considered the best times to visit for those who want to enjoy a balance of pleasant weather, fewer crowds, and lower travel costs. These seasons provide excellent opportunities for outdoor activities, cultural exploration, and enjoying the natural beauty of the country. However, summer remains the prime time for beachgoers, while winter appeals to those looking for a quieter and more unique experience, especially in the mountains.

The best time to visit Albania depends on your personal preferences and the type of activities you're looking to enjoy. Whether you prefer the warm beaches of summer, the mild and green landscapes of spring, the colorful harvests of autumn, or the snowy mountains of winter, Albania has something to offer yearround. Knowing the seasonal weather patterns and knowing what to expect during each time of the year will help you plan your trip in a way that aligns with your interests and ensures you have the most enjoyable experience possible.

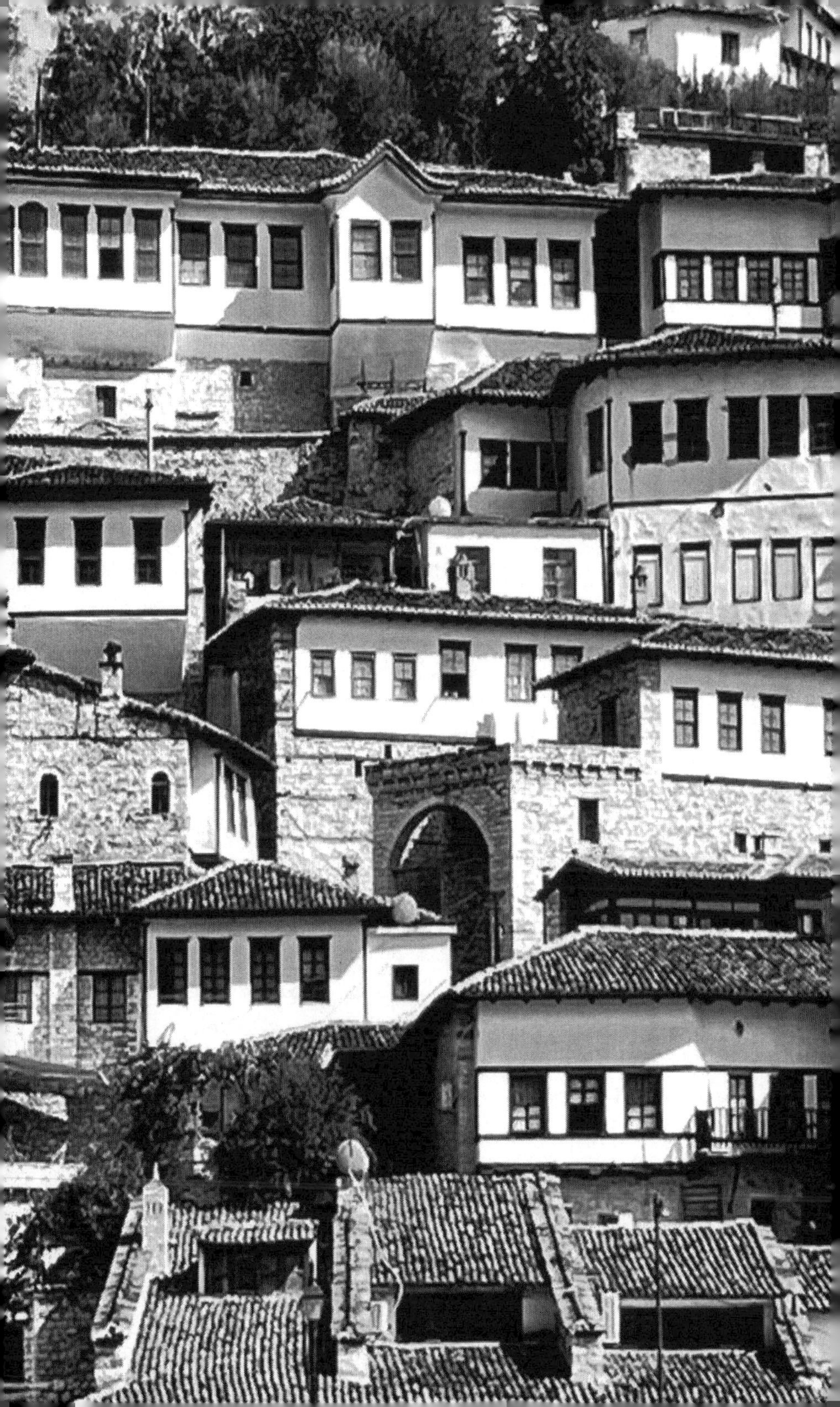

CHAPTER 2

TIRANA: THE HEARTBEAT OF MODERN ALBANIA

Must-see Sights in Tirana

Tirana, the capital of Albania, is a city rich in history, culture, and modern energy, offering visitors a unique blend of old and new. Among the many sights to explore, three landmarks stand out for their historical significance and cultural importance: Skanderbeg Square, the Et'hem Bey Mosque, and The Pyramid of Tirana. Each of these places tells part of the story of Albania's past, from its centuries of struggle for independence to its more recent communist history. Together, they offer a deeper Knowing of the country and its people, making them must-see stops for anyone visiting Tirana.

Skanderbeg Square

Skanderbeg Square is not only the main plaza in Tirana but also the heart and soul of Albania's capital city. It holds immense cultural, historical, and social significance, and has become an iconic landmark for both locals and visitors alike. Skanderbeg Square is named after the Albanian national hero, Gjergj Kastrioti, famously known as Skanderbeg, who fought against the Ottoman Empire in the 15th century and is a symbol of Albania's fight for independence and identity.

Located in the center of Tirana, Skanderbeg Square is surrounded by important cultural institutions and historical buildings. The square is vast, covering 40,000 square meters, and its most prominent feature is the equestrian statue of Skanderbeg himself, which stands proudly in the middle of the square, symbolizing Albanian bravery and resistance.

Reaching Skanderbeg Square is easy since it is situated at the very center of the city. If you are staying anywhere near the downtown area, it is within walking distance. For those staying farther from the city center, there are a few options to get there. Tirana's public buses run frequently, and many routes stop near or directly at the square, with bus fares typically costing around 40 Lek (€0.30). Taxis are also widely available in Tirana, and getting to the square by taxi is affordable, though the fare will depend on your starting point. For those traveling from the airport, taking a taxi or the Rinas Express bus, which drops you off near the square, is the best option.

Once at Skanderbeg Square, there is plenty to do and see. The square itself is an expansive pedestrian zone, allowing visitors to explore freely without the interference of traffic. Its open space makes it ideal for leisurely strolls, and the design of the square encourages people to gather, relax, or enjoy events. The large stone surface, designed with stones from all over Albania, reflects the country's diversity and unites the regions of Albania into a single space.

One of the key highlights of Skanderbeg Square is the Skanderbeg Statue, a massive bronze sculpture of the national hero on horseback. The statue was erected in 1968 to celebrate the 500th anniversary of Skanderbeg's death. Many visitors enjoy taking photographs in front of this iconic statue, which stands as a proud reminder of Albania's resilient spirit. The statue has become a symbol of the city itself, and seeing it in person allows visitors to connect with Albania's historical narrative.

Surrounding the square are some of the city's most important landmarks. The National Historical Museum is located directly on Skanderbeg Square and is Albania's largest museum, offering a comprehensive overview of the country's history from ancient times to modern-day events. The museum's facade is adorned with a large mosaic mural, "The Albanians," which depicts key moments in the country's history. The museum is divided into various sections, including archaeology, the Middle Ages, the National Renaissance, and the communist period. Entrance to the museum costs around 200 Lek (€1.70), making it an affordable and valuable way to immerse yourself in Albania's rich history.

Another notable building on the square is the Et'hem Bey Mosque, one of the oldest and most culturally significant buildings in Tirana. Dating back to the 18th century, the mosque is a beautiful example of Ottoman architecture and features intricate frescoes inside, depicting landscapes and nature scenes. During the communist period, all religious practices were banned, but the mosque was quietly reopened in 1991 during a peaceful demonstration, which was a pivotal moment in Albania's religious and political history. Visitors are welcome to enter the mosque, though it is important to dress modestly and be respectful of worshippers. Entry is free, though donations are appreciated to help with the upkeep of this historic site.

Adjacent to the mosque is the Clock Tower, another important symbol of Tirana. Built in the early 19th century, the Clock Tower stands at 35 meters tall and offers one of the best views of the city. Visitors can climb the stairs to the top for a small fee of 100 Lek (€0.85), where they will be rewarded with panoramic views of Skanderbeg Square and the surrounding cityscape. The climb itself is relatively easy, and the view from the top makes it a mustdo experience when visiting the square.

Skanderbeg Square is not only a place for historical and cultural exploration, but it is also a hub for events and public gatherings. The square often hosts concerts, cultural festivals, and public celebrations, particularly during national holidays and important dates in Albania's calendar. If you happen to visit during a holiday, such as Independence Day (November 28) or Liberation Day (November 29), you will witness the square coming to life with music, lights, and crowds of people celebrating Albania's history and culture.

There are also several cafes and restaurants around the square, making it a great place to sit down and enjoy a coffee or a meal while soaking in the atmosphere. Albanian cafes are central to social life, and having a coffee while watching the world go by is an essential part of the local experience. Many visitors choose to relax at one of the outdoor seating areas, where you can enjoy views of the square and surrounding buildings.

Skanderbeg Square is also conveniently located near the Tirana International Hotel, a popular choice for tourists due to its proximity to the city's main attractions. The hotel often offers great views of the square, particularly from its upper floors, giving guests the opportunity to observe the square's lively atmosphere from above.

As the central point of Tirana, Skanderbeg Square is a key starting point for exploring other areas of the city. From the square, you can easily reach other nearby attractions such as the Pyramid of Tirana, Blloku neighborhood, and the Grand Park of Tirana.

Et'hem Bey Mosque

The Et'hem Bey Mosque in Tirana is one of the most historically significant and culturally rich landmarks in Albania's capital city. It is not only a place of worship but also a symbol of Albania's resilience and heritage, reflecting the country's Ottoman past and its peaceful transition into a modern European state. Built in the late 18th century by Molla Bey and later completed by his son, Haxhi Et'hem Bey, the mosque stands as one of the finest examples of Ottoman architecture in Albania and has survived Albania's turbulent history, including the communist regime that sought to ban all forms of religious practice.

Located in the heart of Skanderbeg Square, the mosque is ideally positioned, making it a convenient and accessible stop for anyone visiting Tirana. Its central location means that it's within walking distance from many hotels, restaurants, and other attractions in the city. If you're staying in the downtown area, you can easily reach the mosque on foot in just a few minutes. For those staying further away, Tirana's public buses run frequently to and from Skanderbeg Square, with fares around 40 Lek (€0.30) for a one-way trip. Alternatively, taxis are available throughout the city, and fares are generally affordable, making it easy to reach the mosque from any part of Tirana.

Visiting the Et'hem Bey Mosque offers a unique opportunity to explore a piece of Albania's religious and architectural history. Though modest in size compared to some larger mosques around the world, the Et'hem Bey Mosque is famous for its intricate and highly detailed frescoes, which are a rare feature in Islamic architecture. These frescoes depict scenes from nature, such as trees, waterfalls, and bridges, in stunning colors that are both vibrant and delicate. The level of detail and artistic skill displayed in the frescoes is exceptional, making the mosque a must-see sight for anyone with an interest in art and architecture.

What makes the mosque even more significant is its role in Albania's modern history. During the communist era, Albania was declared an atheist state, and all religious practices were banned by the government. However, in 1991, at the end of the communist regime, the Et'hem Bey Mosque became a symbol of peaceful resistance when a group of brave citizens entered the mosque to pray in defiance of the authorities. This act, which occurred without violence, marked the reopening of religious practices in Albania and was a pivotal moment in the country's return to religious freedom. Today, the mosque is open to visitors and worshippers alike, representing not only a place of spirituality but also a monument to the resilience and strength of the Albanian people.

When visiting the mosque, it's important to remember that it is still an active place of worship, so respect for the customs and traditions is essential. Modest dress is required for both men and women, with women asked to cover their heads with a scarf upon entering. Scarves are typically provided at the entrance for those who may not have one with them. Shoes must be removed before entering the mosque, as is customary in Islamic places of worship. The mosque is open to visitors during nonprayer hours, and while there is no official entrance fee, donations are appreciated, as they help with the maintenance and preservation of this important historical site.

Once inside, take the time to admire the beautiful interior. The calm and serene atmosphere of the mosque provides a stark contrast to the busy streets outside, making it a peaceful retreat from the bustle of the city. The frescoes that line the walls and the ceiling are mesmerizing, with their detailed depictions of landscapes and floral patterns. These frescoes are particularly unusual for an Islamic structure, as most mosques avoid figurative depictions. The uniqueness of this artwork adds to the charm and beauty of the Et'hem Bey Mosque.

As you explore the mosque, consider the historical events that have taken place here. Standing in the mosque where citizens once gathered in defiance of the government's religious bans can be a powerful and moving experience. The mosque's significance extends beyond its religious function—it tells the story of Albania's struggle for freedom and the importance of preserving cultural and religious heritage in the face of adversity.

After visiting the mosque, it's worth exploring the surrounding area, as there are several other important landmarks nearby. The Clock Tower, which stands right next to the mosque, is another must-see sight. Built in the early 19th century, the Clock Tower offers visitors the chance to climb to the top for a small fee of around 100 Lek (€0.85). The views from the top are spectacular, providing a bird'seye view of Skanderbeg Square and the surrounding city. From this vantage point, you can see the entire square, including the National Historical Museum, the Skanderbeg Statue, and many of the city's iconic buildings.

The New Bazaar (Pazari i Ri) is also just a short walk away, offering visitors the chance to experience Tirana's vibrant market life. Here, you can find fresh produce, local delicacies, and handmade crafts that reflect the culture and traditions of Albania. It's the perfect place to pick up souvenirs or enjoy a coffee while observing the lively atmosphere of the marketplace.

Visiting the Et'hem Bey Mosque is a must for anyone interested in Albania's rich history, culture, and art. Its location in the heart of Skanderbeg Square makes it easily accessible, and its blend of spiritual and historical significance ensures that it will leave a lasting impression on all who visit. Whether you're captivated by the stunning frescoes, moved by the mosque's role in Albania's fight for religious freedom, or simply seeking a peaceful moment of reflection in the city, the Et'hem Bey Mosque offers a memorable and enriching experience.

Clock Tower

The **Clock Tower of Tirana** is one of the most iconic landmarks in Albania's capital, and it holds great historical and cultural significance. Built in the early 19th century, it stands as a symbol of the city's growth and development. Located in the very heart of **Skanderbeg Square**, the Clock Tower has become an essential stop for tourists seeking to explore Tirana's past and experience its modern urban life. Its strategic position next to the **Et'hem Bey Mosque** makes it part of a key cluster of historical attractions, and its towering presence provides an unforgettable view of the city for those who make the climb to the top.

Constructed by Haxhi Et'hem Bey, the same individual responsible for the mosque, the Clock Tower was completed in 1822. Standing 35 meters tall, it was the tallest building in Tirana for many years and remains one of the city's most distinctive structures. The original clock mechanism was imported from Venice, a nod to Albania's historical ties with the wider Mediterranean world. Over the years, the Clock Tower has undergone various renovations, including the installation of a new clock system and some minor architectural changes. Despite these updates, it retains its historic charm and serves as a reminder of Tirana's evolving landscape over the centuries.

The **Clock Tower** is located in **Skanderbeg Square**, right next to the **Et'hem Bey Mosque** and across from the **National Historical Museum**. This central location makes it easily accessible from anywhere in Tirana. For visitors staying in or around the city center, the Clock Tower is just a short walk away. The pedestrian friendly nature of the square allows for a relaxed stroll, and the tower itself is hard to miss as it stands prominently in the skyline. If you're staying further away from the city center, Tirana's public buses provide easy access to the square, with routes stopping nearby for as little as 40 Lek (€0.30). Taxis are also readily available, and given the central location, the fare to reach **Skanderbeg Square** from most parts of Tirana is reasonable.

Upon reaching the Clock Tower, one of the most exciting activities is the opportunity to climb to the top. Although the tower is modest in height compared to modern buildings, its elevated position provides visitors with panoramic views of Tirana and the surrounding area. The ascent is made via a spiral staircase, which, while narrow, is manageable for most visitors. As you make your way up, there's a sense of stepping back in time, surrounded by the original stonework and architecture. The climb is part of the charm, offering a gradual buildup of anticipation as you approach the top.

At the top of the Clock Tower, you are rewarded with stunning views of **Skanderbeg Square**, the surrounding landmarks, and the cityscape stretching out toward the horizon. From here, you can see the **National Historical Museum**, the **Et'hem Bey Mosque**, and even the modern parts of Tirana that blend into the distance. The contrast between the historical buildings and the newer urban developments provides a unique perspective on how Tirana has evolved over time. The view also offers a great photo opportunity, and many visitors choose to take a few moments to capture the beauty of the square from above.

The entry fee for climbing the Clock Tower is modest, typically around 100 Lek (€0.85). This small fee is well worth the experience of standing atop one of Tirana's oldest and most cherished landmarks. Given the affordability, it is accessible for all types of travelers, making it an experience that should not be missed while exploring the city.

While the Clock Tower itself is the main attraction, the area surrounding it is filled with other activities and sights to enhance your visit. After descending from the tower, take the time to explore **Skanderbeg Square** in more detail. The square is a pedestrian friendly zone, ideal for walking, relaxing, and taking in the atmosphere of the city. You can also explore the **National Historical Museum**, which is located just a few steps away. This museum offers an in-depth look at

Albania's history, from ancient times through the communist era, and provides a comprehensive context for understanding the country's cultural heritage.

Directly next to the Clock Tower is the **Et'hem Bey Mosque**, another essential stop. The mosque, with its intricate frescoes and rich history, offers a serene contrast to the busy square outside. For those interested in religious and cultural history, visiting both the Clock Tower and the mosque provides a fuller picture of Tirana's development through the centuries.

If you're visiting in the evening, the Clock Tower takes on a different ambiance as **Skanderbeg Square** becomes illuminated with lights. The square is beautifully lit, and the Clock Tower, standing tall against the night sky, provides a perfect backdrop for a peaceful evening stroll. This is also an ideal time to sit at one of the nearby cafes or restaurants to enjoy a coffee or meal while watching the city come to life around you.

In addition to the historical significance of the Clock Tower, it is also a focal point for modern events. **Skanderbeg Square** is often used for concerts, festivals, and other public gatherings, especially on national holidays. If you happen to be visiting Tirana during one of these events, the Clock Tower offers an elevated view of the festivities below. Being in the heart of the city during these times provides a sense of community and a chance to witness Albanian culture firsthand. The **Clock Tower of Tirana** is more than just a historical structure—it's a symbol of the city's growth, its resilience, and its connection to both its past and future. The climb to the top is not just about the view but also about the experience of connecting with a piece of Tirana's history. Whether you're a history enthusiast, a casual traveler, or someone simply looking for a memorable experience in Tirana, the Clock Tower offers something for everyone.

National Historical Museum

The **National Historical Museum** in Tirana is not only the largest museum in Albania but also one of the most important cultural landmarks in the country. It offers an in-depth look into Albania's complex and rich history, from ancient civilizations to the modern era. A visit to this museum is essential for anyone seeking to understand the story of Albania and its people, making it a must-see sight for any traveler exploring Tirana. The museum is a repository of the country's collective memory, providing a comprehensive view of the key historical events, movements, and figures that have shaped the nation.

The **National Historical Museum** is located at the heart of **Skanderbeg Square**, Tirana's central square, which is already home to many of the city's top attractions. Its prominent position makes it one of the easiest landmarks to find and visit. The building itself is instantly recognizable by the large mosaic mural called "The Albanians" on its facade. This mural, created during the communist era, is a striking representation of Albania's history, featuring important figures from the country's ancient, medieval, and modern periods.

Getting to the museum is straightforward, especially if you are staying in central Tirana. Most visitors will find that walking is the best way to reach the museum, as it's just a short distance from many hotels, restaurants, and other sights in the city center. For those staying further out, Tirana's public buses are an excellent option. The bus system is affordable, with fares costing around 40 Lek (€0.30) for a one-way trip. Many bus routes stop at or near **Skanderbeg Square**, making it easy to reach the museum. Taxis are also readily available, and because of the museum's central location, fares are generally low from any part of the city.

Upon entering the **National Historical Museum**, visitors are welcomed into a vast space that houses thousands of artifacts and exhibits, spanning millennia of history. The museum is divided into several pavilions, each dedicated to a different period or theme in Albania's history. These pavilions guide visitors through the country's journey from the ancient Illyrians, through the medieval period, the Ottoman era, the fight for independence, and the modern struggles during the 20th century, including the communist period.

One of the highlights of the museum is the **Pavilion of Antiquity**, which contains artifacts dating back to the Paleolithic era, showcasing the long and rich history of human settlement in Albania. This section is particularly fascinating, with exhibits featuring tools, weapons, pottery, and other everyday objects used by Albania's ancient inhabitants. The pavilion also includes impressive examples of Illyrian art and culture, including jewelry, coins, and statues that tell the story of Albania's earliest civilizations. Walking through this section is like taking a step back in time, as you learn about the ancient roots of the Albanian people.

Another important section of the museum is the **Pavilion of the Middle Ages**, which focuses on Albania's medieval history, including the period of Ottoman rule. This pavilion contains relics from Albania's medieval kings and nobles, including armor, weapons, and manuscripts that provide insight into life during this era. One of the most notable displays is related to **Skanderbeg**, Albania's national hero who led the resistance against the Ottomans in the 15th century. This section is particularly engaging for visitors interested in military history, as it features detailed accounts of the battles fought to defend Albania's independence during this time.

The **Pavilion of National Renaissance** is another highlight. This section is dedicated to Albania's efforts to break free from Ottoman control in the late 19th and early 20th centuries. It's filled with documents, photographs, and artifacts that tell the story of Albania's fight for national identity and independence. Visitors can learn about the key figures who led the Albanian Renaissance movement and the events that culminated in the declaration of Albania's independence in 1912. The pavilion provides an emotional and inspiring account of the country's efforts to establish itself as a free and independent nation after centuries of foreign rule.

Perhaps the most haunting part of the museum is the **Pavilion of Communist Terror**, which offers a stark and sobering look at the repressive regime that ruled Albania for over four decades in the 20th century. This section details the control, surveillance, and persecution imposed by the regime of Enver Hoxha. Visitors can view disturbing artifacts, such as prison records, photographs of political prisoners, and the tools used by the secret police to maintain control over the population. This pavilion provides a visceral understanding of the difficulties Albanians faced under communist rule and the price many paid for freedom and democracy.

In addition to the historical pavilions, the museum also includes a **Pavilion of Iconography**, which is dedicated to the religious art of Albania. This section contains a beautiful collection of religious icons and frescoes from Albania's Orthodox Christian tradition, many of which were painted by renowned Albanian iconographers during the medieval period. These works of art are not only aesthetically stunning but also provide insight into Albania's religious heritage and the role of Christianity in shaping the country's cultural identity.

Another key area is the **Pavilion of Independence**, which focuses on the establishment of the Albanian state and its challenges throughout the 20th century. This section explores Albania's role in the two World Wars and its complex relationships with neighboring countries during these turbulent times. The pavilion provides a thorough exploration of the country's modern history, including its eventual transition from communism to democracy in the early 1990s. Throughout the museum, visitors will find detailed information in both Albanian and English, making the exhibits accessible to international tourists. Audio guides are available for those who prefer a more guided experience, providing additional context and insight into the exhibits on display.

For those interested in exploring the museum at a more leisurely pace, plan to spend at least a couple of hours here. The sheer size of the museum and the breadth of its exhibits mean that there's plenty to see and absorb. The entrance fee is quite affordable, costing around 200 Lek (€1.70), making it an accessible option for most visitors.

In addition to its permanent exhibits, the **National Historical Museum** frequently hosts temporary exhibitions, lectures, and cultural events. These events often focus on specific aspects of Albanian history or culture, providing visitors with a deeper understanding of the country's heritage. It's worth checking the museum's schedule to see if there are any special exhibitions or events during your visit.

After exploring the museum, visitors can take advantage of its prime location in **Skanderbeg Square** to explore other nearby attractions. Just steps away from the museum are the **Et'hem Bey Mosque**, the **Clock Tower**, and the **Pyramid of Tirana**—all of which are worth visiting. The square itself is a great place to relax and take in the lively atmosphere of the city, with cafes and restaurants nearby offering a perfect spot to unwind after your visit to the museum.

Bunk'Art 1

Bunk'Art 1 is one of the most unique and fascinating places to visit in Tirana, Albania. This massive underground bunker, built during the communist era, has been transformed into a museum that provides a comprehensive and immersive look into Albania's Cold War history and the oppressive regime that ruled the country for over four decades. More than just a museum, Bunk'Art 1 is an experience that takes visitors deep into the heart of Albania's communist past, offering an upclose look at the country's history of isolation, repression, and survival.

Located on the outskirts of Tirana, Bunk'Art 1 is set in a secluded area near the **Dajti Mountain**. The bunker itself was constructed under the orders of the dictator Enver Hoxha during the 1970s, at a time when Albania was preparing for a potential invasion, fearing attacks from both the West and the Soviet Union. This vast underground complex was built to shelter Albania's political and military elite in case of war. It remained a secret for many years, hidden from the general public until it was opened as a museum in 2014. Today, it is not only a symbol of Albania's paranoia during the Cold War but also a reminder of the intense repression experienced by the Albanian people under Hoxha's regime.

Getting to Bunk'Art 1 is relatively straightforward, although it is a little outside the city center compared to some of Tirana's other attractions. If you are staying in the center of Tirana, you can reach Bunk'Art 1 by taking public transport or a taxi. The easiest and most common way to get there is by taking the **Linzë bus**, which departs from **Skanderbeg Square**. This bus route takes you close to the entrance of Bunk'Art 1, and the fare is approximately 40 Lek (€0.30). The bus ride takes around 20 minutes. Alternatively, taking a taxi to Bunk'Art 1 is also a convenient option, and because Tirana's taxi fares are quite affordable, a one-way trip from the city center should cost around 600 to 800 Lek (€5 to €7). Once you arrive at the location, it's a short walk to the entrance of the bunker, which is built into the side of a hill.

Upon entering Bunk'Art 1, visitors are immediately struck by the scale and depth of the bunker. Spanning five floors and containing over 100 rooms, the bunker is a vast underground labyrinth designed to protect the country's most important leaders during a crisis. The bunker includes sleeping quarters, offices, and even a conference hall large enough to hold 200 people. Walking through the long corridors, you can almost feel the heavy atmosphere of secrecy and isolation that once permeated this underground fortress.

As a museum, Bunk'Art 1 is divided into two main themes: the history of Albania's communist period and the daily life inside the bunker. The exhibits are carefully curated, blending photographs, documents, objects, and multimedia presentations to tell the story of Albania's Cold War years.

One of the first things you'll encounter upon entering the bunker is an overview of the bunker's construction, detailing the immense resources and effort that went into building this hidden complex. You'll learn about Enver Hoxha's strict policies of selfreliance and paranoia, which led to the creation of thousands of bunkers across Albania, with Bunk'Art 1 being the most significant.

As you move through the different rooms of the bunker, you'll come across various exhibits that focus on different aspects of Albania's communist history. One of the most striking areas is the room dedicated to Albania's **Sigurimi**, the country's secret police force. The Sigurimi was responsible for surveillance, imprisonment, and the persecution of anyone suspected of dissent or anticommunist sentiment. The exhibit includes photos, surveillance equipment, and personal accounts from former political prisoners, giving visitors a chilling insight into the state's control over its citizens.

Another key section of the museum focuses on Albania's relationship with its communist allies, particularly the Soviet Union and China. These alliances were critical to Albania's development during the early years of the regime, but as Albania became increasingly isolated under Hoxha's rule, these relationships deteriorated. The museum provides detailed explanations of how Albania navigated the complex geopolitics of the Cold War, and how its growing isolation eventually led to widespread poverty and repression.

One of the most fascinating aspects of visiting Bunk'Art 1 is the opportunity to explore the actual living and working spaces that were intended for Albania's top officials. The bedrooms, meeting rooms, and command centers have been preserved as they were originally designed, offering a glimpse into what life would have been like for those who sought refuge in the bunker. These rooms are stark and functional, with minimal decoration, reflecting the utilitarian mindset of the communist regime. Walking through these spaces, you get a real sense of the fear and paranoia that shaped Albania's leadership during the Cold War.

In addition to the historical exhibits, Bunk'Art 1 also serves as a cultural space, hosting contemporary art installations and performances in some of its larger rooms. This blending of past and present adds another layer to the visitor experience, as modern artists use the space to reflect on Albania's history and create new interpretations of its legacy. The contrast between the stark, functional architecture of the bunker and the creative energy of the contemporary art installations creates a thought-provoking environment that encourages reflection and discussion.

The experience at Bunk'Art 1 is further enhanced by the multimedia presentations found throughout the museum. Video screens and audio guides are available to provide additional context for the exhibits, allowing visitors to delve deeper into specific events or figures in Albania's history. Many of the multimedia exhibits include firsthand testimonies from those who lived through the communist era, providing a personal perspective on the challenges faced by the Albanian people during this dark period.

The entrance fee to Bunk'Art 1 is relatively affordable, typically around **500 Lek (€4.30)**. This price includes access to all of the exhibits and galleries within the bunker. Audio guides are also available for an additional fee, and these are highly recommended for visitors who want to gain a deeper understanding of the history presented throughout the museum.

To make the most of your visit to Bunk'Art 1, it's advisable to set aside at least two to three hours to fully explore the exhibits and take in the atmosphere of the bunker. The sheer size of the complex and the depth of the exhibits mean that there is a lot to see and absorb, so taking your time will ensure you get the most out of the experience.

After visiting Bunk'Art 1, consider extending your trip to explore the **Dajti Mountain** area, as the bunker is located near the base of this beautiful natural landmark. The **Dajti Ekspres Cable Car** is located nearby and offers a scenic ride up the mountain, providing breathtaking views of Tirana and the surrounding countryside. This can be a great way to unwind and reflect on your experience at Bunk'Art 1 while enjoying some of Albania's stunning natural beauty.

Bunk'Art 1 is a must-see sight for anyone visiting Tirana. It offers an immersive and deeply informative look into Albania's Cold War history and the repressive communist regime that shaped the country for much of the 20th century. Located just outside the city center, the bunker is easily accessible by public transport or taxi, and its affordable entrance fee makes it an accessible attraction for all visitors. Whether you're interested in history, politics, or architecture, Bunk'Art 1 provides a unique and memorable experience that will leave you with a deeper understanding of Albania's past and its journey toward freedom.

Bunk'Art 2

Bunk'Art 2 is one of the most significant historical and cultural landmarks in Tirana, offering an intimate look at Albania's dark past under its communist regime. This underground bunker has been transformed into a museum dedicated to the history of the Albanian secret police, known as the **Sigurimi**, and the repressive measures the state used to control its people during the years of isolation. Unlike **Bunk'Art 1**, which primarily focuses on the Cold War and military history, **Bunk'Art 2** delves deeply into the human cost of Albania's surveillance state. Visiting Bunk'Art 2 is an immersive and often chilling experience that sheds light on one of the most difficult chapters in Albania's history.

Bunk'Art 2 is located in the center of **Tirana**, near **Skanderbeg Square**, making it easily accessible for visitors. The bunker is housed in what used to be an emergency shelter for government officials during the communist era. The entrance is discreet but impossible to miss once you spot the large metallic bunker door—a reminder of the utilitarian and paranoid architecture of the time. This central location means that reaching Bunk'Art 2 is relatively simple. If you're staying anywhere near the city center, it's just a short walk from most key attractions, including the **Et'hem Bey Mosque** and the **National Historical Museum**. Public buses that pass-through Skanderbeg Square are also an option, with fares typically around 40 Lek (€0.30). Alternatively, taxis are widely available and inexpensive, costing about 300–500 Lek (€2.50–€4) depending on your starting point.

Once inside **Bunk'Art 2**, visitors are immediately taken back to Albania's communist era. The bunker itself is a cold, stark space, designed for function rather than comfort. The original architecture has been preserved, allowing visitors to experience what it might have been like for those who worked and sheltered in this underground space. The walls are thick, the corridors narrow, and the lighting is dim, all contributing to a feeling of claustrophobia and isolation that mirrors the oppressive nature of the regime that built it.

As a museum, **Bunk'Art 2** is divided into various sections that document the rise and operations of Albania's secret police, the **Sigurimi**, and the impact their surveillance had on the lives of ordinary Albanians. The exhibits are a mix of photographs, documents, personal testimonies, and objects used by the Sigurimi to monitor, control, and often persecute citizens. Many of the items on display—such as listening devices, interrogation tools, and secret files—bring to life the terrifying reality of living under constant state surveillance.

One of the most poignant aspects of **Bunk'Art 2** is its focus on the individuals who were targeted by the regime. The museum pays tribute to the thousands of Albanians who were arrested, imprisoned, tortured, or executed for their perceived disloyalty to the communist state. Detailed accounts of political prisoners are displayed, along with personal artifacts like letters, clothing, and even items smuggled into or out of prisons. These stories offer a deeply personal view of the trauma experienced by Albanians during this time and highlight the courage of those who resisted the regime, even at great personal cost.

As you walk through the bunker, you'll also come across rooms dedicated to different aspects of the **Sigurimi's** operations. There are sections on how the secret police infiltrated religious institutions, educational establishments, and even families to root out dissent. This level of state control was pervasive, with neighbors spying on neighbors and family members often forced to inform on one another. These exhibits underscore how the fear of being constantly watched was an everpresent reality for people living in communist Albania.

Another key exhibit focuses on the tools of surveillance used by the **Sigurimi**. This includes primitive listening devices, hidden cameras, and recording equipment. Despite the simplicity of the technology compared to modern surveillance systems, these tools were highly effective in sowing fear and maintaining control. The museum provides detailed explanations of how these devices were used to monitor conversations in private homes, workplaces, and public spaces. For anyone interested in the history of espionage or state surveillance, this section of the museum is particularly fascinating.

Throughout **Bunk'Art 2**, multimedia displays enhance the visitor experience. There are video presentations showing archival footage of life in Albania under the communist regime, including speeches by Enver Hoxha and footage of public demonstrations of loyalty to the state. There are also audio installations that allow visitors to hear the voices of those who lived through the era, including survivors of the regime's prisons and labor camps. These multimedia elements provide a powerful and immersive experience, helping visitors to connect with the human side of the history being told.

Despite the oftendark subject matter, **Bunk'Art 2** is not without hope. The museum also highlights Albania's eventual path to freedom, detailing the fall of the communist regime and the country's slow but steady transition to democracy in the early 1990s. Exhibits covering the protests, uprisings, and international pressures that led to the regime's collapse are deeply moving, reminding visitors that Albania's story is one of resilience and perseverance.

The museum is well-organized, and all exhibits are presented in both **Albanian and English**, making it accessible to international visitors. To enhance your experience, audio guides are available for a small additional fee, allowing you to delve deeper into the specific exhibits and understand the historical context more fully.

The entrance fee for **Bunk'Art 2** is around **500 Lek (€4.30)**, making it an affordable and worthwhile experience for visitors of all backgrounds. Given the depth of the exhibits and the size of the bunker, it's recommended to set aside at least **one to two hours** to fully explore the museum. For those who want to engage with the material in greater detail, more time may be necessary, especially if you plan to watch all of the video presentations or listen to the various audio installations.
\

After your visit to **Bunk'Art 2**, you may want to reflect on what you've seen. There are several cafes nearby where you can sit and process the experience. The museum is emotionally intense, and many visitors find that they need some time to absorb the gravity of Albania's recent history. The location of **Bunk'Art 2** in the center of Tirana also makes it easy to continue your exploration of the city. Nearby attractions such as **Skanderbeg Square**, the **National Historical Museum**, and the **Et'hem Bey Mosque** are all within walking distance, allowing you to seamlessly transition from the bunker's underground world into the vibrancy of modern Tirana.

For those interested in Albania's Cold War history and its communist past, **Bunk'Art 2** is an essential stop. It complements the larger **Bunk'Art 1** by focusing more intimately on the domestic impact of Albania's repressive regime, offering a more personal and focused narrative on how the regime maintained its control through fear and surveillance. Together, these two museums provide a complete picture of one of the most difficult periods in Albania's history.

Pyramid of Tirana

The **Pyramid of Tirana** is one of the most intriguing and visually striking landmarks in Albania's capital city. This structure, which was originally built as a monument to Enver Hoxha, the country's communist dictator, has since become a symbol of Albania's transition from its communist past to its modern-day identity. Despite its controversial history, the Pyramid has remained a key part of Tirana's urban landscape, drawing tourists and locals alike with its unique architecture and evolving purpose. A visit to the Pyramid offers a glimpse into Albania's past, as well as a look at its ambitions for the future.

Located in the **city center of Tirana**, the Pyramid stands along **Deshmoret e Kombit Boulevard**, one of the main thoroughfares of the city. Its position makes it easily accessible from other key sites, such as **Skanderbeg Square**, the **National Historical Museum**, and **Et'hem Bey Mosque**. The building's unique design—a sloping, concrete structure that resembles a futuristic pyramid—sets it apart from the surrounding modern and traditional architecture. The Pyramid's history and its current state reflect the rapid and dramatic changes Albania has undergone in the past few decades.

Reaching the **Pyramid of Tirana** is simple due to its central location. If you're staying near **Skanderbeg Square** or anywhere in the heart of Tirana, you can easily walk to the Pyramid in 10 to 15 minutes. The city's bus system also offers convenient access, with many routes stopping nearby for the typical fare of 40 Lek (€0.30). For those staying further out, taxis are a quick and inexpensive option, with fares generally ranging between 300 and 500 Lek (€2.50 to €4), depending on your starting point. Once you arrive, you'll immediately notice the imposing structure and its unconventional form.

The Pyramid was originally designed in the late 1980s by a team of architects, including the daughter of Enver Hoxha, as a museum dedicated to the late dictator. Completed in 1988, just three years after Hoxha's death, the Pyramid was intended to glorify his life and rule, serving as a central cultural landmark that celebrated Albania's communist achievements. However, within just a few years, Albania's communist regime collapsed, and the Pyramid's purpose changed almost immediately. It became a symbol of the country's uncertain transition into democracy, a physical reminder of a past many sought to move beyond.

Today, the Pyramid is largely seen as a relic of the communist era, but it has been repurposed for various uses over the years. For a period, it served as a cultural center, hosting exhibitions, conferences, and even a nightclub. It was also used as a temporary NATO base during the Kosovo War in the late 1990s, reflecting the changing political landscape of the region. Over time, the Pyramid fell into a state of disrepair, and debates about whether to demolish or restore the building have raged for years. Despite these challenges, the Pyramid has remained a significant cultural and architectural landmark in Tirana.

One of the most unique aspects of visiting the Pyramid is the ability to **climb its exterior**, which has become an unofficial activity for locals and tourists alike. The sloping sides of the Pyramid make it relatively easy to scale, although the surface can be slippery and uneven, so it's important to take caution if you decide to make the climb. Reaching the top of the Pyramid offers an excellent view of Tirana, with the surrounding cityscape unfolding below you. The view provides a different perspective of the city, allowing you to see everything from the bustling **Deshmoret e Kombit Boulevard** to the greenery of **Grand Park** in the distance.

While climbing the Pyramid is one of the most popular things to do, it's important to note that it's technically discouraged by authorities, as the structure is not in the best condition. However, this hasn't stopped adventurous visitors from making the ascent. For many, the climb has become symbolic of Albania's post-communist transformation—a mix of rebellion, freedom, and creative expression. If you choose to climb, be sure to do so carefully and respect any safety warnings.

In recent years, there have been plans to fully restore the Pyramid and repurpose it as a digital technology and innovation hub. This project, aimed at transforming the Pyramid into a center for tech startups and digital education, reflects Albania's forwardlooking ambitions. The restoration work began in 2021, and the building is expected to become a key part of Tirana's cultural and educational landscape once again. This transformation will breathe new life into the structure, making it an even more significant attraction for future visitors. During your visit, you might witness construction work or the early stages of the Pyramid's rebirth, which adds another layer of historical significance to the experience.

Although there is no official **entry fee** to visit the Pyramid's exterior, if you choose to explore any future exhibitions or cultural events inside once the restoration is complete, it's possible that there will be entrance fees for specific activities. In the past, entrance to exhibitions or events held inside the Pyramid ranged from 200 to 500 Lek (€1.70 to €4.30), depending on the nature of the event. However, these prices are likely to vary based on the Pyramid's evolving role in the city.

After visiting the Pyramid, there are plenty of nearby attractions to round out your exploration of Tirana. Directly across from the Pyramid is **Taiwan Park**, a green area with cafes and a large fountain, where you can relax and take in the atmosphere of the city. Just a short walk away is **Blloku**, the trendy neighborhood that was once closed off to the public during the communist regime. Today, Blloku is the heart of Tirana's nightlife and restaurant scene, making it the perfect place to grab a meal or a drink after visiting the Pyramid.
Another nearby landmark is the **National Gallery of Arts**, which showcases both modern and contemporary Albanian art. The gallery is a great stop for those interested in seeing how Albania's artistic community has evolved since the fall of communism. This combination of historical, cultural, and

contemporary elements makes the area surrounding the Pyramid one of the most dynamic parts of Tirana.

Visiting the **Pyramid of Tirana** is more than just a trip to a historical site—it's an opportunity to reflect on Albania's turbulent history and its journey toward a brighter future. Whether you're drawn to the architectural curiosity of the Pyramid, the chance to climb its slopes, or its evolving role as a cultural center, the Pyramid offers an experience that is both thought-provoking and unforgettable.

Mount Dajti National Park & Dajti Ekspres Cable Car

Mount Dajti National Park and the **Dajti Ekspres Cable Car** are two of the most popular and scenic attractions in Tirana, offering visitors a perfect blend of natural beauty, outdoor activities, and breathtaking views. Situated just east of Tirana, Mount Dajti National Park serves as the city's natural escape from the hustle and bustle of urban life. With its towering peak and vast expanses of forested terrain, the park provides visitors with endless opportunities for hiking, picnicking, and simply enjoying the outdoors. The **Dajti Ekspres Cable Car**, which transports visitors from the city to the mountain, is an experience in itself, providing panoramic views of Tirana and the surrounding countryside as it climbs to the summit.

Mount Dajti stands at an impressive 1,613 meters and is part of the **Dajti Mountain Range**, which forms a natural backdrop to Tirana. The national park covers approximately

330 square kilometers and is home to a rich variety of wildlife, including birds, mammals, and plant species. It's a haven for nature lovers and those seeking a peaceful retreat from the city. The Dajti National Park was established to protect this important ecosystem, and today it's one of the best-preserved natural areas in the region. For both locals and tourists, a trip to Mount Dajti is an essential part of experiencing the best of Tirana's natural offerings.

To reach **Mount Dajti National Park**, the easiest and most exciting way is to take the **Dajti Ekspres Cable Car**, which departs from the outskirts of Tirana and travels up the mountainside. The cable car base station is located in the village of **Linzë**, just a 15minute drive from the city center. If you're staying in the central part of Tirana, the most convenient way to get there is by taxi, which usually costs around **600 to 800 Lek (€5 to €7)** depending on traffic and your starting point. Alternatively, you can take the **Linzë bus** from **Skanderbeg Square**, which will drop you near the base of the cable car. The bus fare is around **40 Lek (€0.30)**, making it a budget friendly option for those looking to save on transportation costs.

The **Dajti Ekspres Cable Car** is the longest cable car ride in the Balkans, stretching nearly 4.7 kilometers and offering a 15minute journey up the mountainside. As you ascend, you'll be treated to stunning views of the city of Tirana, the surrounding valleys, and the rugged landscape of the Dajti Mountain Range. The cable car's large glass windows provide an unobstructed view, allowing you to take in the full beauty of the scenery. The ride itself is smooth and comfortable, making it suitable for all ages. For many visitors, the cable car ride is one of the highlights of the trip, as the perspective from above gives you a whole new appreciation of the area's natural beauty.

The cost of a roundtrip ticket for the **Dajti Ekspres Cable Car** is around **800 Lek (€6.80)** for adults, while children, students, and seniors benefit from reduced fares, typically costing around **500 Lek (€4.30)**. This price includes both the ride up the mountain and the return journey, making it an affordable way to explore the park while enjoying the unique experience of traveling by cable car.

Once you reach the top of **Mount Dajti**, you'll find yourself surrounded by the stunning natural landscape of the national park. The air is crisp and cool, especially compared to the warmer temperatures in Tirana below, making it a refreshing escape from the city. The first thing many visitors do is take a moment to enjoy the panoramic views of Tirana and the Adriatic Sea in the distance. On a clear day, the view stretches as far as **Durres** and even further along the Albanian coast. The viewing platforms near the cable car station are perfect for taking photos, and many visitors choose to relax here for a while, taking in the serene atmosphere.

Hiking is one of the most popular activities in Mount Dajti National Park, with trails ranging from easy walks to more challenging routes that take you deeper into the park. One of the easiest and most popular trails leads to **Tujani Peak**, which stands at 1,580 meters and offers an incredible vantage point for views of the surrounding landscape. The hike to Tujani Peak takes around **1.5 to 2 hours** each way, depending on your pace, and is suitable for most fitness levels. Along the way, you'll pass through dense forests, rocky outcrops, and open meadows, all while enjoying the fresh mountain air.

For those seeking a more relaxed experience, the park also has designated **picnic areas** where you can enjoy a meal surrounded by nature. These areas are equipped with tables and benches, making it easy to settle down for a leisurely afternoon in the great outdoors. Many visitors bring their own food, but there are also restaurants and cafes near the cable car station that offer traditional Albanian cuisine and refreshments. One of the most popular spots is the **Ballkoni Dajtit** restaurant, which features a large outdoor terrace with sweeping views of the valley below. Here, you can enjoy a meal while taking in the stunning scenery, making it a memorable dining experience.

For visitors looking for a bit of adventure, Mount Dajti offers several other activities to keep you entertained. One of the most exciting options is the **Dajti Adventure Park**, an outdoor activity center located near the cable car station. The adventure park features **zip lines**, **rope courses**, and **climbing walls**, making it a great option for families and thrill seekers. The courses are designed to cater to different age groups and skill levels, so whether you're a beginner or an experienced adventurer, you'll find something fun to do. Entrance fees for the **Dajti Adventure Park** vary depending on the activity, but prices generally range from **600 Lek (€5)** for a basic course to **1,500 Lek (€12.80)** for a full experience that includes multiple activities.

During the winter months, Mount Dajti also becomes a popular destination for **snow activities**, including **sledding** and **snowshoeing**. While the area doesn't have a formal ski resort, the snow-covered slopes and trails offer plenty of opportunities for winter fun. If you're visiting Tirana during the colder months, taking the cable car up to Mount Dajti to experience the snow-covered landscape is a magical experience that contrasts sharply with the city's more temperate climate.

For history enthusiasts, there are also a few **World War II bunkers** scattered throughout the park that can be explored. These bunkers were built during the communist era as part of Albania's national defense strategy and now serve as a reminder of the country's Cold War history. While the bunkers are not official tourist sites, they can be found along some of the hiking trails, and they offer an interesting insight into Albania's past.

In terms of practical tips, it's important to note that Mount Dajti National Park can get quite cold, especially in the early morning and late afternoon, so it's a good idea to bring a jacket or warm clothing, even if you're visiting during the warmer months. Comfortable walking shoes are also essential, particularly if you plan to hike or explore the trails.

After a day spent exploring the park, the **Dajti Ekspres Cable Car** provides a relaxing and scenic way to descend back to the city. As the sun begins to set, the cable car ride offers one final opportunity to enjoy the sweeping views of Tirana bathed in the golden light of sunset. It's the perfect way to end a day spent immersed in nature.

Grand Park of Tirana and Artificial Lake

The **Grand Park of Tirana** (known locally as **Parku i Madh i Tiranës** or **Parku i Liqenit**) is one of the most serene and picturesque attractions in the heart of Albania's capital. Spanning more than 230 hectares, this vast green space provides a peaceful escape from the city's hustle and bustle. It is not only a place where locals and tourists alike go to relax, exercise, and enjoy nature but also a significant cultural and historical site with many important landmarks scattered throughout the park. At its center lies the **Artificial Lake of Tirana**, a manmade reservoir that adds to the beauty and tranquility of the park, making it a popular destination for both leisurely walks and outdoor activities.

Located just a few kilometers from **Skanderbeg Square**, the **Grand Park** is easily accessible from anywhere in Tirana. You can reach the park by foot if you're staying in the central part of the city, as it's about a 15 to 20 minute walk from the city center. Alternatively, public buses such as the **Green Line** or the **Tirana e Re** line make frequent stops near the park's main entrances. Bus tickets are inexpensive, typically costing around **40 Lek (€0.30)** for a one-way trip. For those preferring a faster option, taxis are readily available throughout Tirana, and a ride from the center to the park costs around **300 to 500 Lek (€2.50 to €4)**. The park has several entrances, with the most popular ones being located near **Mother Teresa Square** and **Blloku**.

The **Grand Park** offers a perfect retreat for those looking to relax amidst nature. With its beautifully maintained lawns, shaded pathways, and abundant trees, the park provides an ideal environment for a leisurely walk, jogging, or simply sitting and reading a book. The **Artificial Lake** is the centerpiece of the park, with a walking path that encircles the water, offering visitors stunning views of the lake, as well as the surrounding greenery. The lake is a popular spot for locals to gather, especially on weekends, when families and groups of friends come to enjoy picnics, boat rides, and outdoor games.

One of the main attractions of the **Grand Park** is its walking and cycling trails. The park has over 10 kilometers of paved paths that are perfect for joggers, cyclists, and those who enjoy a quiet stroll. The wide, treelined paths provide plenty of shade, making it an enjoyable experience even during the warmer months. For cycling enthusiasts, bike rentals are available in the park, allowing visitors to explore the vast expanse at their own pace. Rentals typically cost around **300 Lek (€2.50)** per hour, making it an affordable way to experience the park.

Another feature that makes the **Grand Park** a must-see sight is its numerous picnic areas. Scattered throughout the park, these areas are equipped with benches and tables, making them ideal spots for a relaxing outdoor meal. Many visitors bring their own food, but there are also several cafes and kiosks within the park where you can purchase snacks, drinks, and ice cream. These areas often get lively during the weekends, with families and friends coming together to enjoy the green space, making it a great opportunity to observe local life.

In addition to its natural beauty, the **Grand Park** is home to several important cultural and historical landmarks. One of the most notable is the **Presidential Palace**, which is located on the northern edge of the park. While the palace itself is not open to the public, it is an impressive sight from the outside, and its well-maintained grounds are worth a visit. Nearby is the **Tomb of the Unknown Soldier**, a memorial dedicated to the soldiers who died during World War II, and a solemn reminder of Albania's history and its struggles for independence.

Another landmark within the park is the **Saint Procopius Church**, a small and peaceful Orthodox church nestled among the trees. Built in 1942, the church is a lovely example of modern religious architecture and provides a tranquil spot for reflection. Visitors are welcome to enter the church and explore its interior, which features beautiful icons and religious artwork.

For those interested in contemporary art, the **Memorial to the AntiFascist Resistance** is another highlight within the park. This striking monument commemorates Albania's resistance during World War II and is a powerful reminder of the country's fight against occupation. The memorial's abstract design, with its tall, angular stone pillars, contrasts with the natural surroundings, creating a dramatic visual impact.

In recent years, the **Artificial Lake** has become a hub for recreational activities, particularly water sports. Visitors can rent **pedal boats** or **kayaks** and take them out onto the lake, offering a fun and relaxing way to experience the water. Prices for boat rentals are quite reasonable, typically starting at **500 Lek (€4.30)** for a 30minute ride. The calm waters of the lake make it an ideal spot for beginners or families with young children, and the experience provides a unique perspective on the park's natural beauty.

For those traveling with children, the **Grand Park** offers plenty of family friendly activities. There are several **playgrounds** located throughout the park, where kids can enjoy swings, slides, and climbing structures. The playgrounds are safe and well-maintained, making them perfect for families who want to spend an afternoon outdoors. The open grassy areas also provide ample space for children to run around and play ball games, making it a great place for families to spend quality time together.

Another unique feature of the park is its **Botanical Garden**, located near the **Artificial Lake**. The garden is home to a wide variety of plant species native to Albania, as well as several rare and exotic plants from other parts of the world. A visit to the Botanical Garden is not only a relaxing experience but also an educational one, as information boards provide details about the different plant species and their significance in Albania's ecosystem. Entrance to the garden is usually free, making it an accessible activity for all visitors.

For those looking for a bit of fitness or exercise, the park is also home to several outdoor **fitness stations**. These stations are equipped with basic workout equipment such as pullup bars, benches, and resistance machines, allowing visitors to get in a workout while enjoying the fresh air. The fitness areas are popular with both locals and tourists and are often used by joggers and fitness enthusiasts as part of their routine. The scenic surroundings make exercising in the park an enjoyable experience, and there's no charge to use the equipment.

As you explore the park, you'll also find several **statues** and **sculptures** scattered throughout the grounds. These works of art add an element of culture and history to the park and are worth stopping to admire. Many of the sculptures reflect Albania's history and its journey through different political regimes, providing a thought-provoking contrast to the natural environment.

If you're visiting Tirana during the summer months, the park also hosts a variety of **outdoor events**, including **concerts**, **theater performances**, and **art exhibitions**. These events are often held at the **Amphitheater of Tirana**, a modern openair theater located within the park. The amphitheater has become a cultural hub for the city, and attending a performance here is a great way to experience Albania's contemporary arts scene. Tickets for events vary depending on the performance but are generally affordable, making it accessible to a wide range of visitors.

One of the most pleasant aspects of visiting the **Grand Park** is the chance to simply relax by the **Artificial Lake** and take in the views. Many visitors choose to sit along the lake's edge, enjoying the peaceful atmosphere and watching the swans and ducks that inhabit the water. The park's many benches provide comfortable seating areas, allowing you to take a break and soak up the beauty of your surroundings.

The Colorful Blloku District: A Hub for Nightlife and Cuisine

The Blloku District in Tirana is one of the most lively and lively areas of the city, and it has become a key destination for both locals and tourists seeking to experience the best of Albania's nightlife, dining, and urban culture. What makes Blloku particularly fascinating is the contrast between its presentday energy and its intriguing historical background. Once an area strictly offlimits to ordinary citizens during Albania's communist period, Blloku has transformed into a thriving hub where people gather to enjoy modern cafes, stylish bars, trendy restaurants, and a lively nightlife scene. Today, Blloku stands as a symbol of Tirana's rapid modernization, offering a glimpse into the dynamic character of the capital city.

During the communist era, Blloku was a secluded area reserved exclusively for members of Albania's ruling elite. It was home to Enver Hoxha, the longtime dictator of Albania, and other high-ranking officials in the communist government. For many decades, ordinary Albanians were not allowed to enter the neighborhood, as it was a place of luxury and privilege reserved for the country's political leadership. The district was heavily guarded, and its isolation from the rest of Tirana gave it an aura of mystery. Despite being located in the heart of the city, Blloku was a world apart, with high walls, security checkpoints, and an air of exclusivity.

When the communist regime fell in the early 1990s, the gates of Blloku were opened, and the area quickly became accessible to the public for the first time in decades. This marked the beginning of Blloku's transformation into the lively, open district that it is today. The contrast between its past as a forbidden zone and its current role as a center of social life makes it an especially interesting area to explore. The vestiges of its communist history are still visible in some places, including Hoxha's former residence, a modest house that stands as a relic of Albania's authoritarian past amidst the modern development that has sprung up around it.

For visitors to Tirana, Blloku offers an exciting and dynamic atmosphere. The district is known for its colorful buildings, lively street art, and trendy establishments that line its streets. As you walk through Blloku, you'll notice the stylish architecture and design of the cafes, restaurants, and shops, many of which feature sleek, modern interiors that wouldn't be out of place in other major European cities. This contemporary feel, combined with the district's history, creates a unique blend of old and new that is quintessentially Tirana.

One of the primary reasons people flock to Blloku is for its excellent selection of restaurants and cafes. Whether you're looking for traditional Albanian cuisine, Mediterranean dishes, or international food, Blloku offers a wide range of dining options to suit all tastes. The district is home to some of the city's best restaurants, where skilled chefs serve up high-quality meals in beautifully designed spaces. Albanian cuisine itself is a blend of flavors and influences from the Mediterranean, the Balkans, and the Ottoman Empire, and Blloku is one of the best places to sample these dishes. From grilled meats and fresh seafood to delicious vegetarian options, you'll find a variety of traditional and contemporary Albanian dishes on the menus.

In addition to traditional fare, Blloku has become a hotspot for international cuisine. You'll find Italian trattorias, sushi bars, French patisseries, and even vegan and health-conscious eateries, reflecting the district's cosmopolitan flair. The food scene in Blloku is constantly evolving, and new restaurants are always popping up, catering to both local tastes and the growing number of international visitors. The district is especially known for its outdoor dining culture, with many cafes and restaurants offering alfresco seating that allows diners to enjoy their meals while taking in the lively street scene around them. Whether you're grabbing a quick bite or settling in for a long, leisurely meal, the atmosphere in Blloku is always lively and welcoming.

Blloku also has a reputation for being a center of nightlife in Tirana. As the sun sets, the district comes alive with the sounds of music, laughter, and conversation as people head out to enjoy the city's lively evening scene. The streets are lined with stylish bars, lounges, and nightclubs, each offering something a little different depending on your mood. Whether you're in the mood for a quiet drink at a rooftop bar with a view of the city or looking to dance the night away at a highenergy club, Blloku has it all.

The bar scene in Blloku is particularly diverse. You'll find everything from cozy, intimate wine bars to chic cocktail lounges that serve up inventive drinks crafted by skilled mixologists. Some of the bars in the district have adopted a more laidback, bohemian vibe, with soft lighting, comfortable seating, and a relaxed atmosphere that makes them perfect for unwinding after a day of sightseeing. Other venues are trendier, with a focus on modern design, contemporary music, and a fashionable crowd. The variety means that there is something for everyone, whether you're looking for a quiet night out with friends or a lively evening of socializing with locals and fellow travelers.

For those interested in dancing and live music, Blloku's nightclubs and music venues offer plenty of options. The district is home to some of the best-known clubs in Tirana, where you can hear everything from Albanian pop and Balkan beats to international dance music. Live bands and DJs regularly perform at various venues, and the party atmosphere in Blloku is known to last well into the early hours of the morning. The nightlife in Blloku is not just about the music, though—it's also a place where people come to see and be seen, making it one of the most fashionable areas of the city.

Beyond its dining and nightlife, Blloku is also a center for arts and culture. The district's streets are adorned with colorful murals and street art, giving the area a lively, artistic energy. Many of the cafes and bars in Blloku also double as cultural spaces, hosting art exhibitions, poetry readings, and live performances. The district has become a creative hub for Tirana's young artists and musicians, who see Blloku as a place where they can express themselves and showcase their work. This artistic spirit adds another layer of richness to the area, making it not just a place to eat and drink, but a place to engage with the city's cultural scene.

In recent years, Blloku has also become a popular area for shopping, with a growing number of boutique stores and designer shops opening in the district. Here, you'll find everything from highend fashion to locally made artisanal products. The shops in Blloku reflect the district's youthful and trendy vibe, offering a mix of international brands and independent labels. Whether you're looking for unique souvenirs or stylish clothing, Blloku provides plenty of opportunities to indulge in a little retail therapy while exploring the city.

One of the things that make Blloku particularly appealing is the sense of energy and optimism that permeates the area. After decades of isolation during the communist era, the district has become a symbol of Tirana's transformation and its embrace of modernity and openness. The people who frequent Blloku—whether locals or tourists—come from all walks of life, and the district is a true melting pot of ideas, creativity, and culture. The lively atmosphere, combined with its historical significance, makes Blloku a must-see for anyone visiting Tirana. It offers a window into both the city's past and its future, as it continues to evolve as a center for social life, creativity, and cultural exchange.

Blloku is far more than just a neighborhood for eating and drinking. It's a place where Albania's history, culture, and modern life intersect in fascinating ways. From its roots as a secretive enclave for the communist elite to its presentday role as a lively hub for nightlife, cuisine, and art, Blloku takes the essence of Tirana's transformation. Whether you're sampling traditional Albanian dishes, enjoying a cocktail at a rooftop bar, or simply wandering the colorful streets, Blloku offers an unforgettable experience that reflects the spirit of the capital city and its people.

Museums and Galleries to Explore

Albania is a country with a deep and complex history that stretches back thousands of years, and its museums and galleries offer a unique opportunity for visitors to explore this rich cultural and historical heritage. From ancient artifacts that tell the story of Albania's early civilizations to exhibitions that shed light on the country's more recent communist past, Albania's museums provide valuable insights into the nation's identity and evolution.

House of Leaves – Museum of Secret Surveillance (Shtëpia me Gjethe)

The House of Leaves (Shtëpia me Gjethe), also known as the Museum of Secret Surveillance, is one of the most compelling and thought-provoking museums in Tirana, Albania. It provides a haunting glimpse into Albania's dark past under the communist regime, where state surveillance and oppression were everyday realities. This museum is dedicated to the secret police's methods of monitoring and controlling the Albanian population, revealing how paranoia, fear, and distrust permeated every level of society. It stands as a testament to the lives of those who were persecuted, imprisoned, or worse, during the communist era. Visiting the House of Leaves is an intense, but educational experience that immerses visitors in a time when privacy was almost nonexistent, and suspicion was a tool of the state.

The House of Leaves is located in the heart of Tirana, just a short distance from Skanderbeg Square, the main square in the city. Specifically, it is situated on Dëshmorët e 4 Shkurtit Street, a quiet, leafy street not far from other key landmarks such as the National Bank of Albania and the National Historical Museum. Despite its unassuming appearance, the building played a significant role during Albania's communist period, when it served as the headquarters for the Sigurimi, the feared secret police of the regime. Its nickname, "House of Leaves," comes from the dense ivy that covers the building, giving it an almost hidden, secretive quality—a fitting exterior for the covert activities that once took place within its walls.

Getting to the House of Leaves is quite easy due to its central location. If you're staying anywhere near the city center or Skanderbeg Square, it's only a short walk to the museum—typically about 10 minutes. The area is well connected by public transport, and buses that run through Skanderbeg Square can drop you off close to the museum. A bus ride costs around 40 Lek (€0.30). If you prefer taking a taxi, rides within the city center are affordable, typically costing around 300 to 500 Lek (€2.50 to €4) depending on the distance.

Upon arriving at the House of Leaves, the first thing you'll notice is the building's discreet and somewhat eerie appearance. The ivy-covered exterior creates a sense of concealment, which ties into the museum's theme of secrecy and hidden surveillance. Once inside, you'll be transported back in time to an era when the Albanian government used every means at its disposal to monitor and control its citizens. The museum is spread over several rooms, each focusing on different aspects of the regime's surveillance tactics, from wiretapping and eavesdropping to interrogation and imprisonment.

One of the most striking things about the House of Leaves is how it lays bare the machinery of the secret police. The exhibits include authentic surveillance equipment, such as wiretapping devices, hidden microphones, and radio equipment, all used to spy on private conversations in homes, workplaces, and even places of worship. You'll also find detailed explanations of how this technology was used to create a network of informants, with ordinary citizens often coerced into spying on their friends, neighbors, and even family members. The use of such devices allowed the regime to instill fear and suspicion, ensuring that no one felt safe from the watchful eyes of the state.

As you explore the museum, you'll also encounter a wealth of archival material that provides insight into the daily operations of the Sigurimi. This includes surveillance reports, photographs, and letters that reveal the extent of the secret police's reach. Many of these documents have been declassified, allowing visitors to see firsthand how individuals were targeted, investigated, and persecuted. These exhibits are accompanied by detailed descriptions, both in Albanian and English, making it easy for international visitors to understand the historical context and the severity of the regime's actions.

The House of Leaves also delves into the human cost of Albania's surveillance state. One of the most moving parts of the museum is its focus on the lives of those who were imprisoned, tortured, or killed for their opposition to the regime or for simply being suspected of dissent. Personal testimonies from survivors, as well as accounts from the families of those who disappeared or were executed, provide a deeply personal perspective on the era's repression. You'll learn about the conditions in Albania's notorious labor camps, where political prisoners were forced to work under brutal conditions, often for years, with little hope of release. The museum does an excellent job of balancing the technical aspects of surveillance with the human stories behind it, making the experience both informative and emotionally powerful.

One of the key features of the House of Leaves is its use of multimedia to enhance the visitor experience. Audio recordings, video footage, and interactive displays are used throughout the museum to bring the exhibits to life. For example, you can listen to real recordings of conversations that were secretly monitored by the Sigurimi, giving you a chilling sense of how invasive the surveillance was. There are also video interviews with former prisoners and survivors, who recount their harrowing experiences during the regime. These multimedia elements help to create a more immersive experience, allowing visitors to engage with the history in a more meaningful way.

The museum's layout is carefully designed to guide visitors through the different stages of Albania's surveillance history. You'll begin by learning about the establishment of the Sigurimi in the early years of communist rule and how the secret police became an integral part of the regime's control over the population. As you move through the rooms, you'll see how surveillance evolved over the decades, becoming more sophisticated and widespread. The final rooms of the museum focus on the fall of the communist regime in the early 1990s and the eventual declassification of the Sigurimi archives, which revealed the full extent of the state's surveillance operations.

While the House of Leaves is a museum that deals with heavy subject matter, it's an essential stop for anyone interested in understanding Albania's recent history. It provides a sobering look at the lengths to which totalitarian regimes will go to maintain power and control, as well as the impact such repression has on individuals and society as a whole. The museum's exhibits are presented in a clear and accessible way, making it suitable for visitors of all backgrounds, whether you're a history enthusiast or simply someone wanting to learn more about Albania's past.

In terms of pricing, entry to the House of Leaves is reasonably affordable. Tickets typically cost around 700 Lek (€6) for adults, while students, seniors, and groups may benefit from reduced rates. Audio guides are also available for an additional fee, and these are highly recommended if you want a deeper understanding of the exhibits, as they provide extra context and detail about the items on display. The audio guide is available in multiple languages, including English, making it a valuable resource for international visitors.

To make the most of your visit, it's recommended to set aside at least 1 to 2 hours to fully explore the museum. The compact size of the museum allows for an in-depth experience without feeling overwhelming, and the multimedia exhibits help to break up the more static displays, ensuring that your attention is engaged throughout the visit.

After touring the House of Leaves, you might want to take some time to reflect on what you've seen. The museum's proximity to Skanderbeg Square and other attractions makes it easy to continue your exploration of Tirana. Nearby cafes and restaurants offer a comfortable place to sit and process the experience while enjoying a drink or a meal.

The House of Leaves is not only one of the most important museums in Tirana but also one of the most thought-provoking. It offers a deep and often unsettling look into Albania's history of state surveillance and oppression, revealing the devastating impact of the communist regime on the lives of ordinary people. Its central location, affordable entry fee, and comprehensive exhibits make it a must visit for anyone interested in learning more about Albania's past. A visit to the House of Leaves is a moving experience that will leave you with a greater understanding of the country's journey through one of its darkest periods, and how it has emerged on the other side.

National Gallery of Arts (Galeria Kombëtare e Arteve)

The **National Gallery of Arts** (Galeria Kombëtare e Arteve) in Tirana is one of Albania's most prominent cultural institutions, offering visitors a deep dive into the country's rich artistic heritage, spanning from the late 19th century to contemporary works. As the foremost art gallery in Albania, it houses an extensive collection of paintings, sculptures, and visual art that reflect the country's history, its struggles, and its everevolving identity. This gallery is an essential stop for anyone interested in Albanian culture, providing insight into both traditional and modern artistic expressions.

The **National Gallery of Arts** is located on **Bulevardi Dëshmorët e Kombit**, one of the central and most important boulevards in Tirana. Its location places it in the heart of the capital, making it easily accessible from other key landmarks such as **Skanderbeg Square**, **Pyramid of Tirana**, and **Grand Park**. The gallery is situated next to the **Prime Minister's Office** and other government buildings, adding to its significance within the cultural and political context of the city.

If you are staying near **Skanderbeg Square**, you can easily reach the gallery on foot, as it is about a **10 to 15minute walk** from the square. The wide boulevards and pedestrian friendly sidewalks make for a pleasant walk-through Tirana's city center. Alternatively, you can take one of the many public buses that pass by **Dëshmorët e Kombit Boulevard**. The bus fare is typically **40 Lek (€0.30)**, and buses are frequent and easy to navigate. For those who prefer more direct transportation, taxis are readily available throughout the city, with fares ranging between **300 and 500 Lek (€2.50 to €4)** for short trips around the city center.

Upon arrival at the **National Gallery of Arts**, the first thing you'll notice is the modernist architecture of the building, which was constructed in the 1970s during the communist era. The building's clean, simple lines and concrete facade reflect the aesthetics of the period, while the artwork inside tells a much more complex and layered story of Albania's artistic journey through times of political upheaval, censorship, and liberation.

One of the highlights of the **National Gallery of Arts** is its extensive collection of **socialist realism art**, which was the dominant style during Albania's communist era, from the mid20th century to the early 1990s. Under the regime of Enver Hoxha, art was heavily regulated and used as a tool of state propaganda, with strict rules on what could be depicted and how. The socialist realism works in the gallery showcase heroic depictions of Albanian workers, soldiers, and peasants, often idealized to promote the values of the communist state. These works are not only artistically significant but also provide a window into how art was manipulated to serve political purposes. Visitors will gain an understanding of how the regime shaped the cultural narrative and controlled artistic expression during this time.

In contrast to the socialist realism works, the gallery also features an impressive collection of **contemporary Albanian art**. Following the fall of communism in the early 1990s, Albanian artists were finally able to express themselves freely, leading to an explosion of creativity. Contemporary works in the gallery include paintings, sculptures, and mixed media pieces that explore themes of identity, memory, and Albania's transition from isolation to openness. These modern works reflect the challenges and opportunities that came with the country's newfound freedom, making the collection a powerful testament to Albania's evolving artistic identity.

In addition to its permanent collection, the **National Gallery of Arts** regularly hosts **temporary exhibitions** featuring works by both Albanian and international artists. These exhibitions cover a wide range of artistic styles and themes, from modern installations to retrospectives on key figures in Albanian art. If you are visiting the gallery during one of these temporary exhibitions, it's a great opportunity to see fresh, cuttingedge art and get a sense of how Albania fits into the broader global art scene. Information on upcoming exhibitions is usually posted on the gallery's website, so it's worth checking in advance if there's a particular show that might interest you.

One of the most memorable aspects of visiting the gallery is its **sculpture garden**, located just outside the building. This openair space features several largescale sculptures, many of which reflect the monumental style favored during the communist era. Walking among these statues gives visitors a sense of the power and presence that art held during this period, with many pieces symbolizing strength, unity, and the collective effort of the Albanian people. It's also a peaceful place to relax and take in the surrounding environment after spending time inside the gallery.

For those looking to deepen their experience, the **National Gallery of Arts** offers **guided tours** in both Albanian and English. These tours are an excellent way to gain more context about the artwork on display, particularly regarding the historical and political background that shaped much of the collection. The guides are knowledgeable and passionate about the art, providing insights that you might miss if exploring on your own. Prices for guided tours vary, but they are generally affordable and add significant value to the visit. The gallery also frequently hosts **workshops** and **lectures** that focus on various aspects of art and culture. These events are aimed at both locals and tourists, offering opportunities to learn more about specific techniques, artistic movements, or individual artists. If you're someone who enjoys engaging with art on a deeper level, attending one of these workshops or talks can be an enriching experience. Information about these events is usually available on the gallery's official website or posted at the entrance.

When it comes to pricing, entrance to the **National Gallery of Arts** is very reasonable. General admission is typically around **500 Lek (€4.30)** for adults, with reduced rates for students, seniors, and groups. Children under a certain age often enter for free, making it a family friendly activity. The gallery also offers discounted prices for certain temporary exhibitions or special events, ensuring that it remains accessible to a broad audience.

Once inside, you can expect to spend at least **1 to 2 hours** exploring the various rooms and exhibits. The gallery is large enough to offer a wide variety of works but not so overwhelming that it becomes exhausting. Whether you're a seasoned art lover or someone with a casual interest, the collection is diverse enough to hold your attention and provide a meaningful experience.

After visiting the gallery, you might want to take a stroll along **Bulevardi Dëshmorët e Kombit**, which is home to several other important landmarks, including **Mother Teresa Square** and the **University of Tirana**. There are also numerous cafes and restaurants nearby, making it easy to find a spot to relax and reflect on your visit. The nearby **Taiwan Park** is another great option for a post gallery break, offering green space and a fountain where you can unwind.

Tirana Mosaic (Mozaiku i Tiranës)

The **Tirana Mosaic** (Mozaiku i Tiranës) is one of the most significant archaeological finds in Albania and offers a unique glimpse into the ancient history of the country. This mosaic is a rare remnant from the Roman and Byzantine periods, revealing the deep historical layers beneath Tirana's modern-day appearance. Although relatively small compared to some of Tirana's larger attractions, the **Tirana Mosaic** holds great cultural and historical importance. It offers visitors the chance to step back in time and explore a piece of Albania's ancient past through intricate artwork that has survived centuries of change and development.

The **Tirana Mosaic** is located in a relatively quiet residential area, about **2 kilometers** from **Skanderbeg Square**, the main square in Tirana. Specifically, you'll find the mosaic on **Rruga Naim Frashëri**, which is a short distance from the bustling center of the city. Despite its central location, the mosaic site feels somewhat secluded, adding to the sense of discovery when you visit. Because it's tucked away in a more residential part of Tirana, many visitors are pleasantly surprised by this hidden gem in the middle of the urban landscape.

Getting to the **Tirana Mosaic** is quite simple. If you're staying near **Skanderbeg Square**, it's about a **20 to 25minute walk** from the square. The route is easy to follow and passes through some of the quieter parts of the city. For those who prefer public transportation, several bus lines run in the direction of the mosaic, including the **KinostudioKombinat line**. The bus fare is **40 Lek (€0.30)**, making it an affordable option for getting around. If you're taking a taxi from the city center, the fare should be around **300 to 500 Lek (€2.50 to €4)**, depending on traffic and your starting point. Once you arrive, you'll find that the mosaic site is well marked with signage in both Albanian and English, making it easy to locate.

The **Tirana Mosaic** was discovered in 1972 during construction work, revealing what is believed to have been part of a Roman villa or early Christian Basilica dating back to the **3rd century AD**. Over the years, further excavations have uncovered more mosaics and remnants of walls, indicating that this site was once a significant structure in ancient times. The mosaics themselves are incredibly detailed and feature intricate patterns made from small stones, tiles, and glass. The motifs include geometric shapes, floral patterns, and symbols that reflect the religious and cultural influences of the time.

When you visit the **Tirana Mosaic**, you'll be able to see the beautifully preserved fragments of the ancient floor, which offer insight into the artistry and craftsmanship of the Roman and Byzantine periods. Although much of the original structure has been lost to time, the mosaic remains a remarkable testament to the skill of the artisans who created it. The central section of the mosaic is the most well-preserved, and it's easy to imagine what the larger complex might have looked like when it was first built.

One of the key features of the mosaic is its **Byzantine influence**, as it is thought that the site continued to be used during the early Christian period. The intricate designs reflect the aesthetic preferences of the time, with an emphasis on symmetry and symbolism. The mosaics are a mix of vibrant colors, including shades of red, blue, green, and white, which have managed to survive centuries beneath the ground. Walking around the mosaic site, you can get a closeup view of these details, making it a fascinating experience for anyone interested in art history or archaeology.

Although the **Tirana Mosaic** is a relatively small site, it offers visitors an intimate and educational experience. Information boards are placed around the mosaic to provide historical context, detailing the origins of the site and its significance in Roman and Byzantine history. These explanations are available in both Albanian and English, making it accessible to international visitors. The site itself is enclosed, which helps to protect the mosaic from the elements while still allowing visitors to get an upclose look at the artwork.

For those looking to learn even more about the site, the **National Historical Museum** in Tirana features additional artifacts and exhibits related to the **Tirana Mosaic** and the ancient history of Albania. A visit to both the mosaic site and the museum can provide a more comprehensive understanding of the country's ancient past and how it connects to modern-day Tirana.

One of the best ways to enjoy your visit to the **Tirana Mosaic** is to combine it with a walk through the surrounding neighborhood. This area of Tirana is less touristy than the central parts of the city, giving you a chance to see local life up close. Nearby, you'll find small cafes and shops where you can relax after your visit, making it a pleasant outing that blends history with a more laidback experience of the city.

The entrance fee to the **Tirana Mosaic** is typically very modest, costing around **200 to 300 Lek (€1.50 to €2.50)** for adults. Reduced rates are often available for students, seniors, and groups. For the price, you get to experience a significant piece of Albanian history in an intimate setting, making it an affordable and valuable addition to any itinerary in Tirana.

To make your visit more memorable, consider bringing a camera to capture the intricate details of the mosaic, but be mindful of any photography restrictions that may be in place to protect the site. The natural lighting around the mosaic changes throughout the day, and the early morning or late afternoon light often creates the best conditions for photographing the site. In addition, taking time to read the information provided onsite will give you a better appreciation of the history behind the artwork.

For those with a deeper interest in archaeology, the **Tirana Mosaic** is also part of a broader network of ancient sites throughout Albania. If your travels take you beyond Tirana, you'll find other important archaeological locations such as **Apollonia** and **Butrint**, where you can see even more examples of Roman and Byzantineera art and architecture. Visiting these sites, along with the **Tirana Mosaic**, will give you a fuller picture of Albania's ancient past and its connection to the broader history of the Mediterranean region. In conclusion, the **Tirana Mosaic** is a must-see for anyone interested in Albania's rich historical and cultural heritage. It offers a rare opportunity to experience ancient art up close and provides insight into the Roman and Byzantine periods that shaped much of the region's history. While smaller in scale than some of Tirana's other attractions, the mosaic's historical significance and the artistry it represents make it a unique and valuable stop for visitors to the city. Its central location, affordable entrance fee, and quiet, reflective atmosphere make it a perfect addition to any itinerary, whether you're a history enthusiast or simply looking to explore Tirana's hidden gems.

The Museum of Natural Sciences (Muzeu i Shkencave të Natyrës)

The **Museum of Natural Sciences** (Muzeu i Shkencave të Natyrës) in Tirana, Albania, offers a fascinating and educational experience for visitors interested in the natural world. This museum provides a comprehensive look at Albania's biodiversity, geological history, and environmental sciences, making it a must visit for nature lovers, students, families, and anyone with an interest in the environment. Through its extensive collection of specimens, fossils, and educational exhibits, the museum showcases the richness of Albania's flora and fauna while also offering a glimpse into broader natural history themes.

The **Museum of Natural Sciences** is located in **Rruga Petro Nini Luarasi**, in the **Faculty of Natural Sciences** building, which is part of the **University of Tirana**. Its central location makes it accessible from other key parts of the city, including **Skanderbeg Square**, which is about a **20minute walk** away. The museum is somewhat lesser known compared to Tirana's larger attractions, but this works to its advantage by offering a quieter, more focused experience for those interested in the natural sciences.

Reaching the **Museum of Natural Sciences** is straightforward. For those staying near the city center, walking is a great option, as the route passes through some of Tirana's more academic and residential areas, giving you a sense of the local atmosphere. Alternatively, public buses such as the **KombinatKinostudio line** or the **University of Tirana line** will take you close to the museum, with fares typically around **40 Lek (€0.30)**. If you prefer taking a taxi, a ride from **Skanderbeg Square** or other central locations will usually cost between **300 and 500 Lek (€2.50 to €4)**, making it a relatively inexpensive option.

Once you arrive at the museum, the first thing you'll notice is its location within the **University of Tirana** campus. The university setting adds to the educational atmosphere, and it's not uncommon to see students mingling in the area, giving the museum a lively and intellectually stimulating environment. The building itself has a modest, academic feel, which is fitting for a museum dedicated to natural sciences.

The **Museum of Natural Sciences** houses a wide variety of exhibits, covering topics such as **botany, zoology, geology, paleontology**, and **ecology**. One of the museum's strengths is its focus on Albania's native species and ecosystems, which are highlighted through its extensive collection of animal and plant specimens. The museum's mission is not only to educate visitors about the natural world but also to raise awareness about the importance of conservation and the preservation of Albania's unique biodiversity.

The **zoology section** of the museum is one of its most impressive, featuring a diverse collection of preserved animals, including mammals, birds, reptiles, and insects native to Albania and the surrounding region. Among the highlights are taxidermized specimens of **bears, wolves,** and **lynxes**, as well as rare species such as the **Dalmatian pelican**, which is native to Albania's wetlands. The museum also showcases an extensive array of bird species, both common and rare, giving visitors a chance to learn about Albania's rich avian diversity.

In addition to the zoological displays, the **botany section** features an impressive collection of plant species, including several that are endemic to Albania. These exhibits delve into the ecological importance of Albania's diverse landscapes, from the coastal regions to the mountains, and help visitors understand the unique plant life that thrives in these environments. The museum places a strong emphasis on the role of plants in maintaining the balance of ecosystems and provides detailed information about their uses in traditional medicine, agriculture, and industry.

The **geology and paleontology sections** of the museum are also well worth exploring. Visitors will find an intriguing collection of rocks, minerals, and fossils that shed light on Albania's geological history. Fossils of ancient marine life, such as shells and fish, are displayed alongside more recent discoveries, including **dinosaur footprints** found in the Albanian landscape. These exhibits offer insight into the ancient past of the region, making it clear that Albania's natural history is as rich and varied as its cultural heritage.

One of the museum's standout exhibits is its focus on **marine life**. The Albanian coast, particularly the Adriatic and Ionian seas, is home to a wide variety of marine species, and the museum's displays showcase this biodiversity. Visitors can learn about the fish, mollusks, and crustaceans that inhabit Albania's waters, as well as the environmental challenges facing these ecosystems, such as pollution and overfishing. The museum's commitment to environmental education is evident in these exhibits, as they highlight the importance of protecting Albania's marine environments for future generations.

The **Museum of Natural Sciences** also features exhibits on **ecology** and **conservation**, which emphasize the importance of preserving Albania's natural habitats. These sections explore the challenges faced by Albania's wildlife, including habitat loss, climate change, and human activity. Through interactive displays and educational panels, visitors can learn about current conservation efforts and the steps being taken to protect endangered species and ecosystems. This aspect of the museum is particularly important for raising awareness about the environmental issues facing Albania and the world at large. One of the most enjoyable aspects of the museum is its hands-on, educational approach. Many of the exhibits are designed to be interactive, allowing visitors, especially children, to engage with the material in a meaningful way. Educational programs and workshops are often held at the museum, providing opportunities for students and young visitors to learn more about Albania's natural environment through guided activities and presentations. These programs help foster a sense of curiosity and appreciation for the natural world, making the museum a popular destination for school groups and families.

For those interested in Albania's prehistoric past, the museum's **paleontology section** is particularly fascinating. Here, you can see fossils and reconstructions of ancient species that once roamed the region. These displays offer a glimpse into Albania's geological timeline, showing how the country's landscape has evolved over millions of years. The fossils of extinct species, such as prehistoric mammals and reptiles, are among the highlights of this section, giving visitors a sense of the long history of life in the region.

In terms of pricing, the **Museum of Natural Sciences** is very affordable, with entrance fees typically around **200 to 300 Lek (€1.50 to €2.50)** for adults. Students, seniors, and children usually benefit from discounted rates, and group discounts are often available for school groups or larger parties. The museum also offers guided tours for an additional fee, which can be a great way to gain a deeper understanding of the exhibits. These tours are available in both Albanian and English, making them accessible to international visitors.

For visitors looking to enhance their experience, it's worth noting that the museum is located near **Grand Park of Tirana** and the **Artificial Lake**, two of Tirana's most popular outdoor spaces. After exploring the museum, you can easily take a stroll through the park or relax by the lake, making for a perfect combination of indoor and outdoor activities in the same day. The museum's proximity to the university campus also means that there are several cafes and restaurants nearby, where you can enjoy a meal or a drink after your visit.

Sali Shijaku House Museum

The **Sali Shijaku House Museum** in Tirana, Albania, is a unique and intimate cultural destination that offers visitors an immersive experience into the life and works of one of

Albania's most important and celebrated painters, **Sali Shijaku**. This museum is not just a gallery showcasing his artworks but is also a preserved historical home that reflects Albania's traditional architectural heritage. Visiting the **Sali Shijaku House Museum** provides a deep understanding of the artistic development of Shijaku himself while allowing visitors to appreciate the cultural richness of Albania through the preservation of an old Tirana home and its interior decor.

The **Sali Shijaku House Museum** is located in the **Ali Demi** neighborhood, a residential area of Tirana that is away from the more touristy central areas like **Skanderbeg Square** but still easily accessible. Specifically, the house museum is situated on **Rruga Haxhi Hysen Dalliu**, an unassuming street that hides this artistic gem behind its gates. Because it is located outside the city center, it offers visitors a quieter, more reflective experience compared to other bustling attractions.

Getting to the **Sali Shijaku House Museum** can be accomplished in several ways. If you're staying near **Skanderbeg Square** or in the central parts of Tirana, a taxi ride will take approximately **10 to 15 minutes**, with fares ranging from **300 to 500 Lek (€2.50 to €4)** depending on traffic and your exact location. Public transportation is also available, with buses running along the **KombinatKinostudio line** and stopping nearby. The bus fare is affordable at around **40 Lek (€0.30)**. If you're already in the neighborhood, walking to the museum is a great way to experience the surrounding residential areas and local life.

The **Sali Shijaku House Museum** is housed in a beautifully preserved **Ottomanera home**, which dates back to the early **19th century**. The architecture of the building is one of its standout features, and visitors are immediately struck by the intricate design of the traditional two-story home, complete with **wooden beams, stonework**, and **cobblestone pathways**. The house itself is a perfect example of the kind of traditional homes that were once common in Tirana but are now increasingly rare due to modernization.

As you enter the **Sali Shijaku House Museum**, you are welcomed into a serene courtyard, filled with lush greenery, a small fountain, and vine covered pergolas. The peaceful setting is a stark contrast to the modern city outside and offers a perfect environment for quiet contemplation of the art inside. The house is divided into multiple rooms, each of which serves a different function, from showcasing **Shijaku's paintings** to preserving elements of traditional Albanian domestic life.

One of the main attractions of the museum is the **art collection** itself. **Sali Shijaku** is known for his bold and expressive paintings, which often focus on **Albanian history, mythology**, and **folklore**. His works are characterized by vivid colors and dynamic compositions, with themes that reflect both personal and national struggles. Many of his pieces are largescale paintings depicting significant moments in Albanian history, such as battles for independence and key historical figures. Shijaku's style blends **socialist realism**, which was common during the communist era, with his unique interpretations of Albanian identity and tradition.

Visitors will be able to see some of Shijaku's most famous works up close, including portraits, landscapes, and historical scenes. The collection is displayed in such a way that visitors can trace the evolution of his artistic style over the decades. The house museum also includes some of **Shijaku's personal belongings**, such as his painting tools, sketchbooks, and letters, which offer further insight into his creative process and personal life. The intimate setting of the museum makes this a more personal and reflective experience than one might find in larger galleries, allowing for a deeper connection with the artist and his work.

Another notable aspect of the **Sali Shijaku House Museum** is its focus on preserving **traditional Albanian home life**. The interior of the house has been carefully restored and maintained to reflect the style and layout of an **Ottomanera Albanian home**. Visitors will see traditional furnishings, rugs, and household items that provide a glimpse into how families lived in Tirana during the 19th and early 20th centuries. These artifacts are not just decorative but are part of the narrative of the home and the way it connects to the broader history of Tirana and Albania.

One of the most engaging activities at the **Sali Shijaku House Museum** is participating in **art workshops and cultural events** that are frequently hosted on the premises. These events are designed to promote the arts in Albania and often feature local artists who give talks or lead workshops in painting, sculpture, and other artistic techniques. For visitors, this provides an opportunity to engage with contemporary Albanian art while learning new skills and gaining a deeper appreciation for the country's artistic traditions. The museum also occasionally hosts **exhibitions by other Albanian artists**, making it a living, evolving cultural space.

As for pricing, admission to the **Sali Shijaku House Museum** is typically modest, usually around **300 to 500 Lek (€2.50 to €4)** for adults. Reduced rates may be available for students, seniors, and groups, and children often enter for free. If you plan on attending one of the museum's special workshops or cultural events, there may be additional fees depending on the activity, but these are usually quite reasonable. Guided tours of the museum are available upon request and are highly recommended for those who want to learn more about the history of the house, **Sali Shijaku's life**, and his contributions to Albanian art. The tours are available in both Albanian and English, making the museum accessible to international visitors.

Visitors are encouraged to spend time not just inside the house but also in the **beautiful garden** and courtyard, which provide a tranquil setting for reflection. Many guests find the atmosphere of the house and its grounds to be one of the most memorable parts of the visit, as it offers a peaceful escape from the busy streets of Tirana. It's a great spot to relax, take photographs, or even sketch if you're feeling inspired by the surroundings.

In addition, the museum occasionally offers **art classes** for children, making it a family friendly destination. These classes introduce young visitors to painting and drawing techniques, helping to foster an early appreciation for the arts. The quiet and safe environment of the house makes it an ideal place for families looking for a cultural activity that everyone can enjoy. The **Sali Shijaku House Museum** is not just about the past—it's also a hub for **contemporary Albanian culture**. The museum frequently collaborates with local artists and cultural organizations to host events such as **poetry readings**, **live music performances**, and **film screenings**. These events often take place in the garden during the warmer months, adding an extra layer of vibrancy to the museum's offerings.

The Independence Museum (Muzeu i Pavarësisë)

The **Independence Museum** (Muzeu i Pavarësisë) in Tirana, Albania, is a key cultural institution dedicated to preserving and presenting the story of Albania's long struggle for independence and sovereignty. This museum is particularly important for understanding the historical context of Albania's emergence as an independent state, after centuries of foreign rule and occupation. It stands as a tribute to the Albanian people's resilience, as well as the key figures and events that shaped the nation's path toward freedom. A visit to the **Independence Museum** offers a rich and immersive exploration of Albania's journey to independence, from the Ottoman Empire's decline to the modern-day Republic of Albania.

The **Independence Museum** is located in **Vlorë**, not directly in Tirana, but it remains a critical part of Albania's historical narrative. The **Muzeu i Pavarësisë** in **Vlorë** is tied to the very site where Albania's independence was declared on **28 November 1912** by **Ismail Qemali**. Since it is outside of Tirana, a visit to this museum typically involves a day trip to **Vlorë**, a coastal city in southern Albania. Traveling from Tirana to Vlorë takes about **2 hours by car** or **3 hours by bus**, covering a distance of approximately **150 kilometers**. The museum itself is located in the heart of Vlorë, close to **Flag Square** (Sheshi i Flamurit), a prominent landmark that also holds historical significance as the place where the Albanian flag was raised during the declaration of independence.

To get to the **Independence Museum** from Tirana, there are several transportation options. For those driving, the journey is straightforward along the **SH4 Highway**, which connects Tirana to Vlorë. Alternatively, buses leave from Tirana's main bus terminal to Vlorë several times a day, with a one-way ticket costing around **500 to 600 Lek (€4 to €5)**. The bus ride offers scenic views of the Albanian countryside and coastal areas. Once in Vlorë, the museum is easy to reach by foot from the city center or by local taxi, which is affordable and convenient.

The **Independence Museum** itself is housed in a **19thcentury building**, which has been meticulously preserved to maintain its historical authenticity. The building is where Albania's declaration of independence was signed, and the museum is dedicated to commemorating this monumental event. The architecture of the building reflects the Ottoman influence prevalent in Albania at the time, but its interior has been adapted to serve as a modern exhibition space. As you approach the museum, you'll notice its stately facade, marked by plaques and commemorations that highlight its historical significance.

Upon entering the museum, visitors are greeted by an array of exhibits that vividly depict Albania's path to independence. The **main exhibition hall** is dedicated to the events leading up to **28 November 1912**, when **Ismail Qemali** and other prominent Albanian patriots gathered in Vlorë to declare the country's independence from the Ottoman Empire. This moment marked the beginning of modern Albania and is celebrated every year as Albania's national day.

One of the most striking features of the **Independence Museum** is its extensive collection of **historical documents**, photographs, and personal belongings of the key figures involved in the independence movement. The exhibits feature **original copies of the Declaration of Independence**, along with the pens, inkpots, and desks used by Ismail Qemali and his colleagues. There are also **photographs** and **portraits** of the signatories of the declaration, giving visitors a tangible connection to the people who played pivotal roles in securing Albania's independence.

The museum also offers a **timeline of Albania's fight for sovereignty**, starting with the decline of the Ottoman Empire and covering major uprisings, revolts, and diplomatic efforts that shaped the nation's struggle for freedom. Detailed information is provided about key moments, such as the **Prizren League** of 1878 and the **Congress of Monastir** in 1908, which were crucial in laying the groundwork for the eventual declaration of independence. These exhibits help visitors understand the broader context of Albania's journey to statehood, which involved both armed resistance and strategic diplomacy.

One of the museum's most emotionally impactful sections is dedicated to the **Albanian flag**, a symbol of the country's identity and independence. On display is the **original flag** raised by Ismail Qemali in 1912, which has become an iconic representation of Albania's national pride. The flag is housed in a glass case, accompanied by detailed explanations of its significance and the role it played in unifying the Albanian people during the independence movement.

In addition to the political history, the **Independence Museum** also focuses on the **cultural and social changes** that took place in Albania during this period. Exhibits highlight the growing sense of national identity that emerged in the late 19th and early 20th centuries, including the role of literature, music, and education in fostering a collective Albanian consciousness. There are displays of **traditional Albanian clothing**, manuscripts of early Albanian literature, and musical instruments that reflect the cultural richness of the period.

One of the key experiences at the museum is learning about **Ismail Qemali**, the primary figure behind the independence movement and the first leader of independent Albania. The museum dedicates a significant portion of its space to his life, including personal artifacts such as his **clothing, letters**, and **diplomatic correspondence**. Visitors can trace his journey from an Ottoman bureaucrat to the leader of the Albanian independence movement, gaining insight into his vision for a free Albania and the challenges he faced.

For visitors seeking a more interactive experience, the **Independence Museum** also offers **audio guides** and **guided tours** in both Albanian and English. The guides provide a deeper understanding of the exhibits, offering historical context and interesting anecdotes about the events and figures that shaped Albania's independence. Guided tours are especially recommended for those who want to get the most out of their visit, as they offer a structured and detailed exploration of the museum's collections.

As for pricing, the entrance fee to the **Independence Museum** is typically very affordable, ranging from **200 to 400 Lek (€1.50 to €3.50)** depending on the season and any discounts for students, seniors, or groups. Audio guides and guided tours may incur an additional fee, but these are usually nominal and well worth the cost for the added value they provide. Children under a certain age often receive free entry, making the museum an excellent destination for families looking to educate their children about Albania's history.

After touring the museum, visitors can extend their exploration by visiting nearby **Flag Square**, where a large monument commemorates the declaration of independence. This square is often used for national celebrations, and the **statue of Ismail Qemali** stands proudly as a reminder of the significance of the site. Many visitors take time to reflect here and take photos, as it offers a panoramic view of Vlorë and the surrounding area.

The **Independence Museum** is more than just a collection of artifacts; it is a space for **reflection** and **patriotism**. For Albanians, it serves as a powerful reminder of the sacrifices made to secure the country's freedom, while for international visitors, it provides a rich and immersive understanding of the political and cultural forces that shaped modern Albania. The museum is thoughtfully designed to ensure that visitors of all ages and backgrounds can appreciate the significance of its exhibits.

For those planning a longer stay in Vlorë, the area surrounding the **Independence Museum** offers several attractions worth exploring. **Kuzum Baba Hill**, located nearby, offers a scenic viewpoint over the city, while **Vlorë's beaches** provide a relaxing way to unwind after a day of historical exploration. Local restaurants and cafes offer traditional Albanian cuisine, allowing visitors to experience both the historical and contemporary sides of Vlorë.

In conclusion, the **Independence Museum** is an essential stop for anyone interested in Albanian history, particularly the events leading up to the country's hard-won independence. Its detailed exhibits, historic artifacts, and immersive narrative make it an educational and emotional experience for all who visit. Whether you're a history buff, a curious traveler, or a local looking to reconnect with your heritage, the **Muzeu i Pavarësisë** provides a valuable window into the past and the legacy of Albania's independence. The museum's accessibility, affordable pricing, and proximity to other important sites make it a perfect addition to any visit to Vlorë or Albania as a whole.

Mezuraj Museum (Muzeu Mezuraj)

The Mezuraj Museum (Muzeu Mezuraj) in Tirana, Albania, is a unique cultural space that showcases a wide variety of art and historical artifacts. It serves as a bridge between Albania's rich artistic heritage and its modern identity, offering visitors an intimate look at the country's development through art, sculpture, and historical objects. While not as large as some of Tirana's other museums, Mezuraj Museum's curated collection makes it a must visit for those interested in both traditional and contemporary Albanian art.

The Mezuraj Museum is located on Rruga Kavajës, one of the main streets in Tirana. This central location makes it easily accessible from key points of interest in the city, including Skanderbeg Square, which is about a 10minute drive or a 20minute walk away. The museum's placement in a bustling part of the city allows visitors to explore the nearby shopping areas, cafes, and restaurants either before or after their visit. Public transportation options are plentiful, with several bus lines stopping along Rruga Kavajës, and a taxi from central Tirana will generally cost around 300 to 500 Lek (€2.50 to €4), depending on traffic.

The Mezuraj Museum was established in 2007 and is housed in a modern building, reflecting the museum's commitment to presenting Albania's artistic evolution in a contemporary setting. The museum was founded by Anastas Mezuraj, a passionate art collector, with the goal of creating a cultural space where Albanian history and art could be displayed and appreciated by the public. The museum's collection is a mix of fine arts, sculptures, archaeological finds, and cultural artifacts, offering a diverse exploration of the country's artistic and historical identity.

When you enter the Mezuraj Museum, you are immediately welcomed by a sleek and contemporary interior that contrasts with the traditional art and objects on display. The design of the museum allows visitors to explore the exhibits at their own pace, creating a relaxed and contemplative atmosphere. The museum is spread over multiple floors, with each section dedicated to different aspects of Albanian art and history. Visitors are free to wander through the rooms and galleries, where they will find a wide variety of artwork, sculptures, and historical objects from different periods of Albania's past.

One of the most notable features of the Mezuraj Museum is its extensive collection of fine art. The museum showcases the works of Albanian painters and sculptors, both past and present, providing a comprehensive overview of the development of Albanian art. The paintings range from realist depictions of Albania's landscapes and people to more abstract works that reflect the influence of modern artistic movements. The museum places a particular emphasis on the 20th century, a period during which Albanian art underwent significant changes due to political and social developments.

In addition to its fine art collection, the Mezuraj Museum also features an impressive sculpture gallery. The sculptures on display vary from ancient to modern pieces, showcasing the evolution of sculptural techniques and themes in Albania. Visitors can admire works ranging from classical busts to more avantgarde modern sculptures that reflect contemporary Albanian creativity. The museum provides detailed information about each piece, allowing visitors to gain a deeper understanding of the artists and the cultural context in which the works were created.

Another important aspect of the Mezuraj Museum is its archaeological collection. The museum houses a significant number of artifacts from ancient Illyria, the region that now constitutes modern Albania. These include pottery, tools, jewelry, and coins that offer a glimpse into life in ancient times. The objects on display are well-preserved and accompanied by informative descriptions that provide context for their historical significance. This section of the museum is particularly interesting for those who want to learn more about Albania's ancient roots and its connections to other ancient civilizations in the region.

One of the highlights of the museum's collection is a Roman sarcophagus from the 2nd century AD, which is intricately carved and remarkably well-preserved. This artifact, along with other Romanera pieces, demonstrates the rich cultural exchange that took place in the region during antiquity. Visitors interested in archaeology will find this section of the museum particularly engaging, as it helps to place Albania within the broader context of Mediterranean history.

The Mezuraj Museum also houses a photography collection, which documents Albania's social and political history from the early 20th century to the present day. The photographs provide a visual record of the country's transformation through periods of occupation, communism, and the eventual transition to democracy. This collection serves as a powerful reminder of the resilience of the Albanian people and the cultural shifts that have shaped modern Albania.

For visitors looking to make the most of their experience, the Mezuraj Museum frequently hosts temporary exhibitions and cultural events, including lectures, art workshops, and book presentations. These events are often centered around contemporary Albanian culture and serve as a platform for emerging artists to showcase their work. Attending one of these events can provide visitors with a deeper connection to Albania's current artistic scene and offer opportunities to interact with local artists and intellectuals.

In terms of practicalities, the entrance fee to the Mezuraj Museum is usually around 200 to 400 Lek (€1.50 to €3.50) for adults, with reduced rates for students, seniors, and children. The museum's affordability makes it accessible to a wide range of visitors, and its central location makes it easy to combine with other activities in Tirana. Guided tours are available for an additional fee, and these are highly recommended for those who want to gain deeper insights into the artwork and artifacts on display. The tours are offered in both Albanian and English, making them accessible to international visitors.

The Mezuraj Museum also has a small gift shop where visitors can purchase art books, souvenirs, and works by local artists. The shop is a great place to pick up unique items that reflect Albania's artistic and cultural heritage. For those looking to relax after their visit, there are several cafes and restaurants in the surrounding area, offering traditional Albanian cuisine and refreshments. This makes it easy to spend a few hours exploring the museum before enjoying a meal or a coffee in one of Tirana's vibrant local spots.

One of the best aspects of visiting the Mezuraj Museum is the way it combines both ancient and modern aspects of Albanian culture, making it a comprehensive cultural experience. The museum's mix of art, archaeology, and historical artifacts provides visitors with a wellrounded understanding of Albania's past, while its contemporary exhibitions showcase the vibrancy of its current artistic scene. This balance between history and modernity makes the museum a fascinating destination for anyone looking to explore Albania's cultural heritage in depth.

Whether you are an art enthusiast, a history buff, or simply a curious traveler, the Mezuraj Museum offers something for everyone. Its thoughtful curation and diverse collections make it a must visit for those seeking to understand Albania's artistic evolution and its place in the wider context of European history. The museum's welcoming atmosphere, combined with its informative exhibits, ensures that visitors leave with a greater appreciation for the richness of Albanian culture and the role it has played in shaping the country's identity.

The Mezuraj Museum is a hidden gem in Tirana's cultural landscape, offering visitors a deep dive into the artistic, historical, and archaeological heritage of Albania. With its central location, affordable pricing, and diverse range of exhibits, it is an ideal destination for anyone looking to explore the country's cultural identity. Whether you spend an hour or an entire afternoon wandering through its galleries, the Mezuraj Museum promises a memorable and enriching experience that will leave you with a deeper understanding of Albania's artistic and historical contributions to the world.

COD – Center for Openness and Dialogue (Gallery within the Prime Minister's Office)

The Center for Openness and Dialogue (COD), located within the Prime Minister's Office in Tirana, Albania, is a truly unique space that combines art, culture, and public engagement with government transparency. As a gallery and cultural hub, COD fosters dialogue between the public and the government while showcasing contemporary art exhibitions, historical artifacts, and multimedia projects. This intersection of politics, art, and civil engagement makes it a must visit destination for those looking to explore the modern cultural landscape of Albania.

The COD is located at the heart of Tirana, within the Prime Minister's Office building, which is situated on Deshmoret e Kombit Boulevard, one of the city's most prominent and central streets. Its location is ideal for tourists, as it is within walking distance of major landmarks like Skanderbeg Square, the National Historical Museum, and the Et'hem Bey Mosque. The building itself, a prime example of Fascistera architecture, is imposing yet elegant, and the gallery's presence inside the government headquarters adds an extra layer of intrigue and significance to the space.

Getting to the Center for Openness and Dialogue is very convenient. If you're staying in the center of Tirana, it's just a short walk from most hotels, restaurants, and other attractions. If you're coming from a little farther out, taxis are widely available, and a ride to the Prime Minister's Office from most parts of the city will cost between 300 and 500 Lek (€2.50 to €4). Public buses that run along Deshmoret e Kombit Boulevard will also drop you near the Prime Minister's Office, with fares typically costing around 40 Lek (€0.30).

When entering the COD, visitors are immediately struck by the modern design and open, airy layout of the space. The gallery is situated in the groundfloor area of the Prime Minister's Office, a historically significant building that has been repurposed to promote transparency, dialogue, and accessibility. The initiative for COD was established by Prime

Minister Edi Rama as part of a broader effort to open up government spaces to the public and encourage interaction between citizens and their government.

One of the first things to note about the Center for Openness and Dialogue is that entrance is free, which makes it accessible to everyone, from art enthusiasts and academics to curious travelers and local residents. This focus on openness is central to COD's mission, as the center seeks to invite visitors into the traditionally closedoff space of government, giving them a chance to engage with contemporary issues through art and discussion.

The exhibitions at COD are constantly changing, with a strong emphasis on contemporary art, multimedia installations, and digital exhibitions. The gallery regularly hosts international and Albanian artists, showcasing works that explore themes of politics, history, human rights, and civil society. The COD's exhibitions are designed to challenge viewers and provoke thought, often dealing with complex social and political issues in a visually compelling way. Many of the pieces are interactive, inviting visitors to become part of the dialogue through digital interfaces, video installations, and soundscapes.

Visitors can expect to see an eclectic mix of visual arts, installations, and historical displays. The gallery's flexibility allows it to host everything from solo exhibitions by emerging artists to retrospectives of established figures. One of the unique aspects of the COD is its use of multimedia and technology, which plays a crucial role in making the exhibitions more engaging and immersive. Whether it's through video art, digital projections, or interactive displays, the COD's exhibits are designed to engage a wide range of audiences.

In addition to contemporary art exhibitions, COD also has displays related to Albania's history and its political transformation, including artifacts and documents from the Communist era. These exhibitions often explore themes such as censorship, state control, and the struggle for democracy, offering visitors a nuanced view of Albania's recent past. One notable aspect of COD's historical exhibits is its commitment to transparency. The center often displays previously classified government documents, giving the public a rare opportunity to examine Albania's political history firsthand. This openness is a testament to the government's effort to confront and learn from its past.

One particularly interesting exhibit is the photographic archive of Prime Minister Edi Rama, who is also a noted artist. The archive contains a series of his artistic photographs and sketches, blending his political and artistic careers. This adds an additional personal touch to the space, as visitors are not only engaging with the broader issues at hand but also gaining insight into the creative mind of Albania's current leader.

COD also serves as a public forum for dialogue and discussion. Throughout the year, the center hosts lectures, workshops, panel discussions, and film screenings that focus on topics such as civil rights, governmental transparency, and the role of art in public life. These events are often open to the public and are designed to encourage open conversation about pressing social and political issues. Many of these events are free or have a minimal fee, making them accessible to a wide range of participants.

For those looking to fully immerse themselves in the COD experience, attending one of these public events can be particularly enriching. These discussions and forums provide a platform for civil discourse, where both local residents and international visitors can engage in meaningful conversations about the direction of Albania's political and cultural landscape. The mix of artistic expression and public discourse at COD makes it an ideal destination for anyone interested in how art and politics intersect in contemporary society.

The design of the Center for Openness and Dialogue is worth noting as well. The architects have done an impressive job of maintaining the integrity of the original Fascistera architecture while incorporating modern elements to create a welcoming and dynamic space. The sleek interiors, minimalist design, and large windows that flood the space with natural light create a serene yet thought-provoking environment, perfectly suited to the exhibitions on display. Visitors often remark on the contrast between the austere exterior of the Prime Minister's Office and the inviting, open feel of the gallery within.

For those looking to take home a memento of their visit, the COD shop offers a range of books, art catalogs, and merchandise related to the exhibitions. Many of the books focus on Albanian contemporary art, history, and politics, providing further reading for those interested in deepening their understanding of the country. The shop is a great place to pick up unique gifts or souvenirs that reflect Albania's vibrant cultural scene.

After exploring the Center for Openness and Dialogue, visitors can take a leisurely stroll along Deshmoret e Kombit Boulevard, which is lined with trees, monuments, and government buildings. The area is pedestrian friendly, and there are plenty of cafes and restaurants nearby where you can relax and reflect on your visit. This central part of Tirana is also close to other important cultural landmarks, making it easy to combine a trip to COD with other attractions such as the National Gallery of Arts or the Bunk'Art 2 museum.

The Center for Openness and Dialogue (COD) offers a fascinating glimpse into the intersection of art, politics, and public engagement in Albania. Its location within the Prime Minister's Office adds an additional layer of significance, as it serves not only as a gallery but as a symbol of the government's commitment to openness and transparency. Whether you are drawn to contemporary art, interested in Albania's political history, or simply looking to participate in public dialogue, the COD provides a rich and engaging experience for all visitors.

With free entry, dynamic exhibitions, and a schedule packed with cultural events, the Center for Openness and Dialogue is a must-see destination for anyone visiting Tirana. Its unique blend of art, history, and civic engagement offers something for everyone, from casual tourists to art aficionados and political enthusiasts alike. Whether you spend an hour wandering through the exhibitions or participate in a public forum, the COD is sure to leave a lasting impression and offer valuable insights into Albania's evolving cultural and political landscape.

Parks and Outdoor Spaces: A Relaxing Side of the City

Albania, known for its rich history, lively cities, and stunning landscapes, also offers an inviting selection of parks and outdoor spaces that provide a relaxing contrast to the hustle and bustle of urban life. These green spaces allow both locals and visitors to slow down, enjoy nature, and experience a more tranquil side of the cities.

In the capital city of Tirana, the largest and most popular green space is Grand Park (Parku i Madh). Covering over 230 hectares, this vast park is a favorite spot for locals seeking a place to escape the urban noise and enjoy some fresh air. The park is located just a short walk from the city center, making it easily accessible for tourists who want to take a break from sightseeing. One of the highlights of Grand Park is the Artificial Lake, a manmade body of water that sits at the heart of the park. The lake is surrounded by walking paths, cycling tracks, and open green spaces where visitors can relax, exercise, or simply take in the peaceful surroundings. On any given day, you'll find people jogging, walking their dogs, or enjoying a leisurely bike ride along the paths that wind through the park.

The park's serene atmosphere, with its treelined paths and shaded areas, makes it an ideal place to unwind, whether you're looking to read a book, have a picnic, or just enjoy a quiet moment by the lake. The surrounding greenery and fresh air offer a welcome escape from the city's busy streets, while the lake itself reflects the changing colors of the sky, creating a calming and pretty environment. For families, Grand Park is an especially popular destination, as it provides ample space for children to play and for people of all ages to engage in recreational activities. The park is also home to several cafes where you can sit and enjoy a coffee or a light snack while watching the world go by.

In addition to its natural beauty, Grand Park also has several cultural and historical points of interest. One of the most notable is the Presidential Palace, which is located within the park. While the palace itself is not open to the public, its grounds add to the park's sense of history and importance. Another point of interest is the Park of Heroes, a memorial area that honors Albania's national figures. The park also includes several statues and monuments that commemorate significant moments in Albanian history, providing visitors with an opportunity to reflect on the country's past while enjoying the tranquil surroundings.

Another peaceful green space in Tirana is Rinia Park, which is smaller than Grand Park but equally cherished by locals. Located near Skanderbeg Square, Rinia Park offers a quiet retreat in the heart of the city. The park is well-maintained, with beautifully landscaped gardens, walking paths, and benches where people can sit and relax. It's a popular meeting spot for both young and old, and on sunny days, the park is filled with people enjoying the pleasant weather. Taiwan Complex, a popular entertainment and dining hub, is located on one side of the park, offering visitors the option to enjoy a meal or drink while staying close to nature. The blend of natural beauty and urban convenience makes Rinia Park an attractive place to visit for anyone looking to unwind while remaining in the center of the city.

Outside Tirana, Albania boasts a number of other parks and outdoor spaces that are worth exploring. In the southern part of the country, the coastal city of Saranda is known for its beautiful beaches, but it also has some lovely outdoor spaces where visitors can enjoy nature. Lekursi Castle, located on a hill overlooking the city, offers stunning views of Saranda, the Ionian Sea, and even the nearby Greek island of Corfu on a clear day. While not a traditional park, the area around the castle is perfect for a relaxing hike, and the panoramic views from the top make it a rewarding experience. Visitors can enjoy the fresh sea breeze, take in the breathtaking scenery, and appreciate the peaceful surroundings as they explore the historic ruins.

In the north of Albania, the city of Shkodra is home to one of the country's most beautiful outdoor spaces, Rozafa Castle. The castle, perched on a hill overlooking the city and the Buna River, offers visitors a chance to explore ancient ruins while also enjoying sweeping views of the surrounding landscape. The walk up to the castle is relatively easy, and once at the top, you can take in the beauty of the rivers, lakes, and mountains that stretch out in every direction. The area around Rozafa Castle is a popular spot for both tourists and locals, who come to enjoy the peaceful environment and learn about the history of the site. The combination of nature and history makes it a must visit for anyone traveling to northern Albania.

For those who are interested in exploring Albania's mountains and more remote outdoor spaces, the Albanian Alps offer some of the most stunning scenery in the country. The alpine region is known for its rugged beauty, with dramatic peaks, deep valleys, and crystal-clear rivers. The Valbona Valley National Park is one of the most popular destinations for hikers and nature lovers. Located in the north of Albania, near the border with Montenegro and Kosovo, Valbona Valley is a protected area that showcases the country's natural beauty at its best. The park offers numerous hiking trails that wind through forests, meadows, and along the banks of the Valbona River, allowing visitors to immerse themselves in the unspoiled wilderness. The landscape is particularly breathtaking in the spring and summer months when the valley is filled with wildflowers, and the surrounding mountains are lush and green.

For those looking for a more adventurous experience, the Theth National Park, also located in the Albanian Alps, is another incredible destination. The park is home to the pretty Theth Village, as well as several natural attractions such as the Blue Eye of Theth (a stunning natural spring), and the Grunas Waterfall, which cascades down from a height of 30 meters. Hiking through Theth's pristine nature offers visitors the chance to disconnect from the modern world and fully experience the beauty of Albania's mountains. Theth and Valbona are part of the popular Peaks of the Balkans hiking trail, which is an excellent option for those interested in longdistance trekking through the region.

Back in the urban setting, Durrës, one of Albania's major coastal cities, also offers a mix of cultural heritage and outdoor spaces. While the city is famous for its beaches and ancient Roman amphitheater, the Durrës Beach Promenade provides a relaxing and scenic outdoor space where visitors can take a leisurely walk along the coast. The promenade is lined with cafes and restaurants, making it a pleasant place to enjoy the sea breeze, watch the sunset, or have a meal by the water.

Throughout Albania, parks and outdoor spaces serve as important gathering points for locals, offering a break from the fast pace of everyday life. Whether you're in the capital city of Tirana, exploring historical sites in Shkodra, or hiking through the breathtaking Albanian Alps, the country's green spaces and natural beauty are always close at hand. These areas provide a chance to experience Albania's more peaceful and serene side, allowing visitors to relax, recharge, and connect with nature.

Albania's parks and outdoor spaces reflect the country's commitment to preserving its natural beauty while offering places of recreation and relaxation for both locals and tourists. From the urban parks of Tirana to the wild landscapes of the Albanian Alps, these spaces provide a wonderful opportunity to slow down and enjoy the simple pleasures of being outdoors. Whether you're looking for a quiet spot to enjoy a coffee, a scenic hike through unspoiled nature, or a place to take in panoramic views, Albania's parks and outdoor areas have something to offer for everyone.

Where to Stay: Accommodation Options in Tirana

When planning a trip to Tirana, Albania's lively capital, choosing the right accommodation is a crucial part of ensuring you have a comfortable and enjoyable stay. Tirana offers a wide variety of accommodation options, catering to all kinds of travelers, from those looking for luxury and comfort to those on a budget seeking affordable stays. The city has seen significant growth in its hospitality sector in recent years, and whether you prefer a stylish boutique hotel, a more traditional guesthouse, or a simple hostel, Tirana has something to suit your needs. Knowing the different types of accommodation available will help you make the best choice for your visit, based on your preferences, budget, and the kind of experience you're looking for.

One of the first things to consider when deciding where to stay in Tirana is your location. The city is compact, and most of the major attractions are concentrated in or around the central areas, making it easy to explore on foot. Staying near Skanderbeg Square, the city's central hub, gives you easy access to many of Tirana's top landmarks, including museums, government buildings, restaurants, and shops. If you're looking for convenience and want to be close to the heart of the city, accommodation in or near the city center is ideal. Additionally, the area is well connected to public transportation, which makes getting around easy, even if you want to explore beyond the main tourist spots.

1. Luxury Hotels

If you're looking for an indulgent stay with premium amenities, Tirana's luxury hotels offer comfort, style, and top-notch service. These hotels are typically located in central areas, giving you easy access to major landmarks, restaurants, and shopping districts.

- **Plaza Tirana**: Located in the heart of Tirana near Skanderbeg Square, The Plaza is a 5-star hotel that offers spacious rooms with modern designs, panoramic city views, and an onsite spa. Prices range from €150 to €350 per night. The hotel can be reached by car, taxi, or even by foot if you are staying in central Tirana.

- **Maritim Hotel Plaza Tirana**: This hotel offers luxurious amenities such as a wellness spa, a rooftop bar with stunning views, and gourmet dining. Located centrally, it is a few minutes' walk from major attractions. Prices start from €160 and can go up to €400, depending on the room and season.

- **Rogner Hotel**: Positioned on Tirana's main boulevard, Rogner offers a sophisticated atmosphere with its lush garden, outdoor pool, and fine dining options. Prices typically range from €120 to €300 per night. It's located near public transport routes, making it easily accessible by taxi or bus.

- **Mak Albania Hotel**: Located near the Grand Park of Tirana, this 5-star hotel features elegant rooms, a fitness center, and a pool. It's perfect for guests who wish to combine luxury with nature, as the park is within walking distance. Prices range between €130 and €280 per night.

- **Xheko Imperial Luxury Boutique Hotel**: This hotel combines classic elegance with modern comfort. Situated near the Artificial Lake, it's perfect for those looking to unwind. Rooms range from €100 to €250 per night, and you can easily reach the hotel by taxi or a short walk from the center.

2. Mid-Range Boutique Hotels

Boutique hotels offer a more intimate and personalized experience, often with stylish designs and attention to detail.

These hotels are generally smaller, offering a cozy atmosphere but without sacrificing comfort or convenience.

- **Hotel Opera Tirana**: Located near Skanderbeg Square, this boutique hotel offers contemporary decor, a small fitness center, and personalized service. Prices range between €70 and €120 per night. It's easy to access by foot or taxi.

- **Sar'Otel Boutique Hotel**: Known for its relaxing atmosphere and central location, Sar'Otel offers amenities like an indoor pool and sauna. It's located near Tirana's main attractions, and prices range from €60 to €110 per night. Getting there is easy by foot or public transport.

- **Dinasty Hotel**: A charming boutique hotel located near the Artificial Lake, Dinasty Hotel is known for its classical decor and warm hospitality. Prices range from €80 to €150 per night. You can walk to the nearby park or take a taxi to reach other parts of the city.

- **Lot Boutique Hotel**: With stylish rooms and a quiet atmosphere, Lot Boutique Hotel is located close to cultural sites like the National History Museum. Prices start at around €70 and can go up to €130. It is easily reachable by walking or public transport.

- **Hotel Boutique Vila Verde**: Situated close to the city center, this boutique hotel offers a combination of modern comfort and traditional decor. Rooms cost between €60 and €100 per night, and the hotel is easily accessible by foot, bus, or taxi.

3. Guesthouses and Inns

Guesthouses in Tirana offer a homier, more relaxed setting. Staying in a guesthouse is a great way to experience local hospitality, and they are generally located in quieter areas of the city.

- **Villa 28**: Located in a quiet neighborhood near the city center, Villa 28 offers a comfortable stay with a garden and cozy rooms. Prices range from €40 to €80 per night. You can reach the guesthouse by taxi or a 20-minute walk from central Tirana.

- **Areela Boutique Hotel**: A small, family-run guesthouse that offers a warm and welcoming atmosphere. It's located near the city center, with prices starting at €45 and going up to €70 per night. You can reach it by foot or taxi.

- **Hotel Town House**: Close to Skanderbeg Square, this guesthouse offers clean and spacious rooms with a more personal touch. Prices range from €30 to €60. It's centrally located and accessible by walking or public transport.

- **Boci Hotel**: A family-owned guesthouse with friendly service and traditional Albanian breakfast, Boci Hotel is located near the Grand Park. Prices range from €35 to €60 per night. The guesthouse is accessible by walking or taxi.

- **Hotel Baron**: Located a bit further from the center, Hotel Baron offers a peaceful setting with views of the surrounding hills. Prices start at €30 and go up to €60 per night. The hotel is accessible by taxi or bus.

4. Budget Hostels

For those traveling on a tight budget, Tirana's hostels provide affordable yet comfortable accommodations. Hostels often offer dormitory-style rooms as well as private rooms for travelers who seek budget options without compromising on quality.

- **Mosaic Hostel Tirana**: Situated near the Tirana Mosaic archaeological site, this hostel offers both dorms and private rooms, with prices ranging from €10 for a dorm bed to €30 for a private room. It's easily reachable by foot or bus.

- **Tirana Backpacker Hostel**: This popular hostel is centrally located near Skanderbeg Square and offers budget accommodation in a lively atmosphere. Prices start from €10 for a dorm bed, and private rooms cost around €30. The hostel can be accessed by walking or taxi.

- **Hostel Albania**: Known for its rooftop terrace and social atmosphere, Hostel Albania offers affordable rooms in the city center. Dormitory beds start at €8, while private rooms cost around €25. It's easily reachable by foot or bus.

- **Trip'n'Hostel**: This colorful hostel is close to major attractions like the National Museum. Dorm beds cost around €12, and private rooms start at €25. You can easily walk to the hostel or take a taxi.

- **Destil Hostel**: A trendy hostel with a bar and event space, Destil Hostel is located near the city center. Dorm beds start at €10, while private rooms are around €30. It's easily accessible by foot or public transport.

5. Airbnb and Vacation Rentals

Tirana also offers a growing number of vacation rentals and Airbnb options for those who prefer a more private and flexible stay. From modern apartments to traditional houses, these accommodations provide the comfort of home with added privacy.

- **Central Apartment in Tirana**: This modern apartment is located just a few minutes' walk from Skanderbeg Square and offers all the amenities of a home. Prices range from €40 to €80 per night. It's easily accessible by foot or taxi.

- **Cosy Studio Near the Lake**: For those who want to stay near the Grand Park, this cozy studio offers a peaceful retreat. Prices range from €30 to €60 per night, and it can be accessed by walking or taxi.

- **Old Town House**: Located in the heart of Tirana's historic district, this charming house offers a traditional feel with modern comforts. Prices range from €50 to €90 per night, and it's within walking distance of major attractions.

- **Luxury Loft with City View**: This luxurious loft offers panoramic views of the city and modern amenities. Prices range from €70 to €120 per night. The loft is accessible by taxi or a short walk from the city center.

- **Peaceful Retreat in Tirana**: Located in a quiet residential area, this rental offers a serene escape from the busy city life. Prices range from €40 to €70 per night. You can reach the location by car or taxi.

Tirana offers a wide variety of accommodations to suit every traveler's needs, from luxurious hotels to budget-friendly hostels and cozy guesthouses. The city's compact nature makes it easy to reach any accommodation by walking, taxi, or public transport, allowing visitors to explore Tirana's many attractions with ease. No matter where you choose to stay, Tirana's warm hospitality and vibrant culture will ensure that your experience is both memorable and enjoyable.

CHAPTER 3

EXPLORING THE ALBANIAN RIVIERA: SUN, SEA, AND SERENITY

The Beaches Along the Coast

The Albanian Riviera is one of the most breathtaking coastal stretches in Europe, offering pristine beaches, crystal-clear waters, and a relaxed, tranquil atmosphere that has turned it into a must visit destination for travelers seeking both beauty and serenity. This coastal region, located along the Ionian Sea, is known for its pretty landscapes, where mountains meet the sea, and its charming villages that offer a taste of authentic Albanian life. The beaches of the Riviera are varied, from well-known destinations to more secluded spots, all of which provide a perfect escape for those looking to soak up the sun and enjoy the beauty of nature.

Ksamil Beach

Ksamil Beach is often described as a hidden paradise on the Albanian Riviera. Located in the south of Albania, near the border with Greece, this stunning beach area offers crystal-clear turquoise waters, soft white sand, and breathtaking views. Its serene and inviting atmosphere makes it one of the most visited and beloved spots for both local and international tourists. Ksamil Beach, with its tiny islands scattered off the coast, offers visitors a unique and tranquil escape that rivals some of the best beaches in the Mediterranean.

Ksamil Beach is part of the small coastal town of Ksamil, which lies within Butrint National Park. This region is about 12 kilometers south of Saranda, a major town on the Albanian Riviera, and approximately 20 kilometers from the Greek island of Corfu. Its location within the national park means that it's surrounded by lush greenery and a protected environment, adding to the beach's appeal.

Getting to Ksamil Beach from Saranda is relatively easy, with several transportation options available. The most popular way is by car, and the journey takes around 20 minutes. The road between Saranda and Ksamil is scenic, winding along the coastline and offering spectacular views of the Ionian Sea. For those without access to a car, local buses run regularly between Saranda and Ksamil, costing approximately 100 to 200 Lek (€0.80 to €1.60) one way. Another option is to take a taxi, which can cost around 1000 to 1500 Lek (€8 to €12) depending on the season and demand.

For visitors arriving from Greece, there are ferries from Corfu to Saranda, and once in Saranda, you can follow the same routes to reach Ksamil. The ferry from Corfu takes around 30 to 70 minutes, depending on the type of ferry service, and ticket prices range from €19 to €23 for a roundtrip ticket.

Things to Do at Ksamil Beach

Once at Ksamil Beach, there are plenty of activities and attractions to make your visit unforgettable. The beach itself is composed of small, pristine coves, with sections of sand divided by rocky outcrops. The most famous feature of Ksamil Beach is the group of small islets located just a short distance offshore. Visitors can rent pedal boats or kayaks to explore these islands, which are easily reachable within 10 to 15 minutes of paddling. Renting a kayak or pedal boat typically costs around 500 to 1000 Lek (€4 to €8) per hour.

If you prefer to relax, the beach offers plenty of sunbeds and umbrellas available for rent. Prices vary depending on the season, with sunbeds costing between 500 to 1000 Lek (€4 to €8) for the day. The beach also has designated areas for those who prefer to bring their own towels and enjoy the sand for free.

The calm, shallow waters around Ksamil Beach make it an ideal spot for swimming. The water is warm and crystal clear, offering excellent visibility, which makes it perfect for snorkeling. Snorkeling gear can be rented at nearby kiosks for around 200 to 500 Lek (€1.60 to €4), or you can bring your own. The underwater scenery is full of small fish and colorful sea life, providing an exciting experience for snorkelers.

Another mustdo at Ksamil Beach is to visit the local seafood restaurants, which line the beachfront and serve fresh, locally caught fish and other Albanian delicacies. Grilled fish, shrimp, and octopus are popular dishes here, usually costing around

1000 to 2000 Lek (€8 to €16) per meal. The restaurants also offer beautiful views of the beach and surrounding islands, making them a perfect spot for a relaxing meal after a day in the sun.

For those looking to explore beyond the beach itself, Butrint National Park is just a few kilometers away. The ancient city of Butrint, a UNESCO World Heritage Site, is one of the most important archaeological sites in Albania and provides a fascinating glimpse into the region's history. The site contains ancient Greek, Roman, and Byzantine ruins, including an amphitheater, temples, and a basilica. Entrance to the Butrint Archaeological Park is around 700 Lek (€5.70) for adults, with discounts for students and seniors.

Back at Ksamil Beach, visitors can also enjoy a more leisurely experience by taking a stroll along the shore or exploring the small bays tucked away from the main beach areas. These secluded spots offer even more privacy and tranquility, ideal for those looking to escape the busier parts of the beach.

Nearby Accommodation

There are several accommodation options near Ksamil Beach, ranging from budget friendly guesthouses to more luxurious hotels. Staying in Ksamil gives you the advantage of being within walking distance of the beach, as well as the nearby restaurants and cafes. Prices for accommodation can vary depending on the season, with budget options starting around €20 to €30 per night for a basic room, while midrange hotels cost between €40 to €80 per night. During peak season, it is advisable to book accommodation in advance, as Ksamil is a popular destination and rooms can fill up quickly.

Making Your Experience Memorable

To make your experience at Ksamil Beach truly memorable, consider spending time exploring the surrounding islands by renting a boat or taking a guided boat tour. These tours often last 1 to 2 hours and give you the chance to visit some of the more secluded islets that are difficult to reach by paddleboat. The cost of a boat tour ranges from 1500 to 3000 Lek (€12 to €24), depending on the season and the type of tour.

In the evening, Ksamil takes on a quieter, more serene vibe, with the sound of the waves and the glowing sunset creating a peaceful atmosphere. A sunset walk along the beach is highly recommended, as it offers some of the most beautiful views along the Riviera. Afterward, dining at one of the beachfront restaurants, where you can enjoy local seafood and wine while watching the sunset, is the perfect way to end the day.

In conclusion, Ksamil Beach is a jewel of the Albanian Riviera, offering a blend of natural beauty, tranquility, and adventure. Whether you're looking to relax on the white sands, explore the nearby islets, or enjoy fresh seafood by the sea, Ksamil provides a little bit of everything. Its easy accessibility from Saranda, affordable prices, and stunning scenery makes it a must visit destination for any traveler to Albania. Whether you spend a day or an entire week here, Ksamil Beach is sure to leave a lasting impression and provide you with unforgettable memories of your time on the Albanian Riviera.

Gjipe Beach

Gjipe Beach is one of the most stunning and secluded beaches along the Albanian Riviera, offering visitors a true escape into nature. Nestled between the dramatic cliffs of the Gjipe Canyon and the deep blue waters of the Ionian Sea, Gjipe Beach provides a breathtaking landscape that feels untouched by time. Known for its remote location, crystal-clear waters, and pristine sandy shores, Gjipe Beach is a favorite destination for those seeking peace and tranquility in one of Albania's most beautiful natural settings.

How to Get There

Gjipe Beach is located between the towns of Dhërmi and Himara, two popular stops along the Albanian Riviera. The beach is positioned at the mouth of Gjipe Canyon, which makes it accessible only by foot or boat. This adds to the charm of Gjipe, as it remains one of the more hidden and less crowded beaches along the coast.

There are a few different ways to reach Gjipe Beach, depending on your level of adventure and the time you have:

1. Hiking: The most common and rewarding way to reach Gjipe Beach is by hiking. The hike begins at a parking area near St. Theodore's Monastery, just off the main road between Dhërmi and Himara. From here, the hike to the beach is approximately 2 kilometers long and takes about 30 to 40 minutes on a well-marked path. The trail winds through olive groves, offering stunning views of the coast as you make your way down. It's important to note that the path is mostly downhill on the way to the beach, but the return trip will be uphill, so be prepared for a bit of a workout on the way back. Sturdy shoes and plenty of water are recommended, especially during the hot summer months.

2. By Boat: For those looking to avoid the hike, you can also reach Gjipe Beach by boat. Boats can be rented from nearby beaches such as Dhërmi or Himara, and you can arrange for a drop-off and pickup. Boat rentals typically cost around 3000 to 5000 Lek (€25 to €40), depending on the type of boat and the season. This option allows you to enjoy the scenic views of the Albanian coastline while also providing easy access to the beach.

3. OffRoad Vehicle: Another option is to take an offroad vehicle down the bumpy dirt road that leads from the main highway closer to Gjipe Beach. While you still have to walk the last stretch, this cuts down on the hiking distance, making it easier for those who may not want to walk the entire way. However, the dirt road is rough, so only vehicles suited for offroad conditions should attempt this route.

What to Do at Gjipe Beach

Once you arrive at Gjipe Beach, you'll immediately notice its peaceful atmosphere and stunning natural beauty. The beach is surrounded by high limestone cliffs, giving it a sheltered, secluded feel, with the Gjipe Canyon stretching inland from the shore. The beach itself is a mix of fine sand and small pebbles, and the waters are exceptionally clear, making it an ideal spot for swimming and snorkeling.

Swimming and Snorkeling: The calm, turquoise waters of Gjipe Beach are perfect for a relaxing swim. The water is shallow near the shore, making it family friendly, and it gradually gets deeper as you move farther out. Snorkeling is also a popular activity here, as the clear waters provide excellent visibility, allowing you to explore the underwater world of small fish and marine life. If you bring your own snorkeling gear, you can enjoy this activity for free, but renting equipment in nearby towns will cost around 200 to 500 Lek (€1.60 to €4).

Exploring Gjipe Canyon: Gjipe Beach isn't just about relaxing by the sea—it's also a gateway to adventure. The Gjipe Canyon, which extends inland from the beach, offers incredible hiking opportunities. The canyon is narrow, with towering cliffs on either side, and the hike through it is an exciting way to explore the rugged natural beauty of the area. The hike through the canyon can take anywhere from 30 minutes to 1 hour, depending on how far you want to go. There are caves and interesting rock formations along the way, making it a memorable experience for nature lovers and adventure seekers.

Camping: For those looking to extend their stay and fully immerse themselves in the beauty of Gjipe Beach, camping is a fantastic option. The beach offers a few designated areas where visitors can set up tents, allowing you to spend the night under the stars. Waking up to the sound of the waves and the sunrise over the canyon is a truly magical experience. Camping at Gjipe Beach is free, though you'll need to bring your own tent and supplies, as there are no formal facilities on the beach. This rustic experience is perfect for adventurous travelers who want to disconnect and enjoy nature at its finest.

Kayaking and Paddleboarding: Gjipe Beach is also a great spot for kayaking and paddleboarding. If you've brought your own equipment, you can easily launch from the beach and explore the coastline at your own pace. For those who haven't, kayaks and paddleboards can sometimes be rented from vendors on the beach or in nearby towns like Dhërmi or Himara. Renting typically costs around 500 to 1000 Lek (€4 to €8) per hour.

Photography: The stunning scenery at Gjipe Beach makes it a perfect spot for photography. Whether you're capturing the turquoise waters, the towering cliffs, or the dramatic Gjipe Canyon, there are plenty of opportunities to take breathtaking photos. The natural beauty of the area, combined with its secluded atmosphere, makes for an ideal backdrop, so be sure to bring your camera or smartphone to capture the moment.

Facilities and Prices

Gjipe Beach is known for its remote and undeveloped character, which means that it doesn't have the same level of facilities as some of the more popular beaches along the Riviera. However, there are a few basic amenities available to visitors:

Beach bars: There are a couple of small beach bars on Gjipe Beach that serve cold drinks, light snacks, and simple meals. These are usually seasonal, and the selection is limited to soft drinks, beers, and local snacks such as sandwiches and fruit. Prices are reasonable, with a cold drink costing around 200 to 300 Lek (€1.60 to €2.40) and snacks between 300 to 500 Lek (€2.40 to €4).

Sunbeds and umbrellas: While Gjipe Beach is mostly free for visitors to use, there are a few sunbeds and umbrellas available for rent during the summer months. Renting a sunbed and umbrella for the day will typically cost around 500 to 800 Lek (€4 to €6.50), depending on availability and the season.

No restrooms or showers: It's important to note that Gjipe Beach does not have formal restrooms or shower facilities, so visitors should plan accordingly. The lack of infrastructure is part of the beach's charm, but it's something to keep in mind, especially if you're planning to stay for an extended period or camp overnight.

Making the Most of Your Experience

To make your visit to Gjipe Beach as enjoyable and memorable as possible, there are a few tips to keep in mind:

Bring your own supplies: Given the limited facilities at Gjipe Beach, it's a good idea to bring your own food, drinks, and other essentials, especially if you plan to stay for the day or camp overnight. Make sure to pack plenty of water, as the beach can get very hot in the summer, and shade is limited.

Arrive early: While Gjipe Beach remains relatively uncrowded compared to other beaches in the area, it can still get busier during peak season, particularly in July and August. Arriving early in the morning ensures that you'll have plenty of space to spread out and enjoy the beach before the crowds arrive.

Respect the environment: Gjipe Beach is a pristine and unspoiled natural area, so it's important to be mindful of your impact. Take all of your trash with you when you leave, and avoid disturbing the local wildlife or damaging the delicate natural environment.

Gjipe Beach offers a truly unique and memorable experience for visitors to the Albanian Riviera. With its breathtaking natural beauty, serene atmosphere, and opportunities for adventure, it's a perfect destination for those looking to escape the crowds and enjoy a more tranquil side of Albania's coastline. Whether you're hiking down the scenic trail, exploring the canyon, or simply relaxing by the crystal-clear waters, Gjipe Beach is sure to leave a lasting impression.

Dhërmi Beach

Dhërmi Beach, located along the stunning Albanian Riviera, is widely considered one of the most beautiful and pristine beaches in Albania. Its location between the Ionian Sea and the majestic Ceraunian Mountains provides the perfect blend of golden sands, crystal-clear waters, and a peaceful atmosphere. The scenic setting makes it a popular destination for both relaxation and adventure seekers, offering something for everyone. Whether you're looking for a serene getaway or a vibrant beach experience, Dhërmi Beach is a must-see destination that promises to leave lasting memories.

Dhërmi Beach is situated about 42 kilometers south of the city of Vlorë and 17 kilometers north of Himara. It is part of the larger village of Dhërmi, which is located on the hills overlooking the beach, providing breathtaking views of the entire coastline. You can reach Dhërmi Beach via a few different routes. If you are driving from Tirana, Albania's capital, the journey will take approximately four hours along the SH8 coastal road, which is well paved and offers spectacular views of the Ionian Sea and surrounding landscape. There is a parking area near the beach for those arriving by car, though it can become busy during peak season. Bus services also operate from Tirana to Dhërmi, with the journey taking around five hours and tickets costing between 700 to 1000 Lek (approximately €5 to €8). Although less common, you can reach Dhërmi Beach by boat from nearby towns such as Saranda and Himara, offering a unique way to enjoy the coastline from the water.

Visitors to Dhërmi Beach can enjoy a variety of activities and experiences, making it an ideal destination for any type of traveler. The beach, with its clear blue waters and fine pebbles, is perfect for swimming and sunbathing. The beach stretches over 1.5 kilometers, providing plenty of space for visitors to spread out and find a peaceful spot. Sunbeds and umbrellas are available to rent for between 500 and 800 Lek (€4 to €6.50) per day, allowing you to relax in comfort while soaking up the sun. The beach environment is clean and well-maintained, ensuring a pleasant experience for families, couples, and solo travelers alike.

In addition to swimming and sunbathing, Dhërmi Beach is known for its vibrant beach bars and restaurants, which offer delicious local cuisine and drinks with a view of the sea. Popular spots like Drymades Beach Bar and Splendor Beach Bar provide a range of fresh seafood dishes and refreshing cocktails. Meals at these establishments typically cost between 1000 and 2000 Lek (€8 to €16), while drinks range from 300 to 700 Lek (€2.50 to €5.50), making it affordable to enjoy the local flavors.

For those seeking adventure, Dhërmi Beach offers a variety of water sports and activities. You can rent jet skis, paddleboards, or kayaks, with prices ranging from 500 Lek (€4) per hour for paddleboards to 4000 Lek (€32) for a half-hour jet ski rental. Parasailing is also available, allowing you to take in the stunning coastal views from above, with prices starting at around 5000 Lek (€40). Snorkeling is another popular activity, thanks to the beach's clear waters, where you can spot marine life and explore the underwater world.

In the evening, Dhërmi Beach transforms into a lively nightlife hotspot, with many beach bars hosting DJ sets, live music, and themed parties. Havana Beach Club and Cuba Libre Beach Bar are just a couple of venues known for their exciting atmosphere, where visitors can dance the night away. During the peak summer months, entrance fees to these beach clubs range from 1000 to 2000 Lek (€8 to €16), with drinks priced between 500 and 1000 Lek (€4 to €8).

Beyond the beach itself, the village of Dhërmi is worth exploring. The village, perched on the hillside, offers a glimpse into traditional Albanian life with its stone houses and winding streets. The hike from the beach to the village takes about 30 to 45 minutes and provides panoramic views of the coastline. You can visit historical sites such as St. Stephen's Church and St. Mary's Monastery, both of which date back centuries and reflect the area's rich history. The hike offers not only a cultural experience but also a fantastic opportunity to take in the stunning views of the Riviera.

Dhërmi Beach provides visitors with ample amenities and services to enhance their stay. Public restrooms and outdoor showers are available for a small fee of about 100 Lek (€0.80). Many beach bars also offer facilities for their customers. If you're planning to stay near the beach, there are a variety of accommodation options to suit different budgets. Hotels and guesthouses range from budget friendly options starting at €30 per night to luxury resorts costing upwards of €200. Popular accommodations such as Hotel Imperial and Elysium Hotel offer modern amenities, great views, and convenient access to the beach.

If you plan to visit Dhërmi Beach during the busy summer months, it's a good idea to arrive early in the day to secure a good spot. Peak season runs from July through August, when the beach can become crowded. Bringing cash is recommended, as some smaller beach bars and vendors may not accept credit cards. The village has ATMs, but they can occasionally run out of cash during peak season, so it's better to be prepared.

Dhërmi Beach is an essential stop along the Albanian Riviera for anyone seeking a blend of natural beauty, adventure, and relaxation. Whether you want to swim in the clear waters, explore the charming village, enjoy delicious food and drinks, or experience the lively nightlife, Dhërmi Beach offers an unforgettable experience for visitors.

Jale Beach

Jale Beach, located along the stunning Albanian Riviera, is one of the region's hidden treasures. It is known for its serene atmosphere, crystal-clear waters, and soft sandy shoreline, making it a popular destination for those who want to escape the busier beaches along the coast. Nestled between the more famous Dhërmi and Himara beaches, Jale offers visitors a more tranquil and relaxed experience while still providing plenty of opportunities for fun and adventure. The beach is surrounded by beautiful natural scenery, with the blue Ionian Sea on one side and lush green hills on the other, creating a perfect balance of relaxation and outdoor activities.

To get to Jale Beach, you have several transportation options depending on where you are traveling from. If you are coming from Tirana, the capital of Albania, the best way to reach Jale

Beach is by car. The drive takes approximately four and a half hours along the SH8 coastal road, which winds through the stunning Ceraunian Mountains and offers breathtaking views of the Ionian Sea. Renting a car is a convenient option as it allows you to explore other nearby beaches and attractions at your own pace. There are also buses that operate from Tirana to Himara, and from Himara, you can take a short taxi ride to Jale Beach. The bus journey from Tirana to Himara takes around five to six hours, with tickets priced between 1000 and 1500 Lek (€8 to €12). If you are already staying in one of the nearby towns along the Riviera, such as Dhërmi or Himara, Jale Beach is easily accessible by car or taxi within 20 to 30 minutes. Once you arrive, there is parking available near the beach, although it can become crowded during the summer months.

Jale Beach is known for its calm, turquoise waters, which are perfect for swimming and snorkeling. The beach is sheltered by surrounding hills, so the water is often calm, making it ideal for families with children or those who want to relax in the sea without worrying about strong currents. Snorkeling is a popular activity at Jale Beach because the water is so clear, allowing you to see a variety of marine life beneath the surface. If you don't have your own equipment, there are shops along the beach where you can rent snorkeling gear, with prices typically ranging from 500 to 1000 Lek (€4 to €8) per hour.

For those who prefer to relax and soak up the sun, sunbeds and umbrellas are available for rent on the beach. The cost for a pair of sunbeds and an umbrella is generally between 700 and

1200 Lek (€6 to €10) for the day, depending on the season and the location of the sunbeds. Jale Beach is less commercialized than some of the other beaches along the Riviera, which means that while it is more peaceful, there are also fewer amenities directly on the beach. However, several beach bars and restaurants are within walking distance, offering delicious local cuisine and refreshing drinks to enjoy as you relax by the sea.

Jale Beach is also a great spot for water sports and outdoor activities. Visitors can rent kayaks or paddleboards to explore the coastline from the water, with rentals costing around 500 to 800 Lek (€4 to €6.50) per hour. For a more thrilling experience, jet ski rentals are available, with prices ranging from 3000 to 5000 Lek (€24 to €40) for half an hour. There are also boat trips that depart from Jale Beach and take you to nearby secluded coves and beaches that are only accessible by sea. These boat tours typically cost between 3000 and 5000 Lek (€24 to €40) per person, and they offer a fantastic way to explore the hidden gems of the Albanian Riviera while enjoying the stunning coastal scenery.

In addition to water sports, the surrounding hills and cliffs provide opportunities for hiking and exploring the natural landscape. The trails around Jale Beach offer panoramic views of the sea and the coastline, making them popular with hikers and nature lovers. The hikes are relatively easy and suitable for most fitness levels, making them a great way to spend an afternoon away from the beach. Along the way, you can discover small, hidden coves and admire the diverse flora and fauna of the area. There are no fees to access these hiking trails, and they provide a refreshing contrast to the time spent relaxing on the beach.

If you are looking for something more than just a day trip, Jale Beach also offers accommodation options for those who want to stay longer. There are a few small guesthouses and hotels in the area, offering a range of options from budget friendly to more luxurious stays. Prices for accommodation near Jale Beach typically range from €30 per night for basic guesthouses to €120 or more for beachfront hotels during the peak summer months. Staying at Jale Beach gives you the chance to experience the beauty and tranquility of this part of the Albanian Riviera without the crowds of the larger, more touristy destinations.

In the evenings, Jale Beach takes on a more laidback vibe, with beach bars hosting live music and offering cocktails as the sun sets over the Ionian Sea. These bars are a great place to relax and unwind after a day of swimming and exploring, with prices for drinks ranging from 300 to 700 Lek (€2.50 to €5.50). The calm atmosphere and stunning views make it a perfect spot for couples and those looking to enjoy the peaceful beauty of the Albanian Riviera.

Jale Beach is a must visit destination on the Albanian Riviera for anyone seeking a combination of relaxation, natural beauty, and adventure. Whether you want to swim in the clear waters, explore the coastline by kayak or jet ski, or hike through the scenic hills, Jale Beach offers a wide range of activities for visitors. Its peaceful setting and stunning views make it an ideal spot for both day trips and longer stays, and its proximity to other attractions along the Riviera ensures that you will never run out of things to do. Whether you are a solo traveler, a couple, or a family, Jale Beach promises an unforgettable experience.

Himara Beach

Himara Beach, located on the Albanian Riviera, is one of the most charming coastal destinations in the region. Known for its crystal-clear waters and laidback atmosphere, Himara attracts both locals and international tourists seeking a peaceful yet vibrant beach experience. The town of Himara itself is rich in history, blending a traditional Mediterranean vibe with a modern tourist infrastructure. Surrounded by mountains on one side and the stunning Ionian Sea on the other, Himara Beach offers breathtaking views and an ideal setting for both relaxation and adventure.

Himara Beach is situated in the town of Himara, about 230 kilometers south of Tirana, Albania's capital. Getting to Himara Beach can be done in several ways depending on where you are coming from. If you're traveling from Tirana, the easiest way to reach Himara Beach is by car. The drive takes approximately four to five hours along the coastal SH8 road, which offers stunning views of the mountains and the sea. Many travelers opt for this scenic route to experience the beauty of the Albanian Riviera. If you prefer public transportation, there are regular bus services that run from

Tirana to Himara, which take around six hours, with ticket prices ranging from 1000 to 1500 Lek (€8 to €12). These buses operate daily, especially during the summer months. Alternatively, if you are already in southern Albania, such as in Vlora or Saranda, reaching Himara Beach is faster, with car journeys taking between one and two hours. Taxis are also available, but they are a more expensive option compared to buses.

Once you arrive at Himara Beach, you'll immediately be struck by the beauty of the turquoise waters and the golden sand. The beach is long and spacious, offering plenty of room to lay down a towel or rent one of the many sunbeds and umbrellas available. Prices for renting a pair of sunbeds and an umbrella typically range from 500 to 1000 Lek (€4 to €8) for the day, depending on the location and season. The water is calm and perfect for swimming, making it an ideal destination for families with children. The shallow areas near the shore are safe for younger swimmers, while deeper sections farther out offer excellent conditions for snorkeling.

Himara Beach is known for its exceptional water clarity, and snorkeling is a popular activity here. The underwater scenery, combined with the abundance of marine life, makes snorkeling a memorable experience. You can easily rent snorkeling gear from vendors along the beach, with prices ranging from 500 to 1000 Lek (€4 to €8) per hour. If you are more adventurous, there are also opportunities for scuba diving, where you can explore the deeper parts of the Ionian Sea and see more diverse marine ecosystems. Scuba diving excursions are typically priced around 4000 to 6000 Lek (€32 to €48), depending on the length of the dive and the equipment needed.

For those who prefer staying above water, Himara Beach offers various water sports such as kayaking, paddleboarding, and jet skiing. Renting a kayak or paddleboard is a great way to explore the nearby coves and hidden beaches that are only accessible by water. Rentals typically cost between 500 and 800 Lek (€4 to €6.50) per hour. For a more adrenaline filled experience, jet skiing is also available, with prices ranging from 3000 to 5000 Lek (€24 to €40) for half an hour. Boat tours are another popular option for exploring the coastline, with many local operators offering half day and full day excursions to nearby beaches and islands. These tours usually include stops at secluded spots where you can swim, snorkel, and sunbathe away from the crowds. Prices for boat tours vary but generally range from 3000 to 6000 Lek (€24 to €48) per person, depending on the duration and itinerary.

When you're not in the water, there are plenty of things to do on land as well. Himara town is known for its historic Old Town, which sits perched on a hill overlooking the beach. The Old Town is a fascinating place to explore, with its narrow, winding streets, traditional stone houses, and ancient churches. A visit to Himara Castle, which dates back to the 4th century BC, offers stunning panoramic views of the surrounding landscape and coastline. Entrance to the castle is free, and it's a must-see for anyone interested in the region's history and architecture.

Back at the beach, there are numerous beachfront restaurants and cafes where you can enjoy delicious local food while taking in the sea views. Himara is known for its fresh seafood, with many restaurants serving grilled fish, calamari, and shrimp caught that very day. A meal at a beachfront restaurant typically costs between 1000 and 3000 Lek (€8 to €24), depending on what you order. In addition to seafood, you can also try traditional Albanian dishes such as byrek (savory pie) and tavë kosi (baked lamb and yogurt). Many of these restaurants also serve refreshing drinks, including cocktails, beer, and local wine, making it a perfect place to relax and unwind after a day at the beach.

In the evenings, Himara Beach becomes a vibrant yet peaceful spot, with beach bars and restaurants offering live music and events during the summer months. These establishments are the perfect place to watch the sunset over the Ionian Sea while enjoying a drink or two. Prices for drinks typically range from 300 to 700 Lek (€2.50 to €5.50). The combination of the relaxed atmosphere, stunning natural beauty, and friendly local hospitality makes Himara Beach a favorite destination for both tourists and locals.

Himara Beach is also a great base for exploring other nearby beaches and attractions along the Albanian Riviera. From Himara, you can easily visit other popular beaches such as Livadi Beach, Jale Beach, and Gjipe Beach, all of which are within a short drive. Many visitors choose to spend a few days in Himara to fully experience everything the area has to offer.

For accommodation, Himara Beach offers a wide range of options, from budget friendly guesthouses to more luxurious hotels. Prices for accommodation vary depending on the season, with budget rooms available for as little as €20 per night in the offseason and more upscale hotels costing €80 to €150 per night during the peak summer months. Booking in advance is recommended, especially during the busy summer months when rooms fill up quickly.

Himara Beach is a must visit destination for anyone traveling along the Albanian Riviera. Its combination of crystal-clear waters, stunning natural scenery, and diverse range of activities makes it the perfect spot for both relaxation and adventure. Whether you're snorkeling in the turquoise waters, exploring the historic Old Town, or simply relaxing on the beach with a cocktail in hand, Himara Beach offers something for everyone. Its laidback atmosphere, friendly locals, and beautiful surroundings will make your visit a memorable one.

Llaman Beach

Llaman Beach, located along the stunning Albanian Riviera, is a hidden gem that has grown in popularity among both locals and tourists. Known for its strikingly clear turquoise waters and pebbled shorelines, Llaman Beach provides an idyllic setting for a peaceful and scenic beach day. The beauty of this beach lies in its slightly off-the-beaten-path location, which gives it a more intimate and less crowded feel compared to other beaches in the region. Surrounded by hills and offering picturesque views of the Ionian Sea, Llaman Beach is perfect for those looking to relax in a serene environment while still having access to fun and adventurous activities.

Llaman Beach is situated near the town of Himara, about 2 kilometers south of the town center. It can be easily reached by car, and if you are driving along the coastal SH8 road, the beach is well signposted, making it easy to find. The drive to Llaman Beach from Tirana, Albania's capital, takes approximately 4.5 to 5 hours. If you are coming from the nearby town of Saranda, which is 50 kilometers south, the journey by car takes about 1 hour. For those relying on public transportation, buses run from both Saranda and Tirana to Himara, and from Himara, a short taxi ride or walk can bring you to Llaman Beach. Taxis are readily available in Himara and typically charge between 500 and 1000 Lek (€4 to €8) for the short trip.

Once you arrive at Llaman Beach, you'll immediately be captivated by the crystal-clear waters that make it a haven for swimming and snorkeling. The pebbled shore means the water is free of sand particles, giving it an unparalleled clarity that makes snorkeling a favorite activity here. You can rent snorkeling gear from vendors along the beach, with prices ranging from 500 to 1000 Lek (€4 to €8). For those who enjoy exploring underwater, Llaman Beach offers plenty of marine life to observe, including colorful fish and interesting rock formations.

Swimming in the calm and inviting waters is another key highlight at Llaman Beach. The beach has a gentle slope into the sea, making it an excellent spot for both confident swimmers and families with children. There are sunbeds and umbrellas available for rent, and prices for a set of two sunbeds and an umbrella typically range from 500 to 1000 Lek (€4 to €8) per day. These sunbeds provide a comfortable spot to enjoy the warm Mediterranean sun while taking in the breathtaking scenery.

For those looking to enjoy some adventure, Llaman Beach also offers options for kayaking and paddleboarding. You can rent a kayak or paddleboard for a reasonable price, typically around 800 to 1500 Lek (€6.50 to €12) per hour. Exploring the coastline by kayak is an excellent way to discover the small hidden coves and secluded areas that are otherwise inaccessible from the shore. The calm waters make paddleboarding an equally enjoyable experience, allowing visitors to glide across the water while soaking in the beauty of the surrounding nature.

If you prefer to stay on land, the beach's surrounding hills provide ample opportunity for hiking and exploring. The views from higher up are stunning, offering panoramic vistas of the Ionian Sea and the Albanian coastline. Hiking along these trails allows you to immerse yourself in the natural beauty of the region, making it an excellent complement to a day spent on the beach.

In terms of amenities, Llaman Beach has several small beach bars and restaurants where you can enjoy local Albanian dishes and fresh seafood. Prices are relatively affordable, with meals typically ranging from 1000 to 3000 Lek (€8 to €24) depending on your choice of food. Many of these restaurants serve freshly caught fish, grilled meats, and traditional Albanian salads, providing a delicious break from sunbathing or swimming. The beachfront bars also offer a variety of refreshing drinks, including cocktails, beer, and local wine, which you can enjoy while watching the sunset over the sea.

As evening approaches, Llaman Beach transforms into a more tranquil and romantic setting. While it is not as bustling as some of the larger beaches along the Riviera, its peaceful atmosphere makes it ideal for couples looking to enjoy a quiet evening by the water. There are often live music events or acoustic performances at some of the beach bars during the summer, adding to the laidback and pleasant ambiance.

If you're planning to stay overnight, Llaman Beach offers several accommodation options nearby, from guesthouses to small hotels. Most visitors prefer staying in Himara, where there is a broader range of accommodations, but there are also a few small properties closer to Llaman Beach. Prices for accommodation vary depending on the season, with budget rooms starting at €20 per night in the low season and going up to €80 to €100 during the peak summer months.

Llaman Beach is an excellent destination for those who seek relaxation in a natural setting without the overcrowded feel of more popular tourist spots. The combination of its clear waters, variety of activities, and peaceful surroundings make it a must visit location on the Albanian Riviera. Whether you're spending the day snorkeling, kayaking, or simply lounging on a sunbed, Llaman Beach offers something for everyone. Its relatively secluded nature adds to its charm, ensuring that visitors can enjoy a more private and tranquil beach experience while still being close enough to the amenities of nearby Himara.

For anyone visiting the Albanian Riviera, Llaman Beach is a hidden gem that should not be missed. Its beauty, combined with the range of activities available, guarantees a memorable experience for all types of travelers. Whether you're looking for adventure, relaxation, or a bit of both, Llaman Beach provides the perfect backdrop for a perfect day at the beach.

Porto Palermo Beach

Porto Palermo Beach, located along the Albanian Riviera, is one of the most captivating and serene spots you can visit. Nestled between the towns of Himara and Qeparo, Porto Palermo is famed for its turquoise waters and historical significance, making it an extraordinary blend of natural beauty and rich history. Unlike some of the more crowded beaches along the Riviera, Porto Palermo is relatively quieter, providing an ideal destination for those looking for relaxation in a secluded and picturesque setting.

Porto Palermo Beach is particularly famous for the Porto Palermo Castle, a nearby historical fortress believed to have been built by Ali Pasha of Tepelena in the 19th century. The beach and the castle are located in a bay that offers incredibly clear, calm waters, making it an excellent spot for swimming, snorkeling, and even some diving. The surrounding hills and greenery add to the charm of the beach, making it feel like a hidden paradise.

To get to Porto Palermo Beach, you can either drive or take a bus from nearby towns. The beach is situated about 7 kilometers south of Himara and approximately 52 kilometers from Saranda. If you're coming from Himara, the trip is a quick 10 to 15minute drive along the scenic SH8 coastal road, which offers stunning views of the Ionian Sea as you make your way to the beach. From Saranda, the drive takes just over an hour, and buses regularly operate between Saranda and Himara, stopping along the way, making it easy for those relying on public transportation. For travelers coming from Tirana, the trip by car takes about 5 hours, and it is also possible to take a bus to Himara and continue the journey from there. For visitors using public transport, taxis are available from Himara to Porto Palermo Beach and typically cost between 500 and 1000 Lek (€4 to €8) for the short trip.

One of the standout experiences at Porto Palermo Beach is visiting the nearby Porto Palermo Castle. The fortress is perched on a small peninsula that juts out into the sea, offering panoramic views of the surrounding coastline and mountains. Exploring the castle provides a glimpse into Albania's Ottoman history, and wandering through its ancient walls makes for a memorable cultural experience. The castle is open to the public, and admission is typically around 300 Lek (€2.50). Walking through the castle's stone corridors and looking out from its battlements gives you a sense of what life may have been like during the time of Ali Pasha, and the breathtaking views alone are worth the visit.

For beachgoers, Porto Palermo Beach offers some of the best swimming and snorkeling opportunities on the Riviera. The water is incredibly clear and calm, making it perfect for snorkeling and exploring the underwater world. Visitors can often see a variety of marine life, including fish and other sea creatures, making it a great spot for those who enjoy nature. You can rent snorkeling gear from local vendors for about 500 to 1000 Lek (€4 to €8). The gentle waves and warm waters also make it a safe beach for families with children, while the rocky outcrops and small coves provide plenty of areas to explore and relax away from the main beach.

Unlike many beaches along the Riviera that feature crowded sunbeds and bars, Porto Palermo Beach has a more rustic feel. There are no large beach bars or restaurants right on the beach, which enhances the sense of tranquility and seclusion. However, nearby in Qeparo and Himara, you will find a selection of tavernas and restaurants that serve fresh seafood and traditional Albanian dishes. Meals in these establishments range from 1000 to 3000 Lek (€8 to €24), making it a great place to enjoy a delicious meal after a day of sun and sea. If you prefer a more laidback meal, packing a picnic and enjoying it by the water is also a popular option for visitors.

Kayaking and paddleboarding are other popular activities at Porto Palermo Beach, and renting a kayak typically costs between 800 to 1500 Lek (€6.50 to €12) per hour. Kayaking around the peninsula allows visitors to get a different perspective of the castle and the surrounding coastline, and it's a fantastic way to explore the nearby coves and smaller beaches that are difficult to access by foot. For adventure lovers, kayaking also offers the opportunity to discover hidden gems along the coastline while taking in the incredible views of the Ionian Sea.

While there aren't many organized amenities on the beach itself, Porto Palermo's natural beauty and peaceful environment make it a fantastic place for unwinding. Many visitors bring their own beach chairs and umbrellas, or you can simply lay a towel on the pebbled beach and enjoy the sun. The beach is also popular for photographers, as the unique combination of historical architecture and stunning natural scenery provides endless opportunities for breathtaking shots.

One of the reasons why Porto Palermo Beach feels so special is its relative seclusion. It does not attract as many tourists as the more popular beaches along the Riviera, which means you can enjoy a more private and tranquil experience. This is particularly appealing for couples or solo travelers looking for a romantic or meditative day by the sea. Watching the sunset from the beach or the castle offers an unforgettable experience, as the setting sun reflects off the calm waters and bathes the entire bay in a warm, golden glow.

For visitors who want to extend their stay, the nearby town of Himara offers several accommodation options, ranging from budget guesthouses to midrange hotels. Prices for a room in Himara typically range from €20 to €80 per night, depending on the season and the type of accommodation. While there aren't many options right on Porto Palermo Beach itself, staying in Himara allows you to explore the surrounding area easily while still having access to restaurants and shops.

Porto Palermo Beach is an exceptional destination for those seeking a blend of history, nature, and tranquility along the Albanian Riviera. With its crystal-clear waters, fascinating castle, and peaceful atmosphere, it offers a unique experience for travelers who want to escape the crowds and enjoy the beauty of Albania's southern coast. Whether you're spending the day exploring the castle, swimming in the turquoise sea, or kayaking around the peninsula, Porto Palermo Beach is sure to provide lasting memories for any visitor.

Borsh Beach

Borsh Beach is one of the longest and most serene beaches on the Albanian Riviera, stretching for over seven kilometers along the Ionian Sea. Located in the southern part of Albania, between the towns of Himara and Saranda, Borsh Beach is known for its natural beauty, pristine waters, and quiet atmosphere, making it an ideal destination for those looking to escape the crowds and enjoy a relaxing day by the sea. The crystal-clear waters and unspoiled surroundings give this beach a unique charm, with olive groves stretching down to the water's edge, enhancing the beauty of the landscape.

The beach is located about 40 kilometers south of Himara and 25 kilometers north of Saranda. For visitors traveling from Tirana, the trip to Borsh Beach is approximately 240 kilometers and can take about four to five hours by car. Driving from Himara, the scenic SH8 coastal road provides a stunning journey, offering beautiful views of the Ionian Sea along the way. If you're coming from Saranda, the drive takes about 40 minutes. Public buses regularly travel between Saranda and Himara, and you can stop at Borsh along the way. For those relying on public transportation, it is advisable to get off the bus at the main road and walk down towards the beach, as Borsh Beach is a short distance from the main coastal highway. Taxi services are also available from Saranda or Himara, with costs generally ranging from 1000 to 2000 Lek (€8 to €16), depending on your starting point.

One of the most appealing aspects of Borsh Beach is its tranquil atmosphere. Unlike the more commercialized beaches in the area, Borsh remains largely undeveloped, which adds to its allure for travelers seeking peace and quiet. The long stretch of pebbly beach means there is plenty of space for everyone, even during the busier summer months. It's easy to find a secluded spot to lay down your towel and enjoy the sounds of the sea without feeling crowded by other beachgoers. The beach itself is primarily made up of pebbles, but the water is incredibly clear and perfect for swimming. The gentle slope of the shoreline into the sea makes it a safe and enjoyable beach for families with children, as well as for those who prefer calm waters.

For those looking for a more active experience, there are a number of activities to enjoy at Borsh Beach. Snorkeling is a popular choice due to the clear waters, where you can observe a variety of fish and marine life. The calm sea also makes it an ideal location for paddleboarding and kayaking. Rentals for snorkeling gear, paddleboards, and kayaks can typically be found at nearby beachside stalls, with prices ranging from 500 to 1500 Lek (€4 to €12) depending on the equipment and duration. Kayaking along the coast offers a peaceful way to explore the rocky coves and hidden corners of the beach that are less accessible by foot.

Borsh Beach also offers opportunities to explore its surroundings, especially the Borsh Castle (also known as Sopot Castle), which is located on a hill overlooking the beach. A visit to the castle provides a glimpse into the area's rich history and offers stunning panoramic views of the beach and the surrounding countryside. The ruins of the castle, which date back to ancient times, are a short drive or a moderate hike from the beach. There is no official entrance fee to visit Borsh Castle, and the site remains relatively undiscovered by tourists, which adds to its charm as a peaceful and historical spot.

Alongside the beach, visitors will find several small tavernas and beach bars that serve delicious traditional Albanian cuisine, particularly fresh seafood. Many of these eateries are family owned and offer a cozy atmosphere, where you can enjoy a meal with a view of the sea. Popular dishes include grilled fish, shrimp, calamari, and Borsh's renowned olive oil, which is produced locally from the surrounding olive groves. Prices for a meal typically range from 1000 to 3000 Lek (€8 to €24), making it affordable for most travelers. These restaurants also serve traditional Albanian dishes such as byrek, fërgesë, and qofte, giving visitors a taste of local cuisine.

For those planning to spend an extended period of time at Borsh Beach, there are several accommodation options available. You can find a mix of hotels, guesthouses, and apartments close to the beach, with prices varying depending on the season. In the summer months, it's recommended to book accommodation in advance, as the beach attracts more visitors. Rooms generally range from €25 to €80 per night, with more luxurious options offering sea views and direct beach access. For budget travelers, camping is also a popular choice, with some areas near the beach allowing for tents or campers.

One of the best times to visit Borsh Beach is during the shoulder seasons of late spring and early autumn. The weather is still warm, but the beach is less crowded, allowing you to enjoy the natural beauty of the area in relative solitude. The surrounding hills, covered in olive trees, make for pleasant walks and hikes, and the sunsets over the Ionian Sea are particularly breathtaking during these times of the year. The combination of warm temperatures, crystal-clear water, and fewer crowds makes Borsh Beach a hidden gem for those seeking a more peaceful experience.

If you're looking for a more immersive experience, Borsh Beach is also an excellent place to interact with the local community. The village of Borsh, located nearby, is known for its olive oil production, and many families in the area have been producing olive oil for generations. Some local producers offer tours of their olive groves and olive oil tastings, providing a unique insight into the traditional way of life in this part of Albania. These tours typically cost around 1000 to 1500 Lek (€8 to €12) and are a wonderful way to learn more about the region's culture and history while enjoying the beauty of the landscape.

Borsh Beach is a must visit destination for travelers seeking a peaceful retreat on the Albanian Riviera. Whether you're interested in swimming in the clear waters, exploring the historic Borsh Castle, enjoying delicious local seafood, or simply relaxing on the pebbled beach, Borsh offers something for everyone. Its unspoiled beauty, coupled with its rich cultural and historical significance, makes it a memorable stop on any trip to Albania. Whether you're staying for a few hours or a few days, Borsh Beach promises a truly unforgettable experience.

Qeparo Beach

Qeparo Beach is one of the hidden gems along the Albanian Riviera, offering an idyllic and quiet atmosphere perfect for those seeking relaxation, nature, and a glimpse into traditional Albanian coastal life. Located about 50 kilometers south of the town of Himara and 13 kilometers from the popular Borsh

Beach, Qeparo is split into two parts: the Old Village (Upper Qeparo), situated on the hillside, and the Lower Qeparo, which stretches along the coastline with its peaceful beach. This combination of historical charm and coastal beauty makes Qeparo Beach an essential stop for those visiting the Riviera.

Getting to Qeparo Beach is fairly straightforward if you're traveling by car. From Tirana, the capital city, it's a long but scenic drive of around 220 kilometers, which can take about four to five hours via the SH8 coastal road. This road provides incredible views of the Ionian Sea, passing through other notable coastal towns like Vlora, Dhermi, and Himara before reaching Qeparo. For those already staying in Himara, the drive takes about 30 minutes south along the SH8, a well-maintained highway with winding roads and stunning vistas. If you're relying on public transportation, regular buses run between major cities and coastal villages, including routes from Saranda and Himara, which pass through Qeparo. The bus fare is quite affordable, usually costing between 300 and 500 Lek (€2 to €4) depending on where you're coming from.

Upon arriving in Qeparo, visitors will first be struck by the tranquility of the area. Unlike more bustling beaches on the Riviera, Qeparo Beach retains a calm and unspoiled ambiance, with fewer crowds and less commercial development. The beach itself is a mix of fine pebbles and sand, and the waters are famously clear and calm, making it an excellent spot for swimming and sunbathing. The shallow entry into the sea is perfect for families with children, while the clarity of the water makes it a popular location for snorkeling. Many visitors bring their own snorkeling gear to explore the underwater world along the shoreline, where small fish and other marine life can be observed.

Qeparo is an excellent destination for those who enjoy a balance of both relaxation and light activity. Apart from sunbathing and swimming, the old village of Qeparo, perched on the hill above, is well worth a visit. A short hike or drive up to Upper Qeparo allows you to explore its charming stone houses, narrow cobblestone streets, and panoramic views of the coastline. This part of the village has retained much of its traditional character, with olive groves and terraced gardens surrounding the area. Visitors interested in history and local culture will appreciate wandering through this timeless village, where traces of centuries old architecture and the slow pace of life still linger. The view from the upper village provides an excellent photo opportunity of the entire coastline, including the beach and the surrounding hills.

For those who want to venture out on the water, kayak rentals are available during the summer months, giving you the chance to explore the coastline from a different perspective. Kayaking is a peaceful and scenic activity, with opportunities to paddle along the shore, discover hidden coves, or even make your way down to Borsh Beach if you're up for a longer ride. Kayak rentals typically range from 800 to 1500 Lek (€6 to €12) per hour. The calm waters and pleasant weather during the summer make kayaking a highly enjoyable experience in Qeparo.

One of the main attractions near Qeparo Beach is the impressive Porto Palermo Castle, located just a short drive away. This well-preserved fortress, originally built by Ali Pasha Tepelena in the early 19th century, sits on a small peninsula jutting into the sea, surrounded by crystal-clear waters. The castle offers visitors a chance to explore Albania's history, as well as spectacular views of the sea and coastline from its walls. Entry to Porto Palermo Castle is generally inexpensive, with a typical entrance fee of around 200 Lek (€1.50), and the visit provides a perfect combination of culture, history, and scenic beauty.

Qeparo Beach also offers several traditional Albanian tavernas where you can enjoy fresh seafood and local specialties. These family run restaurants provide an authentic dining experience, serving dishes like grilled fish, calamari, octopus, and shrimp, often paired with freshly prepared salads and Albanian olive oil. Meals are relatively inexpensive, with an average cost of 1000 to 2000 Lek (€8 to €16) per person. For those who prefer something lighter, many beach bars offer snacks, cold drinks, and local wine, allowing you to enjoy your meal right by the water.

As for accommodation, Qeparo has a variety of options ranging from guesthouses and small hotels to rental apartments, most of which are located within walking distance of the beach. Prices for accommodation vary depending on the season and the type of lodging, but you can generally expect to pay between €30 and €70 per night for a room or apartment during the high season. Many of the guesthouses are run by local families who provide a welcoming and personal touch to their hospitality, making it feel like a home away from home.

For nature lovers, Qeparo is also surrounded by scenic hiking trails that lead through olive groves and rolling hills. One popular trail takes you through the ancient olive trees that surround the village, some of which are over 1000 years old. These peaceful walks offer a glimpse into the rural life of Albania and provide a great way to immerse yourself in the natural beauty of the region. Hiking to the upper part of Qeparo Village offers an added bonus: the chance to visit ancient churches and ruins scattered around the hillside, providing a unique blend of nature and history.

The best time to visit Qeparo Beach is from May to October, when the weather is warm and the sea is perfect for swimming. During the peak summer months, the beach sees a little more activity, but it never becomes overly crowded, preserving its quiet and relaxed atmosphere. The shoulder seasons of May, June, and September are especially appealing for those who want to avoid the summer crowds but still enjoy the pleasant weather and warm sea temperatures.

Qeparo Beach is a must-see destination for travelers looking to experience the natural beauty and traditional charm of the Albanian Riviera. Whether you're interested in swimming in the clear waters, exploring the historical upper village, kayaking along the coast, or simply relaxing in a peaceful setting, Qeparo Beach offers a memorable experience. With its stunning landscapes, rich history, and welcoming atmosphere,

Qeparo is the perfect spot for those seeking a tranquil and authentic escape on the Ionian coast. Whether you spend a day or a week here, Qeparo will leave you with lasting memories of Albania's unspoiled beauty.

Livadhi Beach

Livadhi Beach, located on the Albanian Riviera, is one of the most beautiful and tranquil beaches in the region. Situated just a few kilometers from the town of Himara, Livadhi Beach is well-known for its long stretch of white pebbles, crystal-clear waters, and scenic backdrop of olive trees and rolling hills. The beach is around 1.5 kilometers long, making it one of the largest in the area, and its natural beauty makes it a must visit destination for those exploring the Riviera.

To get to Livadhi Beach, there are several options depending on where you're starting your journey. If you're traveling from Tirana, the capital of Albania, the drive is around 220 kilometers and can take approximately four to five hours along the scenic coastal SH8 road. This drive offers breathtaking views of the Ionian Sea and passes through various coastal towns like Vlora, Dhermi, and Himara, each with their own unique charm. Once you reach Himara, Livadhi Beach is just a short drive north, taking around 10 minutes by car. For travelers relying on public transport, buses frequently run from major cities like Tirana, Vlora, and Saranda to Himara. From there, you can take a taxi or even walk to Livadhi Beach, depending on your accommodation. The walk from Himara to

Livadhi is about 30 to 40 minutes and is a great way to take in the beautiful coastal scenery.

Livadhi Beach offers plenty to do for visitors of all ages and interests. For beach lovers, the crystal-clear waters of the Ionian Sea are perfect for swimming, snorkeling, and sunbathing. The water is generally calm, and the beach's long stretch provides plenty of space to relax without feeling crowded, even during peak tourist seasons. For those interested in water sports, Livadhi Beach has various options. You can rent kayaks and paddle along the coastline, exploring hidden coves and rock formations. Prices for kayak rentals usually range from 800 to 1500 Lek (€6 to €12) per hour. Jet skiing is another popular activity, with rentals available for around 3000 Lek (€25) for 30 minutes. These water sports provide an exciting way to experience the beauty of the beach and its surrounding areas.

One of the unique features of Livadhi Beach is its natural setting. The beach is backed by olive groves and hills, giving it a serene and picturesque atmosphere. For those who enjoy nature walks, there are several hiking trails in the area that lead through the olive groves and up into the hills, offering stunning views of the beach and the Ionian Sea. These hikes are relatively easy and are perfect for those who want to take a break from the beach and explore the natural surroundings. The nearby village of Himara is also worth a visit. You can explore the old town, with its narrow streets and historic architecture, or visit the Himara Castle, which offers panoramic views of the coastline.

Livadhi Beach is also known for its excellent selection of beachfront bars and tavernas, where you can enjoy traditional Albanian cuisine and fresh seafood. Many of these establishments are family run and offer a warm, welcoming atmosphere. You can enjoy dishes like grilled fish, shrimp, and octopus, paired with local salads and olive oil made from the surrounding groves. Prices at these tavernas are reasonable, with an average meal costing around 1000 to 2000 Lek (€8 to €16) per person. Beach bars also offer light snacks, cocktails, and cold drinks, allowing you to relax and enjoy the view of the sea while dining.

If you're planning to stay overnight near Livadhi Beach, there are several accommodation options available. You'll find a range of choices, from budget friendly guesthouses to more upscale hotels and apartments. Many of these accommodations are located just a short walk from the beach, offering stunning sea views and easy access to the water. Prices vary depending on the season and the type of accommodation, but you can generally expect to pay between €30 and €80 per night during the summer months. Staying near Livadhi Beach gives you the opportunity to enjoy the quiet, peaceful atmosphere of the area while still being close to the amenities of Himara.

One of the highlights of visiting Livadhi Beach is the opportunity to explore the nearby attractions along the Albanian Riviera. Porto Palermo Castle, located just a short drive south of the beach, is a must-see for history enthusiasts.

This well-preserved fortress, built by Ali Pasha Tepelena, offers incredible views of the sea and coastline, and its strategic position on a small peninsula makes it a striking landmark. Entry to the castle is inexpensive, with tickets typically costing around 200 Lek (€1.50). Exploring the castle provides a fascinating insight into Albania's history while also offering some of the best photo opportunities on the coast.

For those looking for a more active experience, Livadhi Beach is a great base for exploring the surrounding area by boat. Several local operators offer boat tours along the coast, taking you to hidden beaches and sea caves that are only accessible by water. These boat tours typically last a few hours and cost around 3000 to 5000 Lek (€25 to €40) per person. The tours often include stops at isolated beaches where you can swim and snorkel in pristine, uncrowded waters. This is a great way to see more of the Albanian coastline and enjoy a relaxing day on the water.

The best time to visit Livadhi Beach is between May and September, when the weather is warm and sunny, and the sea is perfect for swimming. July and August are the peak tourist months, but even then, Livadhi Beach tends to be less crowded than other beaches on the Riviera. For those looking to avoid the summer crowds, visiting in May, June, or September offers the same beautiful weather with fewer people. The beach remains quiet and peaceful, allowing you to fully appreciate its natural beauty.

Livadhi Beach is ideal for families, couples, and solo travelers looking for a serene and scenic beach experience. Its calm waters and spacious shoreline make it a great place for children to play, while the surrounding nature provides plenty of opportunities for exploration. For couples and solo travelers, Livadhi offers a perfect escape from the more crowded tourist spots along the Riviera, giving you the chance to unwind in a beautiful and peaceful setting.

Livadhi Beach is a must visit destination on the Albanian Riviera. Whether you're interested in swimming, snorkeling, water sports, or simply relaxing by the sea, Livadhi has something for everyone. Its natural beauty, combined with its excellent local cuisine and proximity to nearby attractions, makes it an unforgettable part of any trip to Albania. The beach's tranquil atmosphere, along with the friendly hospitality of the locals, ensures that your time at Livadhi Beach will be a memorable and enriching experience.

Palasë Beach

Palasë Beach is one of the most captivating and scenic spots along the Albanian Riviera, known for its turquoise waters, white pebbles, and serene atmosphere. Located between the Llogara Pass and the small village of Palasë, this beach offers a perfect blend of natural beauty and tranquility, making it a must-see destination for travelers seeking an authentic experience on the Albanian coastline.

Palasë Beach is situated about 35 kilometers south of the city of Vlorë and just a few kilometers from the popular tourist destination of Dhërmi. Its remote location adds to its charm, as it remains relatively untouched by mass tourism, even during the high season. To get to Palasë Beach, travelers have a few options depending on their starting point. If you're coming from Tirana, the drive will take approximately 3 to 4 hours, covering a distance of about 220 kilometers. The most scenic route to take is via the SH8 coastal road, which offers breathtaking views of the Ionian Sea as you pass through the Llogara Pass, one of the most dramatic and beautiful mountain roads in Albania.

For those who do not have their own vehicle, there are buses that run from Tirana and Vlorë to Dhërmi, where you can easily catch a local taxi or even walk the short distance to Palasë. The walk from Dhërmi to Palasë is about 40 minutes to an hour along a relatively easy path that winds through the hillside and offers magnificent views of the sea. Alternatively, there are boat services available from Vlorë or Himara during the summer months that can take you directly to Palasë Beach, offering a scenic and relaxing journey along the coast.

Once you arrive at Palasë Beach, there are several things you can do to make the most of your visit. The crystal-clear waters are perfect for swimming and snorkeling. Because of its remote location, Palasë is often much quieter than other beaches on the Riviera, providing an ideal environment for those who want to relax and enjoy the peaceful surroundings. The water is shallow near the shore, making it suitable for families with children as well. The beach's white pebbles, which gradually turn into soft sand closer to the water, create a unique and picturesque landscape that makes for excellent photography.

If you're seeking more adventurous activities, Palasë Beach offers various water sports, including kayaking, jet skiing, and standup paddleboarding. Kayak rentals are available for around 1000 to 1500 Lek (€8 to €12) per hour, allowing you to explore the coastline at your own pace. Jet ski rentals, which are available during the summer months, cost approximately 3000 Lek (€25) for a 30minute session. These activities provide an exhilarating way to enjoy the beach and its surroundings, especially for those who want to combine relaxation with a bit of excitement.

For visitors who enjoy hiking, Palasë Beach is a great base from which to explore the surrounding hills and mountains. There are several hiking trails that lead from the beach up into the hills, offering panoramic views of the Ionian Sea and the Albanian Riviera. One of the most popular hikes is to the Llogara Pass, which provides stunning views over the coastline and the open sea. The trails are well-marked , and the hikes range from easy to moderately challenging, making them suitable for most visitors. This combination of beach and mountain makes Palasë a unique destination for those who love both the sea and the outdoors.

When it comes to dining, Palasë Beach has a few beach bars and restaurants where you can enjoy traditional Albanian cuisine, fresh seafood, and cold drinks while taking in the sea view. Many of the restaurants are family run and offer a warm, welcoming atmosphere. You can try dishes like grilled fish, calamari, and local specialties like byrek, a savory pastry filled with spinach, cheese, or meat. Prices for meals at the beachside restaurants are reasonable, with most meals costing between 1000 and 2000 Lek (€8 to €16) per person. For those who prefer a more casual dining experience, some beach bars offer light snacks, cocktails, and cold beers, making them ideal spots to relax and enjoy the sunset after a day of swimming and exploring.

In terms of accommodation, Palasë Beach has a few options, including small guesthouses and beachfront villas. Many visitors choose to stay in the nearby village of Dhërmi, which offers a wider range of accommodations, from budget friendly guesthouses to more luxurious hotels. The village is only a short drive or walk from Palasë Beach, making it a convenient base for exploring the area. Prices for accommodations in Dhërmi and Palasë vary depending on the season and the type of lodging, but during the summer months, you can expect to pay between €40 and €100 per night.

One of the highlights of visiting Palasë Beach is the opportunity to explore the surrounding area. The nearby Llogara National Park is a must-see for nature lovers, offering hiking trails, wildlife viewing, and breathtaking views of the Albanian Riviera from the top of the Llogara Pass. The park is home to various species of birds and animals, and it's cool, fresh air provides a pleasant contrast to the hot summer temperatures on the coast. Llogara National Park is also known for its paragliding opportunities, with flights launching from the pass and landing near Palasë Beach. Paragliding is a thrilling way to see the Albanian coastline from a new perspective, and prices for a tandem flight start at around 8000 Lek (€65).

Another nearby attraction is the town of Himara, located just a short drive south of Palasë. Himara is a charming coastal town with a rich history and a picturesque old town. You can visit the Himara Castle, explore the narrow streets lined with traditional stone houses, or relax at one of the many beaches surrounding the town. Himara also has several excellent restaurants and bars, making it a great place to spend an afternoon or evening after visiting Palasë Beach.

The best time to visit Palasë Beach is during the summer months, from May to September, when the weather is warm, and the sea is perfect for swimming. July and August are the busiest months, but even then, Palasë remains relatively quiet compared to other beaches on the Riviera. If you prefer to avoid the crowds, visiting in May, June, or September is ideal, as the weather is still warm, and the beach is even more peaceful.

Palasë Beach is a hidden gem along the Albanian Riviera that offers a perfect blend of natural beauty, tranquility, and adventure. Whether you're looking to relax on the beach, swim in the crystal-clear waters, or explore the surrounding hills and mountains, Palasë has something for everyone. Its remote location and unspoiled beauty make it a must-see destination for those seeking an authentic Albanian beach experience, and its proximity to other attractions like Llogara National Park and Himara adds to its appeal. Whether you're visiting for a day or staying for a longer vacation, Palasë Beach is sure to leave a lasting impression.

Bunec Beach

Bunec Beach is one of the more secluded and peaceful gems located along the stunning Albanian Riviera. Situated between the towns of Saranda and Himara, Bunec Beach offers visitors a unique experience away from the hustle and bustle of the more crowded coastal spots. It stands out for its tranquility, crystal-clear waters, and pebble shoreline, making it an ideal destination for those looking to unwind in a quiet, unspoiled natural setting.

The beach is located approximately 25 kilometers north of Saranda and around 15 kilometers south of Himara, giving it an isolated yet accessible feel. If you're traveling from Tirana, the drive to Bunec Beach will take around 4 to 5 hours, covering a distance of roughly 250 kilometers. The most common route to get there is by car, taking the coastal SH8 road, which runs along the length of the Riviera and offers scenic views of the Ionian Sea. Public transport options such as buses and minibuses that run between Saranda and Himara are available, though renting a car is the most convenient and flexible option. For those arriving in Saranda by ferry or other means, it is easy to find transportation services that can bring you directly to the beach.

Bunec Beach is unique in its relative isolation, allowing visitors to experience the more pristine side of the Albanian coastline. The beach is split by the Bunec River, which flows into the Ionian Sea, creating a serene and picturesque setting. The fresh water from the river meets the salty sea, providing an interesting contrast in temperature for swimmers. Visitors can relax on the pebble beach, swim in the calm, blue waters, or even explore the river and its surroundings. The pebbles give the beach its distinctive look and also keep the waters exceptionally clear, making it perfect for snorkeling. For those who enjoy beachcombing, the shore is often scattered with small, smooth stones, which can be a relaxing activity in itself.

Unlike many of the more developed beaches along the Riviera, Bunec Beach has retained its natural beauty, largely free from largescale tourist infrastructure. This means that it is less crowded even during the peak summer months. Visitors looking for a quiet spot to enjoy the sun, swim, and take in the breathtaking views of the surrounding hills will find Bunec Beach to be a perfect fit.

Despite its remote feel, there are a few small restaurants and beach bars in the area, mostly family run, offering traditional Albanian cuisine, seafood, and refreshments. The prices are generally quite reasonable, with a full meal costing between 800 and 1500 Lek (€6 to €12). These establishments provide the basic amenities needed for a day at the beach without compromising the natural serenity of the area. Many visitors enjoy having lunch or dinner right by the water, with the sound of the waves providing a relaxing backdrop.

For those who prefer to stay active, Bunec Beach offers several opportunities for exploration. The nearby hills are perfect for short hikes, giving you stunning views of the beach and the Ionian Sea. The river that flows into the sea also offers an interesting area to explore, with its cool, fresh water providing a refreshing contrast to the warm sea. While there are no formal hiking trails, visitors are free to wander along the riverbank or through the hills, making it an ideal spot for those who enjoy off-the-beaten-path adventures.

Swimming in the calm waters of Bunec Beach is one of the best activities to do while there. The beach's gentle slope into the sea makes it suitable for families with children, and the clear waters are inviting for anyone looking for a relaxing swim. The peaceful atmosphere makes it easy to spend hours just floating in the water, soaking in the beauty of the surroundings. Snorkeling is another popular activity here, thanks to the excellent visibility provided by the clear waters. While Bunec doesn't have any dedicated snorkeling or diving centers, you can bring your own gear to explore the underwater world along the shore.

For visitors looking to extend their stay, there are several accommodation options nearby. Small guesthouses and family run hotels can be found in the nearby villages, providing a comfortable and authentic Albanian experience. Prices for accommodation are quite affordable, with most guesthouses charging between €25 and €50 per night, depending on the season. Staying in the nearby towns of Lukova or Himara is also a good option for those looking for more amenities and a greater variety of accommodation choices.

If you're planning to visit Bunec Beach, it's important to come prepared. Since it is a relatively undeveloped area, there are fewer conveniences such as beach chairs or umbrellas available for rent, so bringing your own beach gear is recommended. However, this lack of development is part of the beach's charm, as it allows visitors to enjoy the natural environment without the distractions of a busy, commercialized beach. The quiet, laidback atmosphere makes it a great place to spend a whole day, whether you're relaxing by the sea, enjoying a meal at a local restaurant, or exploring the surrounding area.

For those traveling to Bunec Beach during the summer months, the best time to visit is between June and September, when the weather is warm, and the sea is at its most inviting. Even during the peak season, Bunec remains relatively quiet compared to the more popular beaches along the Riviera, making it an excellent choice for those who want to escape the crowds and enjoy a more peaceful beach experience. If you prefer cooler temperatures and fewer visitors, visiting in May or late September is also a good option, as the weather is still pleasant, but the beach will be even more tranquil.

Bunec Beach is a hidden treasure along the Albanian Riviera that offers a serene and relaxing escape from the more crowded and developed beaches nearby. Its natural beauty, combined with its quiet atmosphere and clear waters, make it an ideal destination for those seeking a peaceful retreat. Whether you're swimming in the sea, exploring the river, or enjoying a meal at a beachside restaurant, Bunec Beach provides a unique and memorable experience for anyone who visits. Its location off the beaten path adds to its allure, and for travelers looking to discover a more authentic and unspoiled side of Albania, Bunec Beach is a must-see destination.

Coastal Villages to Visit

The Albanian Riviera is a stunning stretch of coastline along the Ionian Sea, known for its breathtaking beaches, crystal-clear waters, and peaceful atmosphere. While many travelers are drawn to the Riviera for its natural beauty and sunsoaked shores, the small coastal villages that dot this region are equally enchanting. These villages offer a glimpse into the authentic, traditional life of Albania, combining historical charm with a relaxed pace of life that makes them ideal destinations for visitors looking to experience both culture and serenity. Each village has its own unique character, and exploring them provides a deeper Knowing of the region's history, culture, and landscape.

One of the most pretty and culturally rich villages along the Albanian Riviera is Himara, a town that offers a combination of stunning beaches and historical landmarks. Himara is located roughly midway along the Riviera and is famous for its crystal-clear waters, traditional stone houses, and tranquil atmosphere. While the town has become a popular destination for tourists in recent years, it still retains a sense of authenticity that makes it special. The village's charm lies in its blend of old and new, where you can wander through narrow, cobblestone streets, explore ancient churches, and then relax on pristine beaches just a short walk away.

Himara is known for its proximity to some of the Riviera's best beaches, such as Livadhi Beach, which is famous for its wide stretch of sand and calm waters. This beach is ideal for families and anyone looking to spend a relaxing day by the sea, enjoying the warm sun and gentle waves. Himara is also home to Porto Palermo Bay, a beautiful and secluded spot known for its turquoise waters and the Ali Pasha Castle. This historic fortress, perched on a small peninsula, adds a sense of history and intrigue to the natural beauty of the surrounding bay. Visitors can explore the castle and take in panoramic views of the coastline, making Porto Palermo a perfect mix of cultural exploration and seaside relaxation.

The village of Himara itself offers visitors a chance to experience traditional Albanian life. The town's old quarter, known as Old Himara, is located on a hill above the beach and is home to ancient churches, old stone houses, and narrow streets that feel like stepping back in time. The people of Himara are known for their warm hospitality, and many visitors enjoy staying in small guesthouses or family run hotels that offer a more personal and authentic experience. In the evenings, you can dine at local taverns that serve delicious Albanian food, often prepared with fresh seafood and local ingredients, while enjoying views of the sea and mountains.

Further south along the Albanian Riviera is the charming village of Dhërmi, another hidden gem that combines beautiful beaches with a peaceful, laidback atmosphere. Dhërmi is known for its long, pebbly beach and clear blue waters, making it a popular spot for both relaxation and water activities. The beach itself is large enough to provide plenty of space for sunbathing, swimming, and enjoying the sea, even during the busier summer months. While Dhërmi has become increasingly popular with tourists, it has managed to maintain a sense of tranquility and authenticity that makes it stand out from more crowded beach resorts.

One of the highlights of visiting Dhërmi is the opportunity to explore the village itself, which is perched on a hillside above the beach. The village is known for its traditional stone houses and winding streets that offer stunning views of the sea below. As you wander through the village, you'll come across small churches, local cafes, and family-owned guesthouses, all of which contribute to Dhërmi's charm. Many of the houses in Dhërmi date back centuries, and the village's architecture reflects its long history as a center of Albanian culture. Dhërmi is also a great place to enjoy traditional Albanian cuisine, with several restaurants offering fresh seafood, grilled meats, and other local dishes made with ingredients sourced from nearby farms and the sea.

One of the most appealing aspects of Dhërmi is its natural beauty, which extends beyond the beach. The surrounding hills and mountains provide plenty of opportunities for hiking and exploring the countryside. There are several trails that lead from the village into the hills, offering spectacular views of the coast and the Ionian Sea. For those who enjoy outdoor activities, Dhërmi is the perfect base for combining beach time with hiking and nature walks.

Continuing along the coast, you'll find the village of Jale, a smaller and more secluded spot that is perfect for travelers looking to escape the crowds and enjoy a quiet, peaceful beach experience. Jale is a small bay with calm, shallow waters, making it ideal for swimming and relaxing by the sea. The beach is surrounded by green hills, which add to the sense of seclusion and natural beauty. Unlike some of the larger villages along the Riviera, Jale has remained relatively untouched by mass tourism, and its simplicity is part of its charm.

While Jale offers fewer amenities than larger beach towns, it has a few beach bars and cafes where visitors can enjoy a meal or a drink while taking in the view. Many travelers who visit Jale come for the peace and quiet, as the beach is less crowded than others along the coast. For those who enjoy camping, Jale is also a popular spot for pitching a tent and spending the night under the stars. There are several campsites near the beach, making it a great destination for those looking to connect with nature and enjoy a more rustic experience.

Further north along the Riviera, you'll find the village of Vuno, another traditional Albanian village that is known for its historic charm and beautiful surroundings. Vuno is located on a hillside overlooking the sea, and its location provides visitors with stunning views of the coastline. The village itself is small and quiet, with narrow streets, old stone houses, and a peaceful atmosphere that makes it a perfect place to unwind. Vuno is an excellent destination for those looking to experience traditional Albanian life, as the village has remained largely unchanged over the years. Many of the houses in Vuno have been passed down through generations, and the village's slow pace of life offers a stark contrast to the busier coastal towns.

Vuno is also a great base for exploring some of the nearby beaches, such as Gjipe Beach, which is one of the most remote and beautiful beaches on the Albanian Riviera. Gjipe Beach is located at the end of a canyon, and the only way to reach it is by hiking from Vuno or by boat. The hike to Gjipe Beach is relatively easy and offers stunning views of the canyon and the sea. Once you arrive, you'll be rewarded with a secluded beach with crystal-clear waters and a sense of tranquility that is hard to find elsewhere. Gjipe Beach is perfect for those who want to enjoy the natural beauty of the Riviera without the crowds, and its remote location makes it feel like a hidden paradise.

One of the most distinctive features of the Albanian Riviera is the way its villages have managed to preserve their traditional character while offering modern amenities for visitors. Whether you're staying in a family run guesthouse in Himara, camping on the beach in Jale, or hiking to a remote beach from Vuno, the villages along the Riviera offer a perfect blend of culture, history, and natural beauty. Each village has its own unique charm, and exploring them allows you to experience the diversity and richness of Albanian life.

The coastal villages of the Albanian Riviera are much more than just places to visit for their beaches. They offer a deeper connection to the culture and history of Albania, providing visitors with an authentic and memorable experience. From the historic streets of Himara to the tranquil beaches of Jale and the remote beauty of Gjipe, the villages along the Riviera are as diverse as they are beautiful. Whether you're looking for relaxation, adventure, or a glimpse into traditional Albanian life, the coastal villages of the Albanian Riviera offer something for every traveler, making them an essential part of any visit to this stunning region.

The Llogara Pass: A Scenic Mountain Road

The Llogara Pass is one of the most iconic and breathtaking roads in Albania, offering a scenic drive that takes travelers from the lowlands of the coast to the heights of the mountains, providing panoramic views of the Albanian Riviera. This winding mountain pass is not only a key route connecting the coastal towns of Vlorë and Dhërmi, but it is also a destination in itself due to its dramatic landscape, stunning vistas, and the sense of adventure it evokes. For many, driving along the Llogara Pass is one of the highlights of any trip to the Albanian

Riviera, as it combines the beauty of Albania's rugged terrain with the serenity of the Ionian Sea below.

The Llogara Pass reaches an elevation of over 1,000 meters (around 3,300 feet) above sea level, making it one of the highest coastal passes in the Balkans. As you ascend the road, the scenery shifts from the Mediterranean olive groves and beaches to steep cliffs, pine forests, and alpinelike landscapes. This dramatic change in elevation offers travelers a unique opportunity to experience several different ecosystems in a relatively short distance, making the journey as exciting as the destination itself. The road, which stretches for around 20 kilometers, is paved and in good condition, but it is also steep and filled with hairpin turns, making it both thrilling and challenging for drivers. Despite the curves and the elevation, the road is welltraveled, and the effort to navigate it is more than rewarded by the views that unfold with every turn.

One of the most impressive aspects of the Llogara Pass is the sense of grandeur it provides as it rises from sea level and winds its way up into the mountains. As you climb higher, the road offers stunning views of the Ionian Sea, with its deep blue waters stretching out into the distance. On clear days, you can even see the outlines of the nearby Greek island of Corfu across the sea. This vantage point gives travelers a sense of scale and majesty, as the road clings to the mountainside, offering glimpses of tiny villages and secluded beaches far below. The steep cliffs that rise above the road, coupled with the sheer drop to the sea on the other side, create a dramatic and awe-inspiring landscape that is unmatched along the Albanian coast.

The pass is part of the Llogara National Park, a protected area that covers more than 1,000 hectares of forested mountains and alpine meadows. The park is home to a rich variety of wildlife, including deer, foxes, and various species of birds, as well as rare and endemic plants that thrive in the cooler mountain air. The dense pine and oak forests that blanket the slopes of the Llogara Pass create a sharp contrast with the drier, more arid landscape of the coast below, offering a refreshing change in scenery for those traveling along the road. The cool, fresh air of the mountains provides a welcome respite from the heat of the coast, especially during the summer months when temperatures along the Albanian Riviera can soar.

At the highest point of the pass, known as the Llogara Summit, there is a viewpoint where travelers can stop to take in the full expanse of the landscape. The summit offers some of the most spectacular views in all of Albania, with the road stretching out behind you, the Ionian Sea glittering far below, and the rugged peaks of the Ceraunian Mountains rising to the north. This is a popular spot for both tourists and locals to stop, take photos, and simply marvel at the natural beauty of the area. On a clear day, the views from the summit are truly unforgettable, providing a perfect opportunity to appreciate the grandeur of the Albanian coastline and the mountains that tower above it.

One of the unique features of the Llogara Pass is that it serves as a natural boundary between two distinct regions of the

Albanian Riviera. To the north of the pass lies the region around Vlorë, characterized by its more developed coastline, with larger towns, busier beaches, and a more cosmopolitan atmosphere. As you cross over the pass and descend to the south, the landscape becomes more rugged and remote, with smaller, less developed villages and a quieter, more laidback vibe. The southern stretch of the Albanian Riviera, with its hidden beaches, crystal-clear waters, and charming coastal towns like Dhërmi, Jale, and Himara, feels like a different world compared to the busier northern coast, and the Llogara Pass is the gateway to this more tranquil part of the country.

For those who enjoy outdoor activities, the Llogara Pass and the surrounding national park offer numerous opportunities for hiking, birdwatching, and even paragliding. Several well-marked trails lead from the pass into the surrounding mountains, providing hikers with the chance to explore the forested slopes, alpine meadows, and high peaks that make up this stunning landscape. One of the most popular hikes in the area is the trail to Cesar's Pass, a historical route that dates back to ancient times. This trail offers both natural beauty and historical significance, as it was once used by Julius Caesar during his campaign in the Balkans.

The Llogara Pass is also famous for its local cuisine, with several roadside restaurants and guesthouses offering traditional Albanian dishes made from fresh, locally sourced ingredients. Many of these restaurants specialize in grilled meats, such as lamb and goat, as well as locally caught seafood. The cool mountain air and the spectacular views make dining at one of these establishments a memorable experience. Sitting on a terrace overlooking the Ionian Sea while enjoying a meal of freshly prepared Albanian food is one of the highlights of any trip along the Llogara Pass. The restaurants here are known for their hospitality, and many offers cozy accommodations for travelers who wish to stay overnight in the mountains.

For those looking for a more extended stay, there are several hotels and lodges located near the pass, offering comfortable accommodations in a serene mountain setting. Staying overnight in this area allows visitors to fully immerse themselves in the beauty and tranquility of the Llogara National Park, with opportunities for hiking, wildlife watching, or simply relaxing in the fresh mountain air. The cool temperatures and peaceful surroundings make the Llogara Pass a perfect retreat for those looking to escape the heat and bustle of the coast, while still being just a short drive away from some of the best beaches on the Albanian Riviera.

The drive down the southern side of the pass is just as stunning as the ascent. As the road winds its way down toward the coast, the landscape opens up to reveal breathtaking views of the southern Albanian Riviera, with its hidden coves, pebbly beaches, and the azure waters of the Ionian Sea. The descent from the Llogara Pass offers travelers a sense of anticipation, as each bend in the road brings them closer to the beautiful beaches and quiet villages that await along the coast. This part of the journey feels almost cinematic, as the road hugs the mountainside and the sea stretches out endlessly before you.

The Llogara Pass is not just a means of getting from one part of the Albanian Riviera to another; it is an unforgettable experience in its own right. The dramatic landscapes, sweeping views, and natural beauty of this scenic mountain road make it one of the highlights of any trip to Albania.

Water Sports and Activities for Adventure Seekers

The Albanian Riviera is well-known for its stunning beaches, crystal-clear waters, and peaceful atmosphere, but it's also a paradise for adventure seekers, particularly those interested in water sports and outdoor activities. The calm, warm waters of the Ionian Sea and the dramatic coastline that stretches along the Albanian Riviera make it a perfect destination for a wide range of water-based activities.

One of the most popular water sports along the Albanian Riviera is kayaking, a great way to explore the coast's many hidden beaches, caves, and secluded bays. The rugged and rocky coastline of the Riviera is dotted with small, Hardt reach coves that are often inaccessible by foot or road, making kayaking an ideal way to discover these secret spots. Paddling along the coastline allows you to experience the Riviera from a different perspective, taking in the stunning cliffs, crystal-clear waters, and lively marine life that thrive in the region. Kayaks can be rented from various beachside locations, and many companies offer guided tours that take visitors to some of the most scenic and remote areas along the coast.

For example, Ksamil, located near the southern tip of the Albanian Riviera, is known for its calm waters and small islands just off the coast. Kayaking around these islands provides a peaceful and relaxing way to experience the natural beauty of the area while exploring some of its more secluded corners. The shallow waters and gentle waves around Ksamil make it an excellent location for beginners, while more experienced kayakers can venture further out to explore the nearby coastline. Similarly, the waters around Dhërmi and Himara are perfect for kayaking, offering a mix of rocky cliffs, sandy beaches, and hidden caves that are best explored by paddling along the coast.

In addition to kayaking, the Albanian Riviera is an excellent destination for standup paddleboarding (SUP), another popular water sport that allows you to glide along the surface of the sea while taking in the beautiful surroundings. Standup paddleboarding is easy to learn and provides a fun and relaxing way to explore the calm waters of the Ionian Sea. Like kayaking, paddleboarding offers the opportunity to reach more remote areas of the coastline, and the quiet, peaceful nature of the activity allows you to get up close to the marine life that inhabits the waters around the Riviera. Many of the beaches along the coast, including Jale, Livadhi, and Porto Palermo, offer paddleboard rentals, and the gentle waves of the Ionian Sea make it an ideal location for this activity, even for beginners.

For those seeking more thrilling water-based adventures, the Albanian Riviera is also a growing destination for windsurfing and kitesurfing. The strong winds that blow along certain parts of the coast create perfect conditions for these adrenaline pumping sports. Vlorë, one of the largest cities on the Albanian Riviera, is known for its consistent winds and wide, sandy beaches, making it a prime spot for windsurfing and kitesurfing. The combination of the warm water and reliable winds provides excellent conditions for both beginners and experienced surfers alike. There are several schools and rental shops in Vlorë that offer lessons for those new to the sport, as well as equipment rentals for more experienced windsurfers and kitesurfers.

While Vlorë is one of the best-known spots for windsurfing on the Riviera, other beaches along the coast, such as Dhërmi and Himara, also offer good conditions for the sport, particularly during the summer months when the wind is at its strongest. Windsurfing and kitesurfing are ideal activities for adventure seekers who want to combine their love of the sea with the thrill of speed and skill. The wide, open beaches of the Riviera provide plenty of space to enjoy the sport, and the stunning natural scenery makes every ride along the waves a memorable experience.

For those interested in exploring the underwater world of the Albanian Riviera, scuba diving and snorkeling offer the chance to discover the rich marine life and underwater landscapes that lie beneath the surface of the Ionian Sea. The warm, clear waters of the Riviera provide excellent visibility, making it easy to spot colorful fish, sea turtles, and even dolphins in some areas. The coastline is also home to a number of interesting dive sites, including underwater caves, reefs, and shipwrecks, which add an element of mystery and exploration to the experience.

Saranda, located near the southern end of the Albanian Riviera, is one of the best spots for diving, with several dive centers offering guided tours and equipment rentals. The waters around Saranda are known for their diverse marine life and underwater caves, which provide a thrilling experience for both beginner and experienced divers. One of the most famous dive sites in the area is the Bristol Wreck, a World War IIera shipwreck that lies just off the coast of Saranda. The wreck is accessible to divers and offers a fascinating glimpse into history, as well as an opportunity to see how marine life has taken over the sunken vessel. For those who prefer to stay closer to the surface, snorkeling is a great way to explore the underwater world, with many of the best snorkeling spots located near the rocky shores and shallow waters of Ksamil, Jale, and Dhërmi.

Another exciting way to explore the Albanian Riviera is by taking a boat tour, which allows you to see more of the coastline and visit some of the more remote and less accessible beaches. Boat tours are available from many of the larger towns along the coast, including Vlorë, Saranda, and Himara, and they offer a range of options, from leisurely sightseeing cruises to more adventurous excursions that include snorkeling, cliff jumping, and even cave exploration. One of the most popular boat tours along the Riviera is the trip to Karaburun Peninsula and the Sazan Island, both of which are part of the KaraburunSazan Marine Park. This protected area is home to some of the most pristine and unspoiled beaches on the Albanian Riviera, as well as a rich variety of marine life, making it a must visit for nature lovers and adventure seekers alike.

The waters around the Karaburun Peninsula are known for their stunning clarity and lively blue color, and the coastline is dotted with hidden caves and secluded beaches that can only be reached by boat. One of the highlights of a boat tour to this area is the opportunity to explore the Haxhi Ali Cave, a massive sea cave that stretches deep into the cliffs and is accessible only by boat. The cave is named after a famous Albanian pirate and is one of the largest and most impressive sea caves in the region. Exploring the cave by boat is a thrilling experience, as the turquoise water glows with an otherworldly light, and the towering rock walls create an echo that adds to the sense of adventure.

For those who want to add an extra element of excitement to their time on the Albanian Riviera, cliff diving is another activity that has become increasingly popular along the coast. The rocky cliffs that line many of the beaches provide perfect spots for daring adventurers to leap into the deep, clear waters below. While it's important to exercise caution and ensure that the water is deep enough before diving, there are several locations along the Riviera that are known for being safe and popular spots for cliff jumping. The cliffs around Jale and Dhërmi are particularly popular with thrillseekers looking to take the plunge into the sea, and the combination of adrenaline and stunning scenery makes cliff diving an unforgettable experience.

The Albanian Riviera is not just a destination for relaxation and sunbathing; it's also a paradise for adventure seekers and outdoor enthusiasts. Whether you're paddling along the coastline in a kayak, exploring underwater caves while scuba diving, or riding the waves on a windsurfing board, the Riviera offers a wide range of water sports and activities that allow you to experience the natural beauty of the region in an exciting and immersive way. With its diverse landscape, clear waters, and unspoiled coastline, the Albanian Riviera provides the perfect setting for both relaxation and adventure, making it a must visit destination for anyone looking to combine the thrill of outdoor activities with the serenity of the sea.

Best Places to Stay Along the Riviera

The Albanian Riviera is an incredible destination that offers sundrenched beaches, crystal-clear waters, and a sense of serenity that has made it increasingly popular with travelers. Nestled between the Ionian Sea and the rugged Ceraunian Mountains, this stunning stretch of coastline is not only home to breathtaking scenery but also to a variety of accommodation options that cater to all types of travelers. From luxury resorts to budget friendly guesthouses, the Riviera provides a range of places to stay, each offering its own unique experience, whether you're looking for a peaceful escape or a livelier atmosphere. The right choice of accommodation can greatly enhance your stay, allowing you to enjoy the best of what the Albanian Riviera has to offer while providing comfort and convenience.

One of the most popular and well-known destinations on the Albanian Riviera is Ksamil, a small coastal village located near the southern tip of the country. Ksamil is famous for its beautiful whitesand beaches and the small islands just off the coast that can be reached by boat or even by swimming. This area has been described as the "tropical paradise" of Albania, and its beauty has drawn visitors from all over the world. In recent years, Ksamil has developed into a thriving tourist hub, with a variety of accommodation options ranging from luxury hotels to more modest guesthouses.

For those seeking luxury and comfort, Ksamil offers several highend resorts and hotels, many of which are located directly on the beach. These accommodations provide guests with stunning sea views, private beach access, and upscale amenities such as swimming pools, spas, and onsite restaurants. Staying at one of these resorts allows you to enjoy the beautiful surroundings of Ksamil while having all your needs taken care of, making it a perfect choice for travelers who want to relax and unwind in style.

One of the most notable hotels in Ksamil is the Hotel Luxury, which offers modern, spacious rooms with balconies that overlook the Ionian Sea. The hotel is just a short walk from Ksamil Beach, and guests can enjoy the convenience of a private beach area, as well as an onsite restaurant that serves fresh seafood and traditional Albanian dishes. The combination of beautiful views, excellent service, and close proximity to the beach makes Hotel Luxury a top choice for those looking for a high-quality stay in Ksamil.

For travelers on a tighter budget, Ksamil also has a wide range of guesthouses and smaller hotels that offer comfortable and affordable accommodation. Many of these guesthouses are family run, providing a more personal and intimate experience compared to larger resorts. Staying in a guesthouse in Ksamil allows you to experience the warm hospitality of the local community while enjoying easy access to the beaches and attractions of the area. Guesthouses like Vila Bello and Hotel Mira Mare are popular choices, offering clean, comfortable rooms at reasonable prices, often with breakfast included. These accommodations are ideal for travelers who want to enjoy the beauty of Ksamil without breaking the bank.

Moving north along the Riviera, another fantastic place to stay is Dhërmi, one of the most beautiful and tranquil villages on the coast. Dhërmi is known for its long pebbly beach and clear blue waters, which attract both locals and international visitors looking for a peaceful beach holiday. The village itself is perched on a hillside overlooking the sea, and its traditional stone houses and narrow streets give it a charming, oldworld feel. Dhërmi has become a favorite destination for those looking to escape the crowds and enjoy a more laidback atmosphere, and its accommodation options reflect this, with many small boutique hotels, guesthouses, and beachside resorts to choose from.

For those looking for a more luxurious stay in Dhërmi, Elysium Hotel is a standout option. This stylish, upscale hotel is located just a short distance from the beach and offers beautifully designed rooms, many with sea views. Elysium Hotel features a large outdoor pool, a gourmet restaurant, and beautifully landscaped gardens, providing a peaceful retreat where guests can relax and unwind after a day spent at the beach. The hotel's excellent service and luxurious amenities make it one of the top choices for travelers seeking comfort and elegance in Dhërmi.

On the other hand, if you're looking for a more budget friendly option in Dhërmi, there are plenty of guesthouses and smaller hotels that offer excellent value for money. Many of these accommodations are located within walking distance of the beach, allowing guests to enjoy the beauty of Dhërmi while staying in more affordable lodgings. One such option is Hotel Ionian, a family run guesthouse that offers clean, comfortable rooms with stunning views of the Ionian Sea. The friendly, welcoming atmosphere of the guesthouse makes it a great choice for travelers who want to experience authentic Albanian hospitality while staying close to the beach.

Further along the coast, the village of Himara is another fantastic destination for travelers seeking sun, sea, and serenity. Himara is known for its beautiful beaches, traditional village atmosphere, and excellent location for exploring the surrounding coastline. The town itself is divided into two parts: the older village, located on a hill above the beach, and the newer, more modern area along the coast. Himara offers a range of accommodation options, from beachside hotels to traditional guesthouses, making it a versatile destination for all types of travelers.

For those looking for a luxurious stay in Himara, Rapos Resort Hotel is one of the most popular choices. Located directly on the beach, this upscale hotel offers spacious rooms with balconies overlooking the sea, as well as an outdoor pool and a restaurant serving local and international cuisine. The hotel's prime beachfront location and excellent amenities make it a favorite among travelers looking for a high-end experience in Himara.

For a more authentic and affordable experience, staying in one of the traditional guesthouses in Old Himara is a great option. Guesthouses like Vila Blu offer cozy, comfortable accommodations in the historic part of the village, with beautiful views of the sea and the surrounding mountains. These guesthouses provide a more intimate and personal experience, allowing guests to immerse themselves in the local culture while enjoying easy access to the beaches below. The old village of Himara is a peaceful and quiet place to stay, offering a glimpse into traditional Albanian life while still being just a short walk from the modern amenities of the beachside area.

For adventure seekers, Himara is also a great base for exploring some of the hidden coves and beaches along the coast. Livadhi Beach and Porto Palermo Bay are just a short drive away and offer some of the most beautiful and unspoiled beaches on the Riviera. Staying in Himara allows you to easily explore these more remote and less crowded areas, making it an ideal destination for those who want to combine relaxation with adventure.

Another hidden gem along the Albanian Riviera is the village of Jale, a small and relatively undeveloped beach town known for its peaceful atmosphere and beautiful natural surroundings. Jale is perfect for travelers looking for a quiet, off-the-beaten-path destination where they can truly unwind. The beach in Jale is pristine, with clear blue waters and soft sand, and the surrounding hills provide a sense of seclusion and tranquility. While Jale is a smaller and less touristy destination compared to places like Ksamil or Dhërmi, it offers several charming guesthouses and beachfront hotels that provide the perfect setting for a relaxing beach holiday.

For those looking for a comfortable stay in Jale, Folie Marine Beach Hotel is a great option. This small beachfront hotel offers modern rooms with sea views, as well as an outdoor pool and a restaurant that serves fresh seafood. The hotel's peaceful location and excellent service make it a popular choice for travelers who want to enjoy the beauty of Jale while staying in comfortable and modern accommodations.

The Albanian Riviera offers a wide range of accommodation options that cater to all types of travelers, from luxury seekers to budget conscious backpackers. Each village along the Riviera offers its own unique charm and atmosphere, making it easy to find the perfect place to stay, no matter what type of experience you're looking for. With its stunning beaches, warm hospitality, and variety of accommodations, the

Albanian Riviera is truly a destination where sun, sea, and serenity come together to create an unforgettable experience.

Where to Stay: Accommodation Options in Albani Rivera

The Riviera offers a diverse range of accommodation options that cater to various budgets and preferences, from luxurious beach resorts to charming guesthouses and budget-friendly hostels. Each location offers unique access to the stunning beaches and breathtaking views that the Riviera is known for.

1. Luxury Beach Resorts
For travelers looking to indulge in comfort, luxury beach resorts along the Albanian Riviera offer an elevated experience, combining modern amenities with stunning views of the Ionian Sea. These resorts typically offer private beaches, pools, fine dining, and spa facilities, ensuring that your stay is as relaxing as possible.

- **Marina Bay Luxury Resort & Spa (Vlora)**: Located near the city of Vlora, this resort is known for its stunning ocean views, private beach, and top-notch amenities. Guests can enjoy the spa, outdoor pool, and onsite restaurants offering Mediterranean cuisine. Prices range from €120 to €250 per night. You can reach the resort by car or taxi from Vlora city center.
- **Hotel Llogara (Llogara Pass)**: Nestled in the Llogara Pass, this hotel offers a perfect mix of beach and mountain views. It is ideal for those looking to combine outdoor

activities like hiking with a luxury stay. Prices range from €80 to €160 per night. The hotel can be accessed by car via the SH8 road.

- **Drymades Inn Resort (Drymades Beach)**: This beachfront resort provides a serene setting with direct access to the beach, making it perfect for a relaxing getaway. Rooms range from €100 to €200 per night, and you can reach the resort by taxi or private vehicle from Dhermi.
- **Grand Blue Fafa Resort (Golem Beach)**: Located near Durres, this 5-star resort offers a variety of amenities, including multiple swimming pools, a private beach, and wellness facilities. Rooms start from €130 and go up to €300 per night. It is accessible by car or taxi from the nearby city of Durres.
- **Riviera Premium Resort (Ksamil)**: Situated in the heart of Ksamil, this resort offers luxurious rooms with ocean views, fine dining, and access to the crystal-clear waters of Ksamil Beach. Prices range from €150 to €280 per night. You can get here via car or taxi from Saranda.

2. Boutique Hotels

Boutique hotels provide a more intimate, personalized experience compared to large resorts. These accommodations are usually smaller, with stylish designs and often include unique touches, such as locally-inspired decor and personalized service.

- **Elysium Hotel (Dhërmi)**: A boutique hotel perched above Dhërmi Beach, Elysium offers modern rooms

with stunning sea views and a beautiful pool area. Prices range from €90 to €180 per night, and it's accessible by car or taxi from Dhërmi village.
- **Bougainville Bay Resort (Saranda)**: This eco-friendly boutique hotel combines modern architecture with natural surroundings. It offers direct access to the beach and has a rooftop infinity pool. Rooms are priced between €100 and €200 per night. The hotel is easily reachable by taxi or a short drive from Saranda.
- **Hotel Prinos (Himara)**: Located near the beach in Himara, this boutique hotel offers a quiet escape with stylish rooms and close proximity to local restaurants and bars. Prices range from €70 to €150 per night, and the hotel is accessible by car or taxi.
- **Aliko Luxury Suites (Ksamil)**: A charming boutique hotel in Ksamil, offering cozy rooms with a modern touch. The hotel is a short walk from the beach and prices range from €80 to €160 per night. You can reach it by car or taxi from Saranda.
- **Rea Boutique Hotel (Himara)**: A luxury boutique hotel located right on the beachfront, Rea offers stylish rooms with all modern amenities. Prices range from €100 to €180 per night. It is accessible by car or a short walk from the center of Himara.

3. Guesthouses and Inns

Guesthouses and inns are perfect for travelers looking for an affordable, home-like atmosphere. These accommodations offer a more personal touch, often run by local families who provide warm hospitality and insight into the local culture.

- **Guesthouse Arti (Himara)**: A family-run guesthouse located near the beach; this accommodation offers a simple but comfortable stay with access to nearby restaurants. Prices range from €30 to €50 per night. It is easily accessible by foot or car from central Himara.
- **Villa Blue Panorama (Qeparo)**: Offering beautiful views of the sea, this guesthouse is located in the small village of Qeparo. It's ideal for travelers looking for a peaceful retreat. Prices range from €40 to €70 per night, and you can get there by car or taxi from the nearby town.
- **Ionian Sea View Guesthouse (Saranda)**: This guesthouse provides budget-friendly rooms with a balcony and sea view. Prices range from €25 to €60 per night, and it is accessible by foot or a short drive from the center of Saranda.
- **Guesthouse Dhermiu (Dhërmi)**: A small, family-run guesthouse located just a short walk from the beach. Rooms are basic but clean and comfortable, with prices ranging from €30 to €60 per night. You can reach it by car or taxi.
- **Riviera Rooms (Ksamil)**: Located just minutes away from Ksamil Beach, this guest

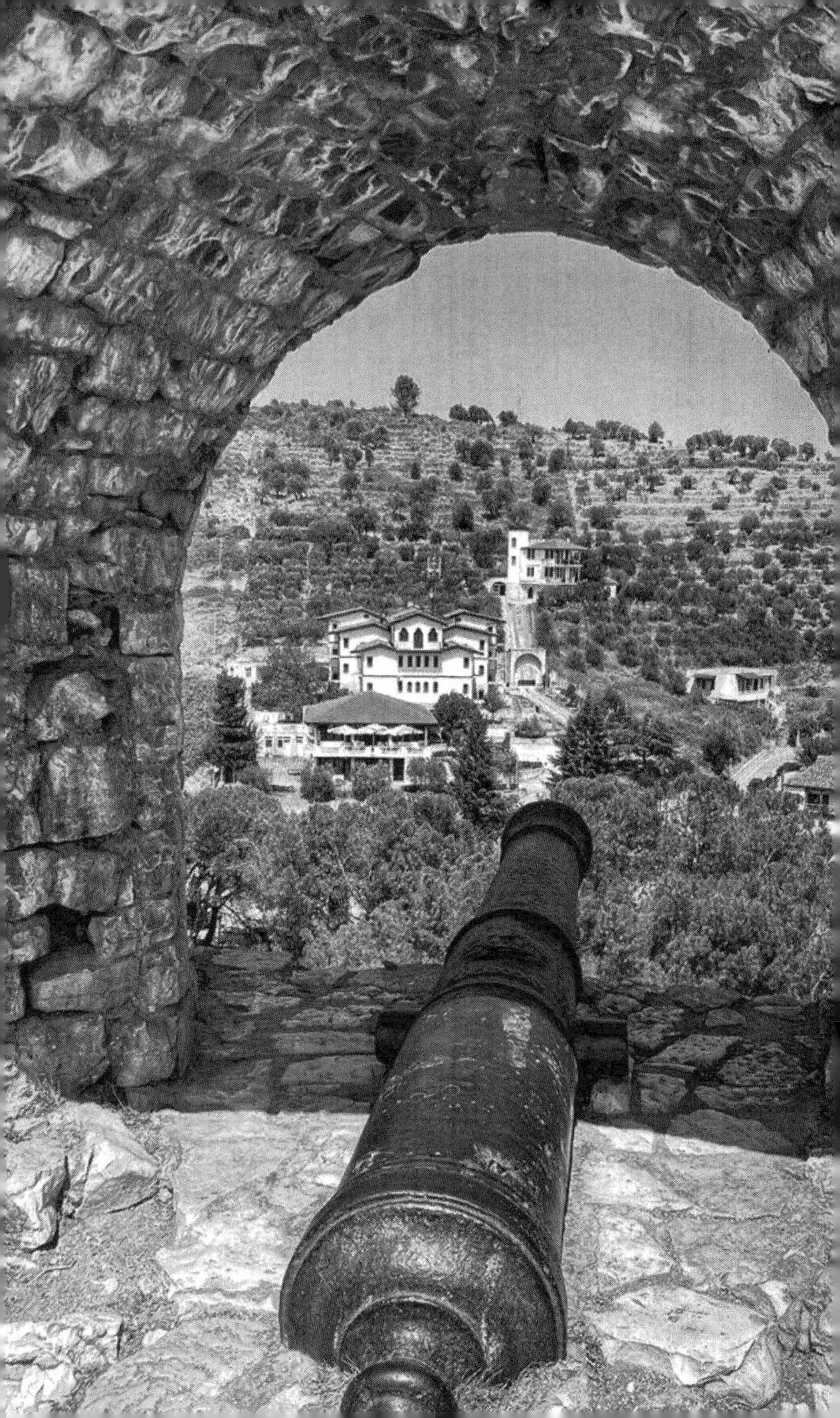

CHAPTER 4

THE ENCHANTING ANCIENT CITIES

Gjirokastër: The Stone City of a Thousand Steps

Gjirokastër, often referred to as the "Stone City of a Thousand Steps," is one of the most fascinating and historically rich cities in Albania. Situated in the southern part of the country, this ancient city is nestled in a valley between the Gjerë Mountains and the Drino River, with its steep, cobbled streets winding up and down the hills. The city is famous for its distinctive Ottoman architecture, with beautiful stone houses that seem to cascade down the mountainside, giving it an appearance like no other. Gjirokastër is not just a city of architectural beauty but also a living museum of Albania's long and complex history. It has been recognized as a UNESCO World Heritage Site since 2005, thanks to its well-preserved buildings and its cultural significance, both regionally and internationally.

One of the most striking features of Gjirokastër is its Ottomanera architecture. The stone houses, many of which date back to the 17th century, are built in a distinctive style with sloping roofs, tall windows, and whitewashed walls. These homes, often referred to as "tower houses," were built by wealthy families during the Ottoman period, and many have been carefully restored to preserve their original beauty.

What makes these houses unique is the way they are constructed out of stone, both for the walls and the roof, giving Gjirokastër its nickname as the "Stone City." The craftsmanship involved in building these houses is evident in their intricate details, from the carved wooden ceilings to the decorated interiors. Walking through the city's steep streets, you can sense the history that has been etched into every stone, as Gjirokastër's architecture tells the story of its past rulers, merchants, and nobility.

Gjirokastër is not only a marvel for its architecture but also for its layout, which reflects the city's historical development. The narrow, winding streets, many of which are too steep for vehicles, create a labyrinthlike environment that invites exploration. The feeling of stepping back in time is strong here, as the city has retained much of its medieval charm, with stone walls, ancient pathways, and grand mansions standing as silent witnesses to the centuries that have passed. The hilly terrain and the many staircases that connect different parts of the city earned Gjirokastër its nickname as the "City of a Thousand Steps." Navigating these streets, you are constantly rewarded with stunning views of the valley below and the surrounding mountains, which seem to change with the light throughout the day.

One of the most important landmarks in Gjirokastër is the Gjirokastër Castle, which towers over the city from its position on a hilltop. This imposing fortress is one of the largest and oldest castles in Albania, and it has played a central role in the city's history. The castle dates back to the 12th century, though much of what remains today was expanded and fortified during the Ottoman period in the 19th century. The strategic location of the castle, overlooking the entire valley, made it a key defensive structure, and it has been used by various rulers throughout the centuries, from the Byzantines to the Ottomans, to control the region.

Exploring Gjirokastër Castle is like stepping into a time capsule, as the fortress offers insight into the city's military and political history. As you walk through its stone walls and massive towers, you can imagine the soldiers who once stood guard, defending the city from invaders. The castle's interior is home to several rooms and halls that have been turned into museums and exhibits, offering a deeper Knowing of the region's past. One of the most interesting parts of the castle is the Gjirokastër Museum, which provides visitors with a comprehensive history of the city and its significance in the Balkans. The museum contains a collection of artifacts, including weapons, traditional clothing, and photographs that tell the story of Gjirokastër's evolution over the centuries. From its early days as a Byzantine outpost to its time under Ottoman rule, the museum offers a detailed look at how the city has changed and developed, while still holding on to its unique identity.

One of the most famous exhibits within Gjirokastër Castle is the collection of military weapons, which are displayed in an openair section of the fortress. These weapons, many of which date back to World War II, include artillery, tanks, and even a downed American airplane, which is believed to have crashed in Albania during the Cold War. This exhibit serves as a reminder of the more recent history of the region and Albania's involvement in global conflicts. The presence of these war relics within the ancient walls of the castle creates a striking juxtaposition between the old and the new, showing how Gjirokastër has been shaped by both ancient empires and modern warfare.

The views from the castle are nothing short of spectacular. From the ramparts, you can see the entire city spread out below, with its stone houses and winding streets leading down into the valley. The surrounding mountains create a dramatic backdrop, and on clear days, you can see for miles in every direction. The contrast between the natural beauty of the landscape and the stone structures of the city creates a breathtaking scene that leaves a lasting impression on anyone who visits. It's easy to see why Gjirokastër Castle has been such an important part of the city's identity for centuries, as it offers both a sense of protection and a symbol of the city's enduring strength.

Another fascinating aspect of Gjirokastër is its status as a UNESCO World Heritage Site. The city was added to the UNESCO list in recognition of its well-preserved Ottoman architecture and its cultural significance. Gjirokastër is one of the few surviving examples of an Ottoman town in the Balkans, and its architecture reflects the influence of the empire that once controlled much of southeastern Europe. The inclusion of Gjirokastër on the UNESCO list has helped to raise awareness of the city's historical value and has contributed to efforts to preserve and restore many of its old buildings. As you walk through the city, you'll notice that many of the traditional stone houses have been carefully restored, ensuring that they will continue to stand for generations to come.

In addition to its architectural and historical significance, Gjirokastër is also known for its role as a center of Albanian culture and literature. The city is the birthplace of Ismail Kadare, one of Albania's most famous writers and a Nobel Prize nominee. Kadare's novels often reflect the history and struggles of the Albanian people, and his connection to Gjirokastër has added to the city's cultural reputation. Visitors to Gjirokastër can visit the house where Kadare was born, which has been turned into a museum dedicated to his life and work. This literary connection adds another layer to the city's rich cultural heritage, as Gjirokastër has inspired not only historians and architects but also artists and writers.

Gjirokastër's importance as a cultural and historical site is further emphasized by its many festivals and events, which celebrate the city's traditions and its place in Albania's national identity. The National Folk Festival, held every five years in Gjirokastër, is one of the most important cultural events in Albania, attracting musicians, dancers, and performers from all over the country. This festival, which takes place in the courtyard of Gjirokastër Castle, highlights the rich traditions of Albanian music and dance, offering visitors a chance to experience the country's lively cultural heritage. The festival is a reminder of the strong connection between Gjirokastër and the wider Albanian cultural identity, as the city continues to play a key role in preserving and promoting the country's traditions.

Gjirokastër is a city that offers a unique blend of history, architecture, and culture, all set against the backdrop of the stunning Albanian landscape. Its stone houses, narrow streets, and towering castle create a sense of timelessness, while its role as a UNESCO World Heritage Site ensures that its beauty and significance will be preserved for future generations. Whether you're exploring the ancient fortress, wandering through the city's steep streets, or simply taking in the views of the valley below, Gjirokastër offers a glimpse into Albania's rich past and a reminder of the enduring strength of its people. For anyone interested in history, culture, or simply experiencing a city unlike any other, Gjirokastër is a destination that should not be missed.

Berat: The City of a Thousand Windows

Berat, often called the "City of a Thousand Windows," is one of the most beautiful and historic cities in Albania. Nestled along the banks of the Osum River and framed by the Tomorr Mountains, Berat's charm comes from its rich cultural heritage and its breathtaking, white Ottoman era houses that seem to rise up the hillsides in perfect harmony with the landscape. With its well-preserved buildings, ancient fortresses, and striking layout, Berat offers visitors a unique glimpse into Albania's past, with layers of history that date back over two millennia. Today, it stands as a testament to Albania's resilience and diversity, earning its place on the UNESCO World Heritage list in 2008.

The most iconic image associated with Berat is its white Ottoman houses, which have earned the city its poetic nickname. These houses are clustered along the slopes of two hills, divided by the Osum River, creating a pretty view that feels like something out of a storybook. As you approach the city, these houses stand out with their rows of large windows, which seem to gaze out over the river and the valley below. The effect of seeing these windows lined up so symmetrically, with their wooden frames and sloped roofs, creates a stunning visual that leaves a lasting impression on visitors. This arrangement of windows, combined with the whitewashed stone walls of the houses, has given Berat its reputation as a city of a thousand windows, with each window serving as a portal to the city's long and storied past.

One of the most fascinating aspects of Berat is the way its architecture reflects its rich history. The Ottoman houses that dominate the skyline of Berat are not only beautiful but also functional, designed to accommodate the unique geography of the city. These homes were typically built on steep hillsides, and their design takes full advantage of the terrain. The lower floors of the houses are built from stone, while the upper floors are made of wood, creating a balanced and harmonious look that blends with the natural surroundings. Inside, these houses were built to be spacious, with large rooms and multiple levels, reflecting the wealth and status of the families that once lived in them. Many of these homes are still occupied today, while others have been converted into museums, guesthouses, and restaurants, allowing visitors to experience the traditional architecture firsthand.

While the Ottoman houses are an integral part of Berat's appeal, the city's history goes back much further than the Ottoman era. One of the most important and impressive landmarks in Berat is the Berat Castle, also known as Kala, which sits high above the city on a rocky hilltop. The castle is one of the oldest and largest in Albania, with its origins dating back to the 4th century BC, when it was a strategic fortress during the Illyrian period. Over the centuries, the castle has been expanded and fortified by the Byzantines, Romans, and Ottomans, each leaving their mark on its architecture and layout.

Exploring Berat Castle is like stepping back in time. The castle walls, which stretch for over a kilometer, are still largely intact, and within the fortress, you'll find an entire village, complete with ancient houses, churches, and mosques. Unlike many other castles, Berat Castle is still inhabited, with families living within its walls, maintaining the traditions of the past while adapting to modern life. This living fortress offers a unique opportunity for visitors to experience a blend of history and contemporary life, as you can walk through its narrow cobblestone streets, visit its old churches, and stop to admire the view from its many lookout points.

One of the most significant structures within the castle is the Church of the Dormition of St. Mary, which houses the Onufri

National Museum. This church dates back to the 18th century and is dedicated to Onufri, one of Albania's most famous icon painters. Onufri's work is known for its lively colors and intricate details, and the museum contains some of his finest examples of religious iconography, along with other icons from the Byzantine and post Byzantine periods. The museum is a must visit for anyone interested in religious art, as it offers a comprehensive collection of Albanian Orthodox icons, many of which were created by some of the most skilled artists of their time.

The view from the castle is truly breathtaking, offering panoramic vistas of the city below, the Osum River, and the surrounding mountains. From this vantage point, you can fully appreciate the layout of Berat and the way its houses seem to rise organically from the hillsides, their windows gleaming in the sunlight. The Kala neighborhood, located within the castle walls, is one of the oldest parts of the city and is a fascinating place to explore. Many of the homes here have been carefully restored, preserving their historical character while offering a glimpse into the traditional way of life in Berat. Walking through the Kala neighborhood, you can visit small shops selling local crafts, stop at family-owned cafes for a taste of traditional Albanian food, and explore the ancient churches and mosques that are scattered throughout the area.

The presence of both churches and mosques within Berat Castle is a testament to the city's long history of religious tolerance and coexistence. Berat has long been a melting pot of cultures and religions, with Christianity and Islam coexisting peacefully for centuries. One of the most famous religious buildings in Berat is the Lead Mosque, which was built during the Ottoman period and remains an important symbol of the city's Islamic heritage. The mosque is named after the lead that was used to cover its dome, and it stands as a reminder of Berat's rich religious diversity.

As you descend from the castle and cross the Osum River, you enter another of Berat's most famous neighborhoods, Gorica. This area, located on the opposite side of the river from the old town, is home to more of Berat's traditional Ottoman houses, as well as several important religious buildings. The Gorica Bridge, which connects the two sides of the city, is one of the most iconic landmarks in Berat and has been a vital crossing point for centuries. The bridge itself is a beautiful piece of architecture, with its stone arches reflecting in the calm waters of the Osum River, creating a picture-perfect scene.

The Mangalem neighborhood, located just below the castle, is another important part of Berat's cultural and architectural heritage. This area is home to many of the city's most beautiful Ottoman houses, and it is here that you'll find some of the most striking examples of Berat's famous "thousand windows." As you wander through the narrow streets of Mangalem, you can't help but feel transported back in time, as the houses, with their wooden balconies and large windows, rise up around you, creating a sense of history and continuity that is palpable in every corner of the neighborhood.

One of the most enjoyable aspects of visiting Berat is simply wandering through its streets and taking in the atmosphere.

Whether you're exploring the winding alleys of the old town, climbing the steps to Berat Castle, or relaxing by the river in the Gorica neighborhood, there's a sense of tranquility and timelessness that pervades the city. Berat's blend of architecture, history, and natural beauty creates a unique experience for visitors, offering a window into Albania's past while showcasing the resilience and creativity of its people.

Berat, with its white Ottoman houses, ancient castle, and rich cultural history, is one of the most enchanting cities in Albania. Known as the "City of a Thousand Windows," it offers visitors a unique combination of architectural beauty and historical significance. The city's well-preserved neighborhoods, such as Mangalem and Gorica, and the impressive Berat Castle provide a glimpse into the city's long history, while its status as a UNESCO World Heritage Site ensures that this cultural gem will be preserved for future generations to enjoy. Whether you're interested in exploring its religious heritage, marveling at its traditional architecture, or simply enjoying the stunning views, Berat is a city that captivates and inspires all who visit.

Archaeological Sites Worth Exploring

Albania is home to many fascinating ancient cities, and among them, Berat stands out not only for its rich cultural heritage but also for its connection to some of the most important archaeological sites in the region. Known as the "City of a Thousand Windows," Berat itself is a treasure trove of history and ancient architecture, but it also serves as a gateway to two of Albania's most significant archaeological sites: Apollonia and Butrint. These ancient cities, both of which played pivotal roles in the development of the region over thousands of years, offer a window into the past and showcase the depth of Albania's historical and cultural landscape. For those interested in ancient history and archaeology, exploring these ruins provides a deeper Knowing of the civilizations that once thrived in this part of the world.

The ancient city of Apollonia is located near the modern city of Fier, about an hour's drive from Berat. Founded by Greek colonists from Corinth in the 6th century BC, Apollonia was one of the most important cities in the region during the ancient period. It was named after the Greek god Apollo, and it quickly grew into a major center of trade, learning, and culture, benefiting from its strategic location along the Vjosa River. The city reached its height during the Hellenistic period, when it became a key player in the region's politics and commerce. Apollonia also had strong ties to Rome, and it was here that Octavian, who would later become Emperor Augustus, was studying when he learned of the assassination of Julius Caesar.

One of the most striking things about Apollonia is its setting. The ruins of the ancient city are spread out over a vast area, surrounded by rolling hills and olive groves, creating a peaceful and scenic environment in which to explore the remnants of the past. As you wander through the site, it's easy to imagine what life must have been like in this bustling city thousands of years ago. Despite the passage of time, many of the structures remain remarkably well-preserved, offering visitors a glimpse into the architectural and cultural achievements of the ancient Greeks and Romans.

One of the most impressive structures at Apollonia is the Bouleuterion, or Council House, which was the political center of the city. This large, rectangular building would have been the meeting place for the city's leaders, who gathered to make decisions and pass laws. The Bouleuterion, along with the Agora, or marketplace, formed the heart of the city's public life, and both areas are still visible today. Walking through the remains of the Agora, you can see the foundations of the shops and public buildings that once lined the square, giving a sense of the bustling commercial activity that would have taken place here.

Another key feature of Apollonia is the Temple of Apollo, which would have been one of the most important religious sites in the city. Although much of the temple has been lost to time, the foundations and parts of the structure are still visible, and it remains a powerful symbol of the city's devotion to the god Apollo. The temple was once surrounded by columns and adorned with statues, and it would have been the focal point of religious life in the city. The theater at Apollonia is another significant ruin, offering visitors a glimpse into the entertainment and cultural life of the city's inhabitants. Although much of the seating has been lost, the layout of the theater is still clear, and it's easy to imagine the crowds that would have gathered here to watch plays and performances.

In addition to its architectural achievements, Apollonia was also a center of learning and philosophy, particularly during the Roman period. The city was home to a renowned school of philosophy, and many young men from prominent Roman families were sent to study here, including the future emperor, Augustus. This connection to Roman history adds another layer of significance to Apollonia, as it played a key role in the development of the region's intellectual and political life.

Exploring the ancient ruins of Apollonia provides a fascinating glimpse into a time when this city was a major hub of culture and commerce. The site is vast, and visitors can spend hours wandering through the remains of the city's buildings, imagining what life must have been like in this thriving metropolis. The combination of well-preserved ruins, beautiful scenery, and the rich history of the site make Apollonia a must visit for anyone interested in the ancient world.

Further south, near the border with Greece, lies another of Albania's most important archaeological sites: Butrint. Like Apollonia, Butrint has been recognized as a UNESCO World Heritage Site, and it is one of the most significant ancient cities in the Balkans. The city's history stretches back more than 2,500 years, and it has been inhabited by a succession of different cultures, including the Greeks, Romans, Byzantines, and Venetians. The ruins of Butrint are located on a small peninsula between Lake Butrint and the Vivari Channel, creating a stunning natural backdrop for the ancient city.

Butrint is known for its exceptionally well-preserved ruins, which offer visitors a comprehensive look at the city's long and varied history. One of the most impressive features of Butrint is its amphitheater, which dates back to the Hellenistic period and was later expanded by the Romans. The amphitheater is still largely intact, and it offers a vivid sense of what life must have been like in the ancient city, where public performances and political events would have drawn large crowds. The seating area, stage, and surrounding buildings are remarkably well-preserved, allowing visitors to walk through the space and imagine the performances that would have taken place here.

Another highlight of Butrint is the Baptistery, which is one of the best-preserved early Christian monuments in the Balkans. The floor of the baptistery is covered with a stunning mosaic, which depicts a variety of animals, birds, and symbolic Christian images. The mosaic is one of the finest examples of early Christian art in Albania, and it provides a fascinating glimpse into the religious life of the city during the Byzantine period. The basilica nearby, with its tall columns and intricate carvings, is another reminder of Butrint's significance as a religious center during this time.

Butrint's strategic location made it an important city throughout its history, and its fortifications reflect the various powers that controlled the city. The city walls, which still stand in many places, were built and rebuilt by successive rulers, from the Greeks and Romans to the Byzantines and Venetians. Walking along the walls, you can see how the city's defenses evolved over time, with each new power adding to and strengthening the fortifications to protect the city from invasion. The Venetian tower, located near the entrance to the site, is a later addition that reflects Butrint's importance as a strategic outpost in the Mediterranean during the Venetian period.

The Butrint Museum, located within the ancient fortress, offers a wealth of information about the history of the site and the various civilizations that have inhabited it. The museum's collection includes artifacts from the Greek, Roman, and Byzantine periods, including pottery, coins, sculptures, and inscriptions. These objects provide insight into the daily life of the city's inhabitants, as well as its connections to the wider Mediterranean world. The museum also tells the story of the site's excavation and restoration, which began in the early 20th century and continues to this day.

One of the most unique aspects of Butrint is its location within a national park, which encompasses the ancient city as well as the surrounding wetlands, forests, and lakes. This natural environment adds to the magic of Butrint, as visitors can explore the ruins while also enjoying the beauty of the landscape. The park is home to a rich variety of wildlife, including birds, reptiles, and fish, making it a haven for nature lovers as well as history enthusiasts. The combination of ancient ruins and stunning natural scenery makes Butrint one of the most enchanting and memorable archaeological sites in Albania.

Berat, along with the nearby ancient cities of Apollonia and Butrint, offers a remarkable journey through Albania's history, from the ancient Greeks and Romans to the early Christian and Byzantine periods. These archaeological sites are not only important for their historical significance but also for the insight they provide into the civilizations that once thrived in this region. Whether you're exploring the scenic ruins of Apollonia or walking through the well-preserved streets of Butrint, these ancient cities offer a deep and meaningful connection to the past, making them essential destinations for anyone interested in the history and archaeology of Albania.

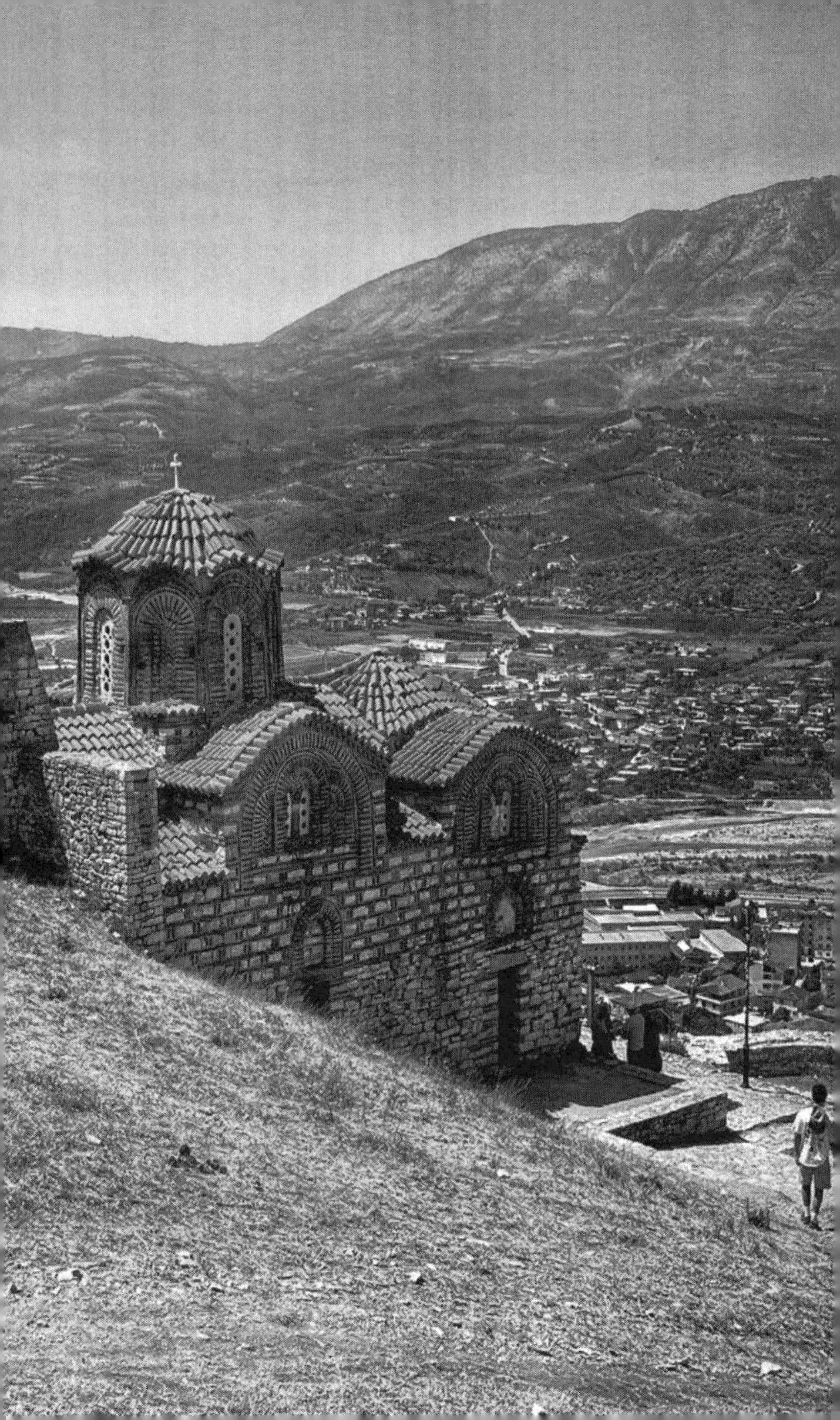

CHAPTER 5

NORTHERN ALBANIA: MAJESTIC MOUNTAINS AND RUGGED LANDSCAPES

The Albanian Alps: Breathtaking Peaks and Valleys

Northern Albania is home to one of the most stunning and untouched regions in Europe—the Albanian Alps. Known for their breathtaking peaks, deep valleys, and rugged landscapes, the Albanian Alps, or Bjeshkët e Namuna, offer a natural beauty that is both awe-inspiring and raw. This mountainous area is characterized by dramatic cliffs, crystal-clear rivers, and lush green meadows, making it a perfect destination for nature lovers and outdoor enthusiasts seeking an adventure off the beaten path.

The peaks of the Albanian Alps rise majestically, with some reaching over 2,500 meters in height, creating a landscape that is both imposing and serene. The area is a haven for hikers and climbers, with numerous trails that wind through the valleys, offering stunning panoramic views at every turn. One of the most popular trekking routes in the Alps is the path between the Valbona Valley and Theth, two of the region's most pretty villages. This trail takes you through dramatic mountain passes, past alpine meadows, and alongside rushing rivers, providing an unforgettable experience for those who make the journey.

The Valbona Valley, in particular, is known for its pristine beauty, with towering mountains surrounding a wide, green valley. The Valbona River cuts through the valley, its clear waters reflecting the peaks above, creating a scene of tranquil beauty that feels far removed from the hustle and bustle of modern life. Theth, another village nestled in the heart of the Alps, is equally enchanting, with its traditional stone houses, waterfalls, and dramatic cliffs. The Grunas Waterfall and Blue Eye are just two of the many natural wonders that visitors can discover in this remote region.

The Albanian Alps are not only a paradise for hikers but also for those interested in Albania's rich cultural heritage. The traditional way of life in the highlands has been preserved for centuries, and visitors to the region can experience the hospitality of the local people, who live in harmony with the rugged landscape. The area's unique history and customs are reflected in its architecture, with many of the villages featuring traditional stone houses with steep, sloping roofs designed to withstand the harsh winters.

The Albanian Alps offer a unique blend of breathtaking natural beauty and rich cultural heritage. With their majestic peaks, deep valleys, and untouched landscapes, they provide an unparalleled experience for those seeking adventure and tranquility in one of Europe's most spectacular regions.

Valbona Valley National Park: Hiking Trails and Nature

Valbona Valley National Park is one of Northern Albania's most captivating natural wonders. Located deep in the Albanian Alps, the park is renowned for its spectacular landscapes, lush greenery, and a network of well-preserved hiking trails that make it a prime destination for nature lovers and adventurers. The Valbona River, with its clear blue waters, runs through the heart of the valley, creating a serene environment framed by the towering peaks of the mountains, some of which reach up to 2,500 meters. The combination of rugged terrain, crystal-clear waters, and rich vegetation offers visitors a peaceful yet thrilling experience in the great outdoors.

The hiking trails in Valbona Valley are some of the most beautiful in Albania, with routes that cater to all levels of experience, from easy walks along the riverbank to more challenging ascents that lead to panoramic views of the surrounding mountains. One of the most popular routes is the Valbona to Theth trail, which connects two of Albania's most pretty mountain villages. This trail takes hikers through alpine meadows, dense forests, and over high mountain passes, offering stunning views along the way. The experience is immersive, with the unspoiled nature and the silence of the mountains creating a perfect escape from urban life.

Apart from hiking, Valbona Valley National Park is home to diverse wildlife, including rare species such as the Balkan lynx, wolves, and brown bears, as well as a variety of bird species. For visitors who appreciate the beauty of undisturbed nature, the park offers an ideal setting for wildlife watching and photography.

Valbona Valley National Park is a treasure of Northern Albania, offering hikers and nature enthusiasts a chance to explore some of the country's most untouched and breathtaking landscapes. With its scenic trails, abundant wildlife, and serene atmosphere, the park provides a perfect opportunity to experience Albania's majestic mountains and rugged natural beauty at its finest.

Theth: Remote Villages and Waterfalls

Theth is a remote and enchanting village in the heart of the Albanian Alps, known for its breathtaking landscapes, traditional stone houses, and stunning waterfalls. Tucked away in a deep valley surrounded by towering peaks, Theth feels like a world apart from modern life. Reaching the village requires a journey through rugged mountain roads, but the reward is an unspoiled natural paradise that offers peace, beauty, and a sense of timelessness. The village is a prime example of Albania's rural charm, where locals still live in traditional homes, and visitors can experience the country's deep rooted mountain culture.

One of the most iconic natural features of Theth is the Grunas Waterfall, which cascades dramatically from the cliffs into a clear pool below. This impressive waterfall, set against the backdrop of the jagged mountains, is easily accessible by foot and is one of the main attractions for hikers and nature lovers. The short hike to the waterfall leads through dense forests and along the valley's river, offering a serene walk through some of the most beautiful natural scenery in Northern Albania. The Grunas Waterfall, with its powerful flow and tranquil setting, perfectly takes the wild and rugged beauty of the Theth region.

Another highlight of Theth is its Blue Eye, a natural spring pool located deep within the mountains. The water is strikingly clear and takes on a mesmerizing blue hue, making it a hidden gem for those willing to venture further into the wilderness. The hike to the Blue Eye is longer and more challenging, but it takes visitors through some of the most pristine parts of the Albanian Alps, with the journey itself being as rewarding as the destination.

Theth offers a perfect escape into the remote, untouched landscapes of Northern Albania. Its waterfalls, natural springs, and traditional mountain life make it a must visit destination for those looking to experience the wild beauty and serenity of the Albanian Alps. Theth provides a rare opportunity to immerse oneself in nature while exploring the rich culture and history of one of Albania's most isolated and scenic regions.

Exploring the Accursed Mountains

The Accursed Mountains, known locally as Bjeshkët e Namuna, are one of the most dramatic and awe-inspiring regions in Northern Albania. These mountains, with their sharp peaks and deep valleys, form part of the greater Dinaric Alps and are often regarded as some of the most rugged and challenging landscapes in Europe. The name "Accursed" might sound ominous, but it speaks to the wild and untamed nature of these mountains, which have long been both a source of wonder and mystery for those who venture into their heights.

Exploring the Accursed Mountains offers a journey into one of the most remote and pristine parts of Albania. The area is a haven for experienced hikers and adventurers, with trails that take you through narrow gorges, alongside fast flowing rivers, and up to towering peaks that offer breathtaking views of the surrounding landscape. The mountains are known for their stark beauty, where jagged cliffs contrast with lush green meadows, and the only sounds you hear are the wind through the trees and the distant rush of waterfalls. This sense of solitude and untouched wilderness is what makes the Accursed Mountains so special for those who seek to explore them.

The region is home to some of the most iconic peaks in Albania, including Maja Jezercë, the highest point in the country, standing at 2,694 meters. For those willing to make the climb, the reward is an unparalleled view of the surrounding peaks and valleys. The journey to reach such heights often involves passing through traditional mountain villages where time seems to have stood still, offering a glimpse into the isolated life of the highlanders who have lived in this rugged landscape for centuries.

The Valbona Valley and Theth are two key entry points for exploring the Accursed Mountains, each offering its own unique access to the region's beauty and hiking trails. Whether it's trekking along ancient shepherd paths, standing at the foot of towering cliffs, or simply soaking in the quiet majesty of the landscape, the Accursed Mountains provide a rare opportunity to experience the raw, natural power of Albania's highlands.

Exploring the Accursed Mountains offers a profound connection to nature, where the sheer scale and untouched beauty of the landscape leave a lasting impression. For those seeking adventure, isolation, and the grandeur of unspoiled wilderness, the Accursed Mountains stand as one of Albania's most remarkable treasures.

Local Traditions in the North: Hospitality and Cuisine

Northern Albania, with its majestic mountains and rugged landscapes, is not only known for its natural beauty but also for the deeprooted traditions of hospitality and cuisine. The people of the northern highlands, often referred to as Malësorë, have long been renowned for their warmth and generosity toward guests. In this remote part of the country, hospitality is considered a fundamental part of the culture, with visitors often welcomed into homes as part of an ageold tradition. When staying in these mountain villages, it's common to be invited to share a meal, where the cuisine reflects the simple yet hearty lifestyle of the region. Northern Albanian food is rich in flavor, with dishes made from fresh, local ingredients, including homemade bread, cheese, and meat. A typical meal might include slow cooked lamb or beef, served with polenta and wild herbs gathered from the surrounding hills. Traditional drinks, such as rakia, are often shared during these meals, further symbolizing the bond of hospitality.

In addition to the warm hospitality, Northern Albania is a paradise for adventure seekers. The region's mountainous terrain provides the perfect setting for a variety of outdoor activities, including hiking, climbing, and mountain biking. The Accursed Mountains and the Valbona Valley are some of the best locations for these activities, offering trails that range from gentle hikes suitable for beginners to challenging routes for experienced adventurers. Hikers can explore ancient shepherd paths, ascend high mountain peaks, and discover secluded valleys, all while being surrounded by stunning views of the Albanian Alps. For climbers, the steep cliffs of the Accursed Mountains offer a thrilling challenge, with several wellestablished climbing routes leading to some of the most breathtaking vantage points in the region.

Mountain biking is another popular activity in Northern Albania, with trails that cut through forests, meadows, and mountain passes. Bikers can experience the region's dramatic landscapes while navigating rough terrain, passing through traditional villages, and stopping at scenic points along the way. Whether it's the thrill of outdoor adventure or the charm of experiencing local traditions, Northern Albania offers a rich and rewarding experience for all who visit. The combination of the people's hospitality, their delicious cuisine, and the variety of adventure activities makes this part of Albania a unique and unforgettable destination.

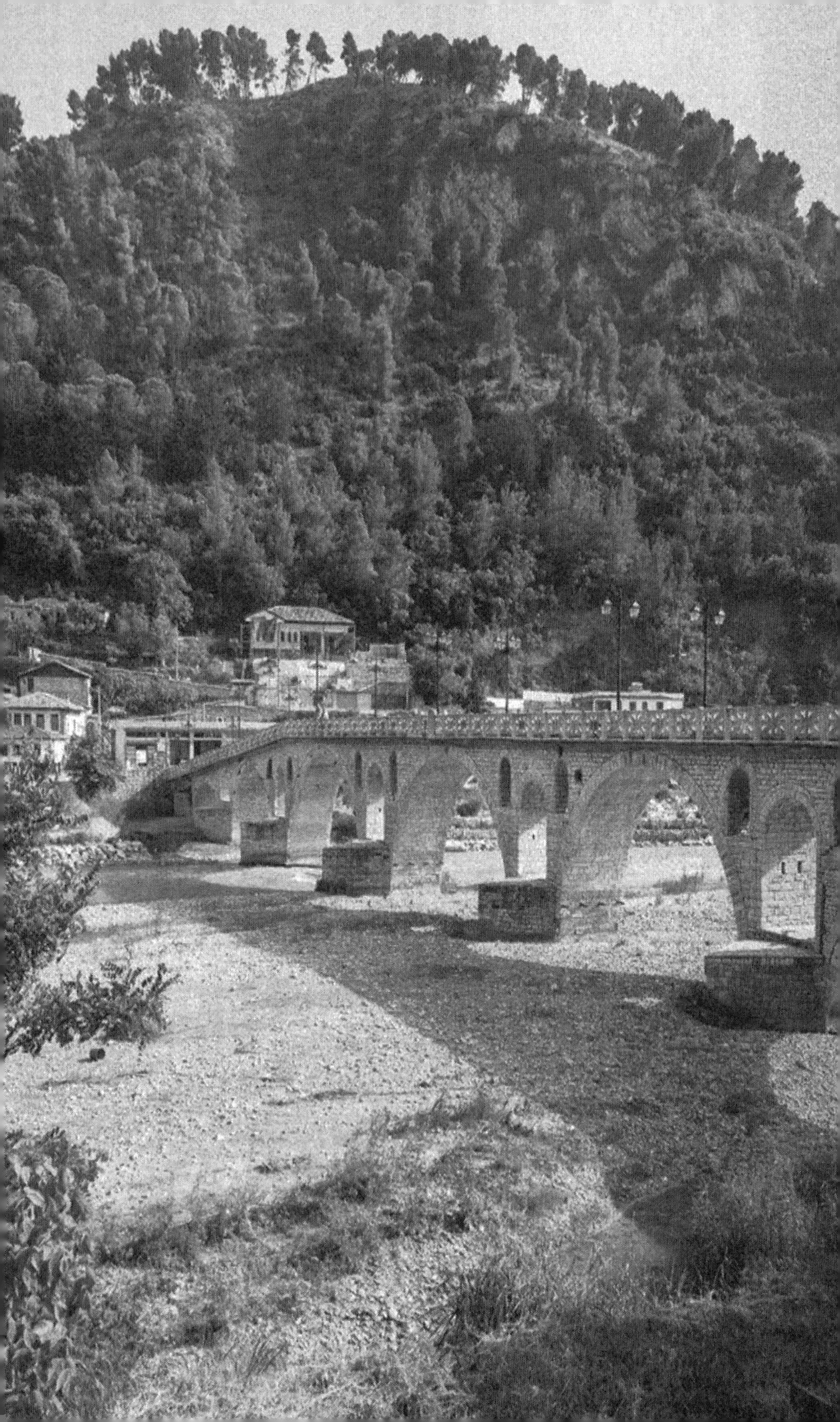

CHAPTER 6

LAKES AND NATURE RESERVES

Lake Ohrid: One of Europe's Oldest Lakes

Lake Ohrid, located on the border between Albania and North Macedonia, is one of Europe's oldest and most unique lakes. Estimated to be around 1.3 million years old, it holds both geological and ecological significance, making it a treasure for scientists and nature enthusiasts alike. Its age and isolation have allowed it to develop an extraordinary ecosystem, with many species found nowhere else in the world. The lake's crystal-clear waters are fed by numerous underground springs, and its depth reaches up to 288 meters, making it one of the deepest lakes in Europe as well. The combination of its age, depth, and biodiversity has earned Lake Ohrid the prestigious designation of a UNESCO World Heritage Site.

Lake Ohrid is surrounded by stunning landscapes, with towering mountains framing its shores and the historic town of Pogradec on the Albanian side, offering pretty views and cultural richness. The lake has long been a source of life and sustenance for the people living around it, and its waters are still vital for fishing, particularly for the famous Ohrid trout, a species unique to the lake. Visitors can enjoy not only the natural beauty but also the historical and cultural heritage of the region, including ancient monasteries, traditional fishing villages, and charming towns that line its shores.

Exploring Lake Ohrid provides a deep connection to nature, as well as an opportunity to appreciate its ancient origins and the unique ecosystems that have thrived for millennia. The combination of stunning scenery, ecological importance, and historical depth makes Lake Ohrid a true gem of the Balkans and one of the most captivating lakes in Europe.

Lake Shkodra: The Largest Lake in the Balkans

Lake Shkodra, also known as Lake Skadar, is the largest lake in the Balkans, spanning the border between Albania and Montenegro. Covering an area of approximately 370 to 530 square kilometers, depending on the season, the lake's size fluctuates due to rainfall and seasonal water levels. This vast body of water is a vital ecosystem, home to a rich variety of wildlife, including over 270 bird species, such as pelicans, herons, and cormorants, making it one of the most important bird habitats in Europe.

The lake is fed by several rivers, with the Buna River acting as its primary outlet, which flows into the Adriatic Sea. The Albanian side of Lake Shkodra is known for its natural beauty, with the town of Shkodër serving as the gateway to the lake. Surrounded by mountains and wetlands, the landscape around the lake is breathtaking, offering visitors opportunities for activities such as boating, fishing, and birdwatching. The region has a rich cultural and historical heritage as well, with ancient fortresses, monasteries, and traditional villages scattered along the lake's shores, adding depth to the experience of visiting this natural wonder.

Lake Shkodra plays a crucial role in the local economy, supporting fishing communities and providing fresh water for agriculture. Its pristine waters and the surrounding protected areas also make it a significant conservation zone. Visitors are often drawn to the peaceful atmosphere of the lake, with its scenic beauty and the diversity of life that thrives both in and around its waters.

Lake Shkodra is not only the largest lake in the Balkans but also a place of incredible ecological and cultural value. Its vast expanse of water, diverse wildlife, and historical landmarks make it a destination that offers both natural beauty and a window into the region's rich past. For those who visit, the lake provides an opportunity to connect with nature while exploring one of the most significant natural sites in the Balkans.

Karavasta Lagoon: A Paradise for Birdwatchers

Karavasta Lagoon, located on the western coast of Albania near the Adriatic Sea, is a natural haven known for its rich biodiversity, making it a paradise for birdwatchers. As one of the largest lagoons in the Mediterranean region, Karavasta spans an impressive area of around 42 square kilometers. Its complex system of saltwater and freshwater habitats attracts a wide variety of bird species, including some of the most endangered in Europe. Among the most famous residents of the lagoon is the Dalmatian pelican, a rare species that finds one of its last breeding grounds in this protected area.

The lagoon is part of the DivjakëKaravasta National Park, which offers visitors a chance to explore its diverse ecosystems, ranging from coastal wetlands to forested areas. Birdwatchers flock to Karavasta not only to catch a glimpse of the Dalmatian pelican but also to observe numerous other species such as herons, egrets, and flamingos. The park is considered one of the most important wetlands in Albania and is internationally recognized under the Ramsar Convention for its significance in preserving biodiversity.

Karavasta's peaceful surroundings and abundance of birdlife make it an ideal destination for nature lovers who seek to experience Albania's unique ecosystems. Visitors can explore the park by following the well-maintained trails, taking boat tours through the lagoon, or simply observing the bird colonies from dedicated viewing platforms. The serenity of the lagoon, combined with its ecological importance, offers a rare opportunity to witness the delicate balance of nature in one of the most pristine environments in the Mediterranean.

Karavasta Lagoon is a treasure for birdwatchers and nature enthusiasts alike. Its vast wetland areas, diverse bird species, and peaceful atmosphere make it a must visit destination for those seeking to experience Albania's rich natural heritage. The lagoon's role as a sanctuary for rare species, like the

Dalmatian pelican, adds to its significance as a key site for wildlife conservation and environmental appreciation.

DivjakëKaravasta National Park: Exploring Untouched Nature

DivjakëKaravasta National Park is one of Albania's most remarkable natural areas, offering a vast expanse of untouched landscapes and rich biodiversity. Located along the country's western coastline, near the Adriatic Sea, the park covers an area of approximately 22,230 hectares. It is best known for the Karavasta Lagoon, the largest lagoon in Albania and one of the most important wetlands in the Mediterranean. The park is a haven for wildlife, particularly bird species, making it a key destination for nature enthusiasts and conservationists alike.

The park's varied ecosystems include coastal wetlands, pine forests, sandy beaches, and salt marshes, all of which contribute to its unique biodiversity. Visitors to DivjakëKaravasta can immerse themselves in the serene beauty of its landscapes while exploring the well-maintained walking trails, which wind through forests and along the edges of the lagoon. The park is especially famous for being home to the rare and endangered Dalmatian pelican, which nests in the lagoon's protected areas. Birdwatchers flock to the park not only for the pelicans but also to observe a wide variety of other species, such as herons, egrets, and flamingos.

Aside from its significance as a birdwatching paradise, DivjakëKaravasta National Park is also a sanctuary for various other wildlife species. Its mix of wetlands and forests provides habitats for mammals, amphibians, and reptiles. The park plays a crucial role in environmental conservation, protecting these fragile ecosystems from human impact while offering a peaceful retreat for those looking to explore nature.

DivjakëKaravasta National Park offers a rare opportunity to experience Albania's untouched natural beauty. With its vast wetlands, diverse wildlife, and tranquil atmosphere, the park is an essential destination for anyone interested in exploring the country's natural heritage. The combination of serene landscapes and rich biodiversity makes it a special place for visitors who want to reconnect with nature and witness the beauty of an unspoiled environment.

CHAPTER 7

CUISINE AND DINING IN ALBANIA

Traditional Dishes You Must Try

Albania offers a rich culinary tradition that reflects its history, geography, and culture. When visiting the country, you'll find that its traditional dishes are an essential part of the experience, providing a deep connection to local customs and flavors. Three dishes stand out as must tries for any tourist: Byrek, Tavë Kosi, and Fërgesë.

Byrek is one of the most popular and widely recognized Albanian dishes, and it's a staple of daily life in Albania. This delicious pastry is made by layering thin sheets of dough, filled with a variety of ingredients that often include cheese, spinach, meat, or even pumpkin. The dough is crisp and flaky, while the fillings provide rich flavors, making it a perfect snack or meal. Byrek can be found in almost every bakery and restaurant across the country, and it's loved for its versatility and taste. Whether you eat it as a quick bite on the go or enjoy it in a more relaxed setting, Byrek offers a true taste of Albania's culinary heritage.

Tavë Kosi is Albania's national dish and is something every visitor should experience. This traditional dish is a baked lamb and rice casserole, prepared in a tangy yogurt sauce that thickens into a custardlike texture during cooking. The combination of lamb, yogurt, and eggs creates a rich, flavorful meal that perfectly balances savory and sour tastes. The origins of Tavë Kosi date back to ancient times, and it remains a favorite for both everyday meals and special occasions. Served hot, it's often accompanied by a fresh salad or bread to complete the meal, and its comforting flavors make it a beloved dish throughout the country.

Another dish you shouldn't miss is Fërgesë, a hearty, flavorful dish made primarily from cheese, tomatoes, peppers, and sometimes meat. It's a simple yet satisfying dish that is typically prepared in an earthenware pot, giving it a distinct, rustic flavor. The cheese, usually cottage cheese or ricotta, melts together with the vegetables to create a creamy, savory blend that's both rich and comforting. Fërgesë can be found in many restaurants and is often enjoyed as a side dish or a light meal. Its warm, flavorful nature makes it a perfect introduction to Albania's rustic cooking traditions.

Trying these traditional dishes—Byrek, Tavë Kosi, and Fërgesë—is an essential part of any visit to Albania. Each offers a unique taste of the country's rich culinary culture, providing a memorable experience for any traveler. From the flaky, savory Byrek to the comforting Tavë Kosi and the flavorful Fërgesë, these dishes reflect the heart and soul of Albanian cuisine.

Wine and Spirits: A Taste of Albanian Vineyards

Albania's winemaking tradition stretches back thousands of years, and today, the country is becoming known for producing a variety of excellent wines and spirits. The combination of fertile soil, favorable climate, and ancient winemaking techniques makes Albanian vineyards a hidden gem for wine lovers. Nestled between the Adriatic and Ionian seas, Albania's diverse terrain creates unique conditions for growing indigenous grape varieties that produce wines with distinct flavors.

Among the local varieties, Shesh i Bardhë (white grape) and Shesh i Zi (red grape) stand out. These grapes, grown primarily in the central and southern regions, give rise to wines that are deeply connected to the country's terroir. The Shesh i Bardhë produces crisp, light white wines with floral and fruity notes, while the Shesh i Zi grape yields robust red wines with rich, earthy flavors. Both are celebrated for their authentic, unadulterated taste, reflecting Albania's dedication to natural winemaking methods.

In addition to wine, Albania is famous for its Rakia, a strong spirit made from distilled grapes or other fruits. Rakia holds a central place in Albanian culture, often served during social gatherings and important events. The flavor of Rakia can vary, depending on the fruit used, with grape and plum varieties being the most common. It is enjoyed both as a premeal aperitif and as a digestive, offering a true taste of Albanian hospitality.

Visiting an Albanian vineyard or winery provides an authentic experience, where visitors can not only taste the country's finest wines and spirits but also learn about the traditional methods used in their production. Many of the vineyards are family owned, passing down their winemaking knowledge through generations. Exploring these vineyards offers a deeper connection to the country's agricultural heritage and the opportunity to enjoy a glass of Albania's finest amidst the scenic landscapes.

Albania's wines and spirits offer a distinct and authentic taste of the region. Whether you're sipping on a glass of Shesh i Zi or enjoying the warmth of Rakia, the country's rich winemaking tradition provides an experience that any traveler can appreciate.

Best Restaurants in Major Cities

Albania's major cities offer a range of dining experiences that cater to all types of tourists, from budget travelers to those seeking fine dining. Each city provides a blend of traditional Albanian cuisine and international flavors, with many restaurants offering amenities such as outdoor seating, stunning views, and family friendly environments.

In Tirana, one of the most recommended spots is Mullixhiu, a high-end restaurant that specializes in traditional Albanian dishes with a modern twist. With a focus on farm totable ingredients, the menu features dishes like byrek, lamb, and a variety of seasonal vegetables. The price range here is on the higher end, making it ideal for tourists looking for an upscale dining experience. Mullixhiu also offers a cozy, rustic ambiance and outdoor seating by an artificial lake, providing a tranquil escape from the city's hustle and bustle. This restaurant is perfect for those who want to explore Albanian cuisine in a refined setting, whether they are food enthusiasts or travelers seeking an immersive cultural experience.

For a more affordable yet authentic dining option, Oda in Tirana is a popular choice. Oda is known for its traditional Albanian dishes served in a homely atmosphere, making it ideal for budget travelers or families. The restaurant's specialties include tavë kosi and grilled meats, with meals typically costing less than €10 per person. The cozy interior, decorated with traditional Albanian artifacts, adds to the charm. It's a great option for tourists who want to experience local cuisine without spending too much, while still enjoying a warm and welcoming environment.

In the coastal city of Durrës, 2 Kitarrat is a midrange restaurant that blends Albanian and Mediterranean flavors, offering a seafood focused menu. Located near the beach, it's perfect for tourists who want to enjoy fresh fish dishes, pasta, and risottos, all while taking in the seaside views. Prices here are moderate, with meals averaging between €15 and €25 per person. The restaurant's casual, family friendly setting makes it a great spot for beachgoers and those looking for a relaxing dining experience by the water.

Shkodër, a city known for its rich history and proximity to the Albanian Alps, has a growing food scene. Tradita Geg & Tosk is a standout restaurant in this region, offering a blend of Northern and Southern Albanian dishes. With a focus on local ingredients, the menu includes hearty options like slowcooked meats and traditional Albanian stews. Prices are midrange, and the restaurant's rustic decor and garden seating make it a charming spot for tourists looking for an authentic, laidback experience. This restaurant is particularly ideal for those interested in exploring the distinct regional flavors of Albania while enjoying a peaceful atmosphere.

Albania's major cities provide a diverse selection of restaurants that cater to a variety of tastes and budgets. From fine dining experiences like Mullixhiu in Tirana to more casual spots like Oda and 2 Kitarrat in Durrës, there's something for every type of traveler. Whether you're seeking authentic local cuisine or a relaxing meal by the coast, Albania's restaurants offer a rich culinary experience that reflects the country's cultural diversity and hospitality.

Street Food and Local Markets

Albania's street food and local markets offer a lively and authentic taste of the country's culinary traditions. In cities like Tirana, Shkodër, and Durrës, street vendors and market stalls are common, serving a wide range of quick, affordable, and delicious foods that reflect the region's flavors and culture. These informal food experiences give tourists a chance to taste Albania's everyday dishes while exploring the bustling atmosphere of local life.

One of the most popular street foods is byrek, a savory pastry made from layers of flaky dough filled with cheese, spinach, or meat. Byrek is an everyday snack for Albanians, often eaten on the go, and can be found at nearly every corner bakery or street vendor. Its light and crispy texture, combined with rich fillings, make it a must try for visitors wanting a quick and tasty bite. Another beloved street food is qofte, which are spiced meatballs usually served with bread and a side of yogurt. Qofte stands are common in markets and offer a satisfying and flavorful option for travelers looking for a heartier snack.

The local markets in Albania are also an essential part of the food experience. Markets such as Pazari i Ri in Tirana and the traditional markets in Krujë or Gjirokastër offer an array of fresh produce, meats, cheeses, and spices. Visitors can stroll through the stalls, sampling local delicacies like olives, goat cheese, and homemade jams, while interacting with friendly vendors. These markets provide a glimpse into the agricultural backbone of the country, with many of the products coming directly from nearby farms. Seasonal fruits and vegetables, as well as traditional cured meats, are among the highlights for tourists who want to experience Albania's food culture at its roots.

Albania's street food and local markets are an integral part of its culinary landscape. Whether you're grabbing a quick byrek from a street vendor or exploring the fresh produce in a bustling market, these experiences offer an authentic and flavorful connection to the country's rich food traditions. For tourists, trying street food and visiting local markets is not only an opportunity to taste the best of Albania but also to engage with the everyday life and culture of its people.

CHAPTER 8

CULTURAL FESTIVALS AND EVENTS

Tirana International Film Festival

The Tirana International Film Festival (TIFF) is one of Albania's most prestigious cultural events, celebrating the art of filmmaking both locally and internationally. Held annually in the capital city of Tirana, the festival draws filmmakers, actors, and cinema enthusiasts from around the world. TIFF has grown significantly since its inception in 2003, becoming a platform for both established and emerging filmmakers to showcase their work in various genres, including feature films, documentaries, animation, and short films. The festival not only highlights Albanian cinema but also promotes global cultural exchange by screening films from diverse countries.

TIFF is known for its rich and dynamic programming, offering a wide array of films that explore different themes and social issues. From avantgarde films to deeply personal stories, the festival fosters creativity and encourages dialogue among filmmakers and audiences. It also includes panel discussions, workshops, and masterclasses, allowing participants to engage more deeply with the art of filmmaking. This makes it not just a film festival but a cultural hub for learning and networking within the industry.

The festival's competitive sections, such as Best Feature Film, Best Short Film, and Best Documentary, offer a platform for recognition, with awards that highlight artistic excellence. For tourists and visitors, attending TIFF offers an opportunity to experience Albania's lively cultural scene and explore Tirana's lively city life, all while engaging with worldclass cinema.

The Tirana International Film Festival is a key cultural event in Albania, celebrating the power of film and its ability to connect people across cultures. It provides a unique blend of artistic talent and global exchange, making it a must attend event for anyone interested in film and culture during their visit to Tirana.

Gjirokastër Folk Festival

The Gjirokastër Folk Festival is one of Albania's most significant and celebrated cultural events, showcasing the country's rich traditions of music, dance, and folklore. Held every five years in the UNESCO World Heritage city of Gjirokastër, this festival draws performers from across Albania as well as neighboring Balkan countries. The festival is a lively display of Albania's cultural heritage, with participants dressed in traditional costumes performing a variety of folk dances and songs that have been passed down through generations.

The festival takes place in the impressive Gjirokastër Castle, an ancient fortress that provides a dramatic backdrop to the performances. The castle's openair setting amplifies the energy and atmosphere of the event, making it a captivating experience for both participants and spectators. For visitors, the festival offers an authentic glimpse into Albania's rural life and the customs that have shaped its national identity.

In addition to the performances, the festival features a rich array of folk instruments, including the lahuta and çifteli, which are integral to Albanian folk music. The event is not only a celebration of Albania's artistic heritage but also serves as a reminder of the country's resilience and unity through its shared cultural expressions.

The Gjirokastër Folk Festival is a must-see event for anyone visiting Albania, especially for those interested in exploring the country's traditions. It offers an immersive experience into the deep-rooted folklore and artistic diversity of the region, leaving visitors with a deeper appreciation of Albania's cultural landscape.

Wine Festivals Across the Country

Albania's Wine Festivals are a lively celebration of the country's longstanding winemaking tradition, held in various regions across the country. These festivals are an opportunity for locals and tourists alike to experience the richness of Albanian wines, many of which are produced from indigenous grape varieties that have been cultivated for centuries. The festivals take place in key wine producing areas such as Berat, Fier, and the coastal region of Vlora, where vineyards are abundant, and winemakers take pride in sharing their finest products.

During these festivals, attendees can sample a variety of wines, including Shesh i Zi and Shesh i Bardhë, two of the country's most notable grape varieties. These events also provide a chance to learn about the traditional methods used in winemaking, with local producers often on hand to discuss their craft. The festivals typically feature food stalls serving traditional Albanian dishes, creating a perfect pairing for the wines on offer. Live music and folk performances further enhance the festive atmosphere, making these events as much a cultural celebration as a gastronomic one.

For wine enthusiasts, the Wine Festivals in Albania offer a unique experience to taste the country's hidden gems and explore its growing reputation as a producer of quality wines. The events also provide a glimpse into rural life and Albanian hospitality, where wine is more than just a drink; it's a symbol of community and tradition.

Albania's Wine Festivals are a must visit for anyone interested in exploring the country's cultural and culinary heritage. They offer an authentic, immersive experience into the heart of Albania's winemaking regions, blending local traditions, fine wines, and festive celebrations.

Summer Music Festivals on the Albanian Coast

The Summer Music Festivals along the Albanian coast have become a major highlight of the country's cultural scene, attracting music lovers from all over the world. These festivals, held in stunning coastal locations such as Dhërmi, Himara, and Ksamil, combine Albania's beautiful beaches with a lively music atmosphere, making for a unique and unforgettable experience. The festivals feature a wide range of music genres, from electronic dance music (EDM) to indie rock and traditional Balkan sounds, creating an eclectic mix that appeals to a diverse audience.

One of the most popular events is the Kala Festival, held in Dhërmi, which has quickly gained a reputation for its worldclass lineup of international DJs and live performances. Set against the backdrop of crystal-clear waters and breathtaking sunsets, Kala offers a mix of daytime beach parties and nighttime performances under the stars. The festival atmosphere is relaxed yet energetic, drawing both locals and international visitors who come to enjoy the music, the coastal beauty, and the festive environment. Another prominent event is ION Festival, which takes place in the same region, further solidifying Albania's reputation as a hotspot for summer music festivals.

These festivals offer more than just music, as many include activities such as yoga sessions, boat parties, and excursions to nearby islands, allowing attendees to fully embrace the natural beauty of Albania's coastline. The affordability of the festivals, combined with the pristine locations, makes them particularly attractive to young travelers and music enthusiasts looking for a unique festival experience in an emerging destination.

The Summer Music Festivals along the Albanian coast provide a perfect blend of great music, stunning beaches, and a lively social scene. For tourists, they offer a chance to experience both the cultural and natural beauty of Albania, making these festivals a must for anyone visiting the country during the summer months.

Local Religious Celebrations and Traditions

Albania's religious celebrations and traditions are a vital part of the country's cultural identity, reflecting its unique history of religious tolerance and coexistence. The country is home to a diverse religious landscape, with a mix of Islam, Christianity, and Bektashism. As a result, religious festivals from different faiths are celebrated with respect and participation from various communities.

One of the most significant religious events is Eid alFitr, marking the end of Ramadan for Albania's Muslim population. This celebration is observed with communal prayers, festive meals, and the giving of charity to those in need. Families gather to share traditional dishes, and the day is marked by a spirit of generosity and togetherness. Similarly, Eid alAdha is celebrated with the tradition of animal sacrifice, and the meat is shared with the less fortunate, reinforcing the values of compassion and charity.

For the Christian population, Easter and Christmas are key religious celebrations. Easter, in particular, is widely observed by the Orthodox and Catholic communities, with midnight services, processions, and the traditional painting of eggs. The rich religious customs surrounding these holidays are deeply tied to family gatherings and community events, with churches filled for special services.

Another unique celebration in Albania is Nowruz, celebrated by the Bektashi community, a mystical branch of Islam. Nowruz marks the Persian New Year and the beginning of spring. It is both a religious and cultural celebration, with gatherings at Bektashi tekkes (shrines), where people come together for prayers, food, and festivities. The Bektashi headquarters in Tirana becomes a focal point for this event, drawing pilgrims and visitors from across the country.

Albania's religious celebrations and traditions offer a unique glimpse into the country's spirit of harmony among different faiths. These events are not just religious in nature but serve as cultural touchpoints that bring together families and communities in a shared celebration of their beliefs and values. For visitors, experiencing these religious festivals offers an authentic view of Albania's deep rooted traditions and its model of peaceful coexistence.

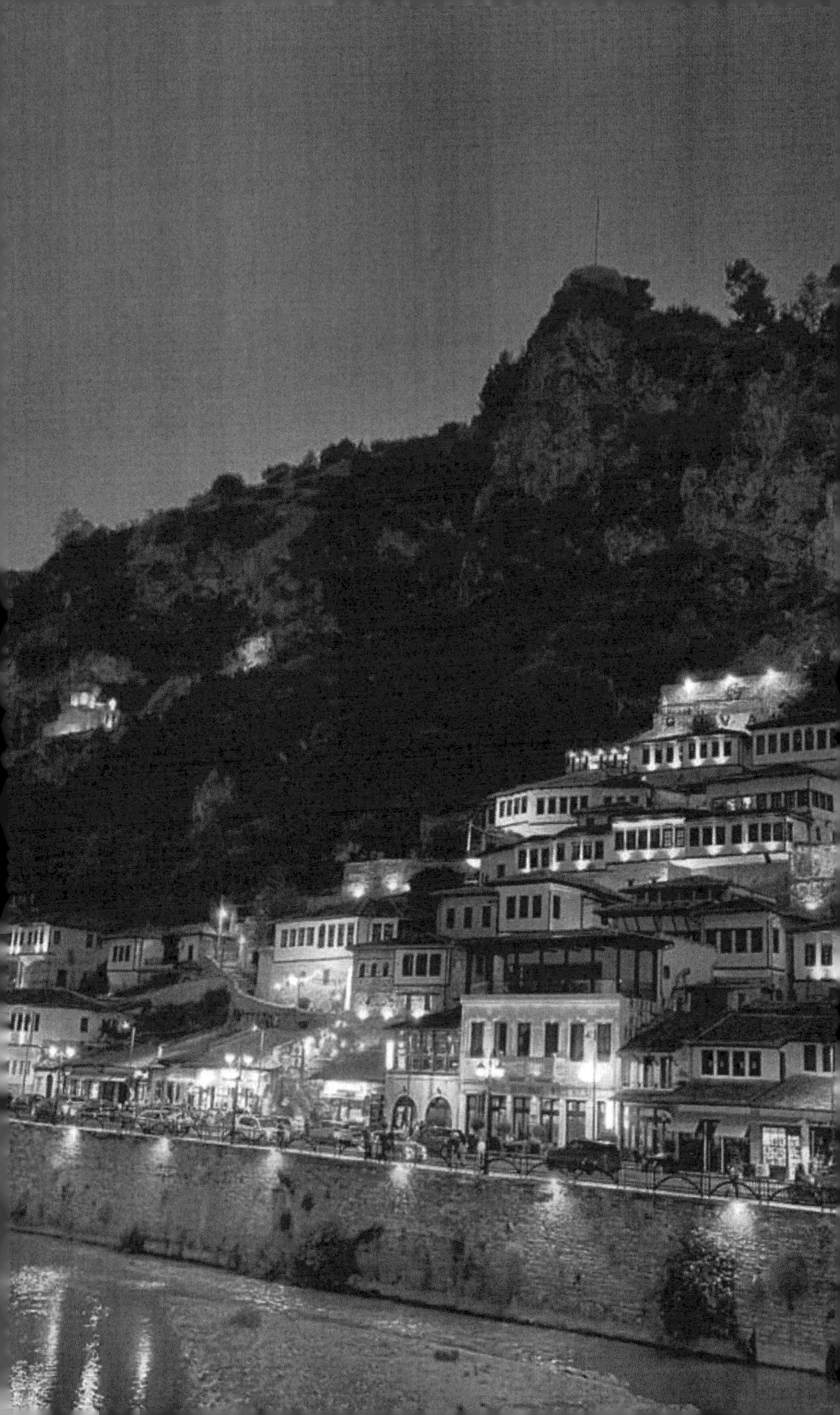

CHAPTER 9

ALBANIA'S HIDDEN TREASURES: OFF-THE-BEATEN-PATH

Vuno: A Pretty Village Untouched by Time

Vuno is a pretty village located on Albania's southern coast, nestled between the mountains and the Ionian Sea. This small, timeless village remains untouched by modern development, preserving its old-world charm and offering a unique glimpse into traditional Albanian life. The stone houses, narrow cobblestone streets, and stunning views of the sea and surrounding hills make Vuno one of Albania's hidden treasures.

Walking through Vuno feels like stepping back in time, as many of the buildings have remained unchanged for generations. The village is known for its tranquil atmosphere and is ideal for those looking to experience authentic, off-the-beaten-path Albania, far from the busy tourist spots. Its serene environment, coupled with the friendliness of the local residents, makes it a perfect retreat for travelers seeking peace and simplicity.

Vuno is also a gateway to some of Albania's most beautiful beaches, such as Jale and Gjipe, which are just a short drive away. These secluded beaches, with their crystal-clear waters and dramatic cliffs, add to the allure of the village. Visitors can enjoy hiking the scenic trails that connect Vuno to these coastal gems, offering breathtaking views along the way.

Vuno is a hidden gem that has preserved its authenticity and traditional way of life, making it one of the most charming and peaceful destinations in Albania. For those seeking an escape from the modern world and a chance to immerse themselves in Albania's rich cultural and natural beauty, Vuno offers an unforgettable experience.

The Forgotten Island of Sazan

Sazan Island, located off the coast of Albania in the Adriatic Sea, is a fascinating and mysterious destination that remains largely untouched by tourism. Known as the "Forgotten Island," Sazan offers a unique glimpse into Albania's hidden past. Once a military base during both World War II and the Cold War, the island is now abandoned, with remnants of bunkers, tunnels, and military buildings scattered across its rugged terrain. This eerie yet captivating atmosphere makes it one of Albania's most intriguing off-the-beaten-path treasures.

Although Sazan has no permanent residents, it is rich in history and natural beauty. The island's strategic position in the Adriatic has made it a focal point for military activity over the years, but today, visitors are drawn to its untouched landscapes and crystal-clear waters. The island boasts a combination of Mediterranean and subtropical climates, which has given rise to unique flora and fauna. Its coastline is dotted with pristine beaches that remain relatively undiscovered, providing an escape from the more crowded coastal areas.

Exploring Sazan is like stepping into another world. The abandoned military infrastructure contrasts sharply with the island's natural beauty, creating a sense of isolation and timelessness. While access to the island is still somewhat restricted, guided tours are available for those curious about its history and wanting to experience its unspoiled landscapes.

Sazan Island is a hidden treasure for adventurous travelers looking to explore one of Albania's most enigmatic locations. With its rich military history, abandoned structures, and untouched natural surroundings, the island offers a unique experience for those willing to venture off the beaten path.

Syri i Kaltër (The Blue Eye): Albania's Natural Wonder

Syri i Kaltër, also known as The Blue Eye, is one of Albania's most captivating natural wonders. This crystal-clear freshwater spring is located in the southern part of the country, near the town of Sarandë, and is famous for its strikingly lively blue color, which gives the spring its name. The Blue Eye is fed by an underground source, and its depth is still unknown, adding to the mystique of this hidden treasure. The center of the spring is an intense blue, resembling a human eye, while the surrounding water appears a bright turquoise, creating a mesmerizing visual effect.

The Blue Eye is surrounded by lush, dense forests, making the journey to this off-the-beaten-path destination an adventure in itself. The area is peaceful, and the natural beauty of the spring, with its cascading water and verdant surroundings, offers a perfect escape from the more touristheavy locations in Albania. While swimming in the spring is technically allowed, the water remains icy cold yearround, adding to the allure for those brave enough to take a dip.

Visitors often come to Syri i Kaltër to marvel at its beauty and enjoy the serene atmosphere, making it a must visit for nature lovers and those seeking to experience one of Albania's most pristine and awe-inspiring landscapes. Whether you're there for a peaceful hike, a refreshing swim, or simply to witness the enchanting beauty of this natural wonder, Syri i Kaltër leaves a lasting impression.

Exploring Remote Monasteries and Churches

Exploring the remote monasteries and churches of Albania offers a unique journey into the country's rich religious heritage, revealing hidden gems tucked away in the mountains and rural landscapes. These ancient sites, often located in hardtoreach areas, have stood for centuries as symbols of Albania's spiritual history and resilience. Many of these churches and monasteries are far removed from the typical tourist routes, making them ideal for travelers seeking a deeper connection to Albania's cultural roots.

One such treasure is the Ardenica Monastery, perched on a hill near the town of Fier. This Orthodox monastery, dating back to the 13th century, is known for its well-preserved frescoes and peaceful surroundings. Visitors are often struck by the monastery's serene atmosphere and the intricate artwork that decorates its walls. Another fascinating site is the Church of St. Mary at Apollonia, located within the ruins of the ancient city of Apollonia. This Byzantine church offers a striking contrast to the surrounding archaeological remains, blending Albania's religious and historical significance.

In the southern part of the country, the Monastery of Saint Nicholas in Mesopotam is a lesser known but captivating site, featuring a blend of Romanesque and Byzantine architecture. Its remote location adds to the feeling of discovery, with few visitors making the trip to this hidden spiritual sanctuary. The Voskopoja Churches, located in a small village in the mountains, also provide a window into Albania's religious art, with beautiful frescoes that date back to the 18th century.

Albania's remote monasteries and churches are among its most valuable hidden treasures. These sites, often overlooked by mainstream tourism, offer a glimpse into the country's deep religious traditions, stunning architecture, and untouched landscapes. For those willing to explore off the beaten path, visiting these sacred places provides a unique and enriching experience, showcasing the spiritual and historical layers of Albania's past.

Remote Hiking Trails for the Adventurous Traveler

Albania's remote hiking trails offer a paradise for adventurous travelers seeking unspoiled landscapes and the thrill of discovery. Tucked away in the mountains, valleys, and rugged coastlines, these trails provide some of the most breathtaking scenery in the Balkans, with fewer crowds and a sense of untouched wilderness. For those looking to step off the usual tourist paths, these hidden gems showcase Albania's natural beauty in its most raw and pristine form.

One of the most famous, yet still relatively isolated, hiking routes is the Valbona to Theth trail, located in the Albanian Alps. This trail takes hikers through dramatic mountain passes, offering stunning views of the jagged peaks and deep valleys that define the region. Along the way, travelers pass by traditional villages, where the lifestyle has remained largely unchanged for centuries. This hike is challenging but rewarding, perfect for those looking for a physical and scenic adventure.

Another incredible trail lies in Llogara National Park, where the coastal and mountain views merge into a breathtaking backdrop. Hikers in this region can ascend through forested slopes and eventually reach panoramic points that reveal both the Ionian Sea and the lush green landscapes of southern Albania. The journey offers both a sense of serenity and exhilaration, making it ideal for nature enthusiasts.

For a more offthegrid experience, the Zagoria Valley in southern Albania presents a lessknown but equally impressive hiking option. This remote area, with its rugged terrain, stone bridges, and quiet villages, is a hidden treasure for those seeking solitude in nature. The trails are steeped in history, and hikers are rewarded with pretty views and a sense of stepping back in time.

Albania's remote hiking trails offer some of the best opportunities for adventurous travelers to explore off-the-beaten-path destinations. Whether trekking through the towering peaks of the Albanian Alps, navigating the coastal cliffs of Llogara, or discovering the tranquil beauty of the Zagoria Valley, these hidden trails provide an unforgettable experience for anyone looking to connect with Albania's wild and untouched nature.

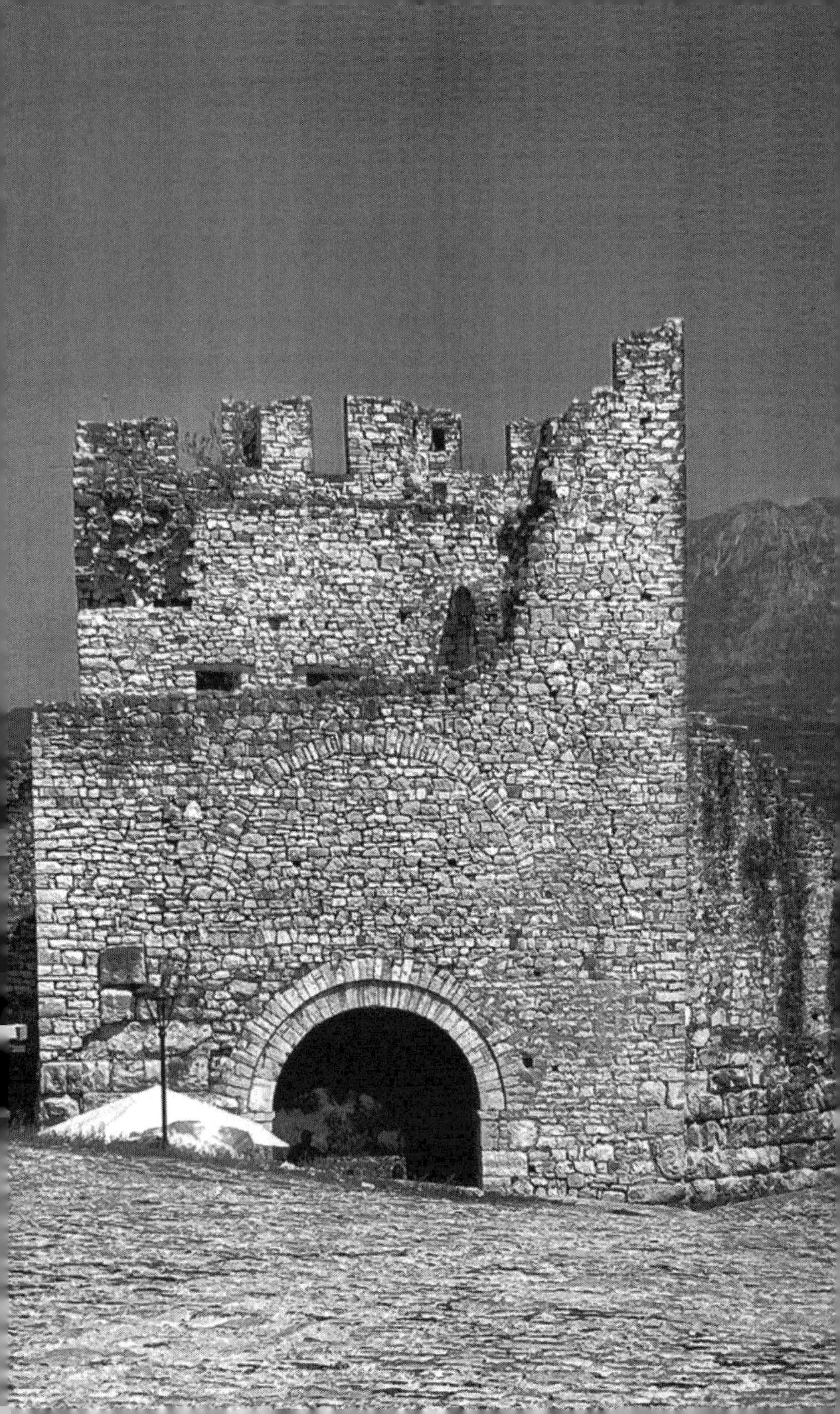

CHAPTER 10

ALBANIA FOR ADVENTURE LOVERS

Kayaking and Sailing on the Albanian Coast

Kayaking and sailing along the Albanian coast offer adventure lovers a unique way to explore some of the most stunning and untouched landscapes in the Mediterranean. With crystal-clear waters, dramatic cliffs, hidden caves, and secluded beaches, Albania's coastline is a paradise for those looking to experience both excitement and tranquility on the open sea.

Kayaking provides an intimate and immersive way to explore the coast, allowing adventurers to navigate through narrow channels, discover hidden bays, and even paddle into sea caves that are inaccessible by larger boats. Popular spots for kayaking include the pristine beaches of Dhërmi and the serene waters around the Karaburun Peninsula, where you can glide through calm seas and take in breathtaking views of the rugged shoreline. The experience is perfect for nature lovers and those seeking a quieter, more personal connection with Albania's coastal beauty.

For those looking for a more expansive journey, sailing along the coast offers a sense of freedom and exploration. The Albanian Riviera, with its turquoise waters and unspoiled beaches, is a perfect destination for sailing enthusiasts.

Popular departure points like Vlora or Sarandë give access to some of the most scenic routes, including trips to the Ionian Islands and along the Butrint National Park coastline. Sailing offers the opportunity to anchor in hidden coves, swim in isolated spots, and experience the coastal landscapes from a completely new perspective.

Both kayaking and sailing allow adventure seekers to enjoy the beauty of the Albanian coast while engaging in an active, exciting experience. Whether paddling through calm waters or charting a course on a sailboat, the combination of stunning scenery, peaceful surroundings, and the thrill of adventure makes Albania's coastline a must visit destination for outdoor enthusiasts.

Paragliding Over the Riviera

Paragliding over the Albanian Riviera offers one of the most thrilling and unforgettable experiences for adventure lovers. Soaring above the stunning coastline, with its crystal-clear waters and dramatic cliffs, gives a unique and breathtaking perspective of the landscape below. The launch point at Llogara Pass, located at an altitude of around 1,000 meters, is particularly popular with paragliders, offering panoramic views of the Ionian Sea and the lush, green mountains that meet the coast.

As you glide through the air, the combination of wind, sea, and sky creates a sense of freedom and exhilaration. The turquoise waters of the Albanian Riviera stretch out below, dotted with hidden coves, sandy beaches, and rocky outcrops, all visible from your bird'seye view. Paragliders can often see iconic landmarks like Dhërmi, Himara, and even the Karaburun Peninsula in the distance. The experience is peaceful yet filled with adrenaline, as you drift through the air with only the sound of the wind around you.

For those seeking adventure, paragliding over the Riviera provides an extraordinary way to explore Albania's natural beauty from an entirely new angle. It's an activity suitable for both beginners, who can fly tandem with experienced instructors, and seasoned paragliders looking to take advantage of the perfect conditions offered by the coastal thermals.

Paragliding over the Albanian Riviera is an adventure lover's dream, combining breathtaking views, excitement, and a unique way to experience the country's majestic coastline. Whether you're an experienced flyer or trying it for the first time, the sheer beauty of Albania from the sky is something that will stay with you long after the flight is over.

Caving and Rock Climbing in the North

Caving and rock climbing in Northern Albania offer an unparalleled experience for adventure lovers seeking to explore the rugged, untouched landscapes of the region. The Albanian Alps, with their towering cliffs, deep valleys, and hidden caves, provide the perfect setting for these adrenaline pumping activities. For those looking to push their limits, the northern region of Albania is full of natural wonders that remain largely undiscovered by mainstream tourism.

Rock climbing in the north takes place against the backdrop of dramatic mountain ranges, offering routes that cater to both beginners and experienced climbers. The steep, limestone cliffs in areas such as Theth and Valbona offer challenging ascents, with the reward being breathtaking panoramic views of the surrounding wilderness. Climbers are often drawn to the vertical walls and craggy peaks, which present technical challenges and the thrill of scaling untouched routes in an environment where nature dominates the landscape.

For those more interested in caving, Northern Albania is home to several impressive caves, such as the Shpella e Pëllumbave and the Shala River Cave, which provide an adventure into the underground world. These caves are known for their intricate rock formations, underground rivers, and expansive chambers, offering explorers a fascinating glimpse into Albania's hidden geological treasures. Equipped with proper gear, adventurers can navigate the dark, cool tunnels, discovering the stalactites and stalagmites that have formed over millennia.

Caving and rock climbing in Northern Albania provide an exciting challenge for thrill seekers and nature enthusiasts. The combination of rugged cliffs, expansive caves, and untouched natural beauty make the region a perfect playground for those looking to experience Albania's wild side. Whether scaling a mountain or exploring deep underground, these activities offer an authentic and exhilarating way to connect with the country's most remote and dramatic landscapes.

River Rafting in Osum Canyon

River rafting in Osum Canyon is an exhilarating experience for adventure lovers seeking to explore one of Albania's most breathtaking natural wonders. Located near the town of Çorovodë in southern Albania, the canyon stretches for around 26 kilometers, with its high cliffs, narrow passages, and crystal-clear waters making it a paradise for rafters. The river runs through the heart of the canyon, offering a thrilling ride through rapids, calm stretches, and some of the most stunning scenery in the country.

Rafting in Osum Canyon is particularly exciting during the spring, when the river is at its fullest due to melting snow from the mountains. Rafters navigate through both gentle and more challenging rapids, all while surrounded by towering canyon walls that reach up to 100 meters in height. The canyon's unique rock formations, waterfalls cascading from the cliffs, and occasional hidden caves add to the sense of adventure. Along the way, rafters are treated to a spectacular view of lush greenery and dramatic rock faces, making the experience as visually stunning as it is thrilling.

For those seeking both adventure and the beauty of nature, river rafting in Osum Canyon is an unforgettable experience. Whether you're an experienced rafter or trying it for the first time, the combination of adrenaline and awe-inspiring scenery makes this one of the best activities for adventure lovers visiting Albania. The canyon's natural beauty and the excitement of navigating its rapids make it a must do for thrill seekers looking to explore the country's wild landscapes.

Diving into the Crystal Waters: Best Scuba Diving Spots

Diving into the crystal-clear waters of Albania offers adventure lovers an unforgettable experience, with some of the best scuba diving spots located along the country's stunning coastline. The Albanian Riviera, particularly near Dhërmi and Himara, is known for its pristine waters and lively underwater landscapes. These diving spots offer incredible visibility, allowing divers to explore the rich marine life, colorful reefs, and unique rock formations that lie beneath the surface.

One of the most popular diving locations is near the Karaburun Peninsula and Sazan Island, where divers can explore underwater caves, ancient shipwrecks, and diverse marine ecosystems. The waters here are teeming with fish, and the dramatic underwater terrain provides an adventurous and exciting environment for both beginner and experienced divers. In addition to the natural beauty, the remnants of historical shipwrecks add an element of mystery and discovery, making each dive feel like an exploration of the past.

The Butrint National Park area, near Ksamil, also offers excellent diving opportunities with its calm, clear waters and unspoiled underwater habitats. This region is less crowded, providing a more peaceful and immersive experience for divers who want to enjoy the tranquility of Albania's underwater world.

Albania's crystal waters offer some of the best scuba diving spots for adventure lovers. With the perfect mix of marine biodiversity, fascinating shipwrecks, and stunning underwater landscapes, diving in these pristine locations provides an unmatched sense of adventure and discovery. Whether you are an experienced diver or new to the sport, Albania's coastline promises a remarkable underwater experience.

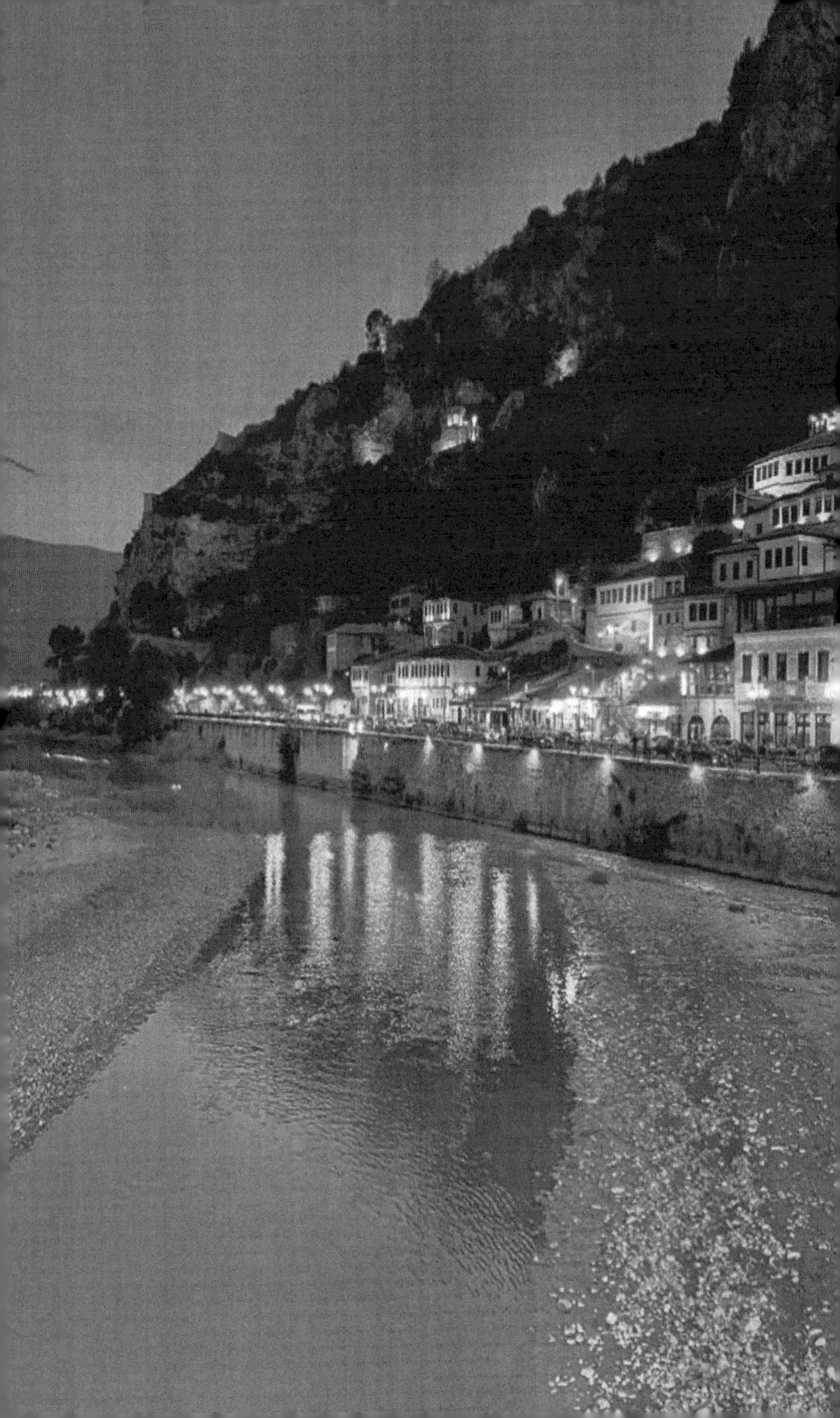

CHAPTER 11

SHOPPING AND SOUVENIRS

Unique Crafts and Handmade Goods to Bring Home

When visiting Albania, tourists have the opportunity to take home unique crafts and handmade goods that reflect the country's rich cultural heritage and artisanal traditions. From intricately woven textiles to finely crafted pottery, Albanian souvenirs are not only beautiful but also tell the story of local craftsmanship passed down through generations.

One of the most distinctive items to bring home is a qilim, a traditional handwoven rug or tapestry. These rugs, often made from wool, are known for their lively colors and geometric patterns. Each qilim is unique, with designs that reflect the region where it was made, making it a meaningful keepsake that takes the essence of Albanian folk art. Many families still produce these rugs by hand, using methods that have been practiced for centuries.

Another popular craft is filigree jewelry, delicately crafted from silver. The intricate designs in this type of jewelry showcase the precision and skill of Albanian silversmiths. Earrings, necklaces, and bracelets made in the filigree style are not only beautiful but also represent a piece of the country's artistic history, as filigree work has been a longstanding tradition in Albania.

Tourists may also want to bring back handmade ceramics, which are often adorned with traditional patterns and motifs. The town of Kruja is particularly known for its pottery, where skilled artisans create both functional and decorative pieces. From painted plates to unique vases, these ceramics make wonderful gifts or personal mementos.

In addition to textiles, jewelry, and pottery, Albania is famous for its wooden carvings. Artisans create everything from decorative boxes to traditional instruments like the lahuta. These pieces reflect the natural materials found in Albania's landscapes and are crafted with meticulous care.

Albania's handmade goods are a reflection of the country's cultural richness and artisanal traditions. Bringing home a qilim, a piece of filigree jewelry, ceramics, or a wooden carving allows tourists to carry a piece of Albania's heritage with them, making their visit to this unique country even more memorable.

Traditional Albanian Carpets and Textiles

Traditional Albanian carpets and textiles are among the most valuable and distinctive items a tourist can bring home from their visit to Albania. These handcrafted pieces are deeply rooted in the country's cultural history and represent centuries of craftsmanship passed down through generations. Known for their lively colors and intricate geometric patterns, these textiles often feature designs that vary depending on the region where they were made, giving each piece a unique identity.

One of the most well-known textiles is the qilim, a handwoven rug that has been a staple in Albanian homes for centuries. Made from wool, these rugs are highly durable and come in a range of sizes and styles, often used as both floor coverings and wall hangings. The detailed patterns on each qilim are not just decorative but hold cultural significance, with symbols representing protection, prosperity, and nature. These pieces are entirely handmade, with many artisans still using traditional wooden looms.

In addition to carpets, Albania is known for producing beautifully woven blankets, linens, and traditional clothing items. These textiles are often adorned with colorful embroidery and intricate stitching that reflect Albania's regional diversity. Particularly in the northern and southern regions, these handmade fabrics are used in daily life but also serve as a representation of the country's artistic heritage.

For tourists, purchasing traditional Albanian carpets or textiles offers more than just a souvenir; it is a way to take home a piece of the country's history and culture. Whether displayed in a home or used as a functional item, these handcrafted pieces provide a tangible connection to Albania's rich artisanal traditions.

Local Markets: A Taste of Albanian Life

Visiting local markets in Albania offers tourists a true glimpse into the daily life and culture of the country. These markets, bustling with activity, are lively hubs where locals gather to buy and sell fresh produce, handmade goods, and traditional Albanian products. Walking through the narrow stalls, tourists can immerse themselves in the lively atmosphere, observing the sights, sounds, and smells that define everyday Albanian life.

The markets are filled with an abundance of fresh fruits and vegetables, many of which are grown in the surrounding countryside. Seasonal produce such as tomatoes, peppers, grapes, and figs are often sold directly by farmers, giving visitors a chance to taste the freshest flavors of the region. Additionally, local cheeses, olives, honey, and cured meats are available, offering a taste of Albania's culinary heritage.

In addition to food, local markets are also the best places to find traditional Albanian crafts, textiles, and handmade souvenirs. Items like byrek pastry, rakia (a traditional Albanian spirit), and artisanal ceramics can all be found in these bustling marketplaces. The Pazari i Ri in Tirana, for example, is a particularly famous spot where tourists can experience both the culinary and artisanal richness of Albania.

For those seeking an authentic experience, exploring these local markets provides a direct connection to Albanian culture, allowing tourists to engage with locals, sample traditional foods, and bring home unique handmade items that reflect the country's lively way of life.

Where to Buy Authentic Souvenirs

For tourists seeking authentic souvenirs from Albania, there are a variety of places where they can find locally crafted items that truly represent the country's rich heritage and culture. One of the best places to start is in the traditional bazaar areas, especially in cities like Kruja and Gjirokastër. Kruja's Old Bazaar, for example, is famous for its wide range of handmade goods, including qilims (traditional rugs), filigree jewelry, and intricately carved wooden items. These markets are filled with small shops where artisans sell their products directly to visitors, ensuring that each purchase supports local craftsmanship.

In the capital, Tirana, tourists can visit Pazari i Ri, a lively marketplace that offers not only fresh produce and local foods but also a selection of handcrafted souvenirs. Here, visitors can find traditional items such as byrek molds, ceramics, and handwoven textiles. For those interested in traditional clothing, embroidered garments and opinga (Albanian leather shoes) are also available.

For more unique and artistic pieces, small galleries and craft shops in Berat and Shkoder offer paintings, local pottery, and vintage souvenirs that reflect the history and culture of these regions. Many of these items are handmade by local artists, making them truly one-of-a-kind gifts or keepsakes.

CHAPTER 12

DAY TRIPS AND EXCURSIONS

From Tirana to Kruja: The Castle and Skanderbeg Museum

A day trip from Tirana to Kruja offers tourists a chance to explore one of Albania's most historically significant cities and its famous Kruja Castle. Located just an hour's drive from the capital, Kruja is steeped in history and is best known as the home of Gjergj Kastrioti, also known as Skanderbeg, the national hero who led the resistance against the Ottoman Empire in the 15th century. The Skanderbeg Museum, housed within the castle, is a highlight of the visit, offering a deep dive into the life and legacy of this legendary figure through its rich collection of artifacts, documents, and exhibits.

The Kruja Castle, perched on a hill with stunning views of the surrounding valleys, provides an immersive experience into Albania's medieval past. Visitors can walk through the ancient walls, explore the remnants of the old city, and imagine what life was like during Skanderbeg's time. The panoramic views from the castle make the trip even more worthwhile, offering sweeping vistas of the Albanian landscape.

In addition to the historical sites, Kruja is home to a lively bazaar, where tourists can browse and purchase traditional

Albanian handicrafts, such as handwoven rugs, filigree jewelry, and other artisanal goods. This adds a cultural touch to the visit, giving tourists the chance to take home a piece of Albania's history and craftsmanship.

A day trip from Tirana to Kruja provides an enriching experience filled with history, culture, and scenic beauty. From the iconic Skanderbeg Museum to the historic castle and bustling bazaar, Kruja is a must visit for anyone looking to explore Albania's rich heritage.

Day Trip to Durrës: Beaches and Roman Amphitheater

A day trip to Durrës, one of Albania's oldest cities, offers a perfect blend of historical exploration and relaxation by the sea. Located just a short drive from Tirana, Durrës is known for its beautiful beaches and rich Roman heritage, making it an ideal destination for tourists looking to experience both culture and leisure.

The city's Roman Amphitheater, one of the largest and most impressive in the Balkans, is a must-see attraction. Built in the 2nd century AD, it once held around 20,000 spectators and is now a fascinating historical site. Walking through the amphitheater, visitors can explore its underground chambers and imagine the grand spectacles that once took place here, from gladiator fights to theatrical performances. The preservation of this ancient structure makes it a key highlight of the trip.

In addition to the historical allure, Durrës is famous for its sandy beaches and lively promenade along the Adriatic Sea. Tourists can relax on the beach, enjoy fresh seafood from local restaurants, and soak up the sun, making it a great spot for both cultural sightseeing and a peaceful day by the water.

A day trip to Durrës provides a well-rounded experience, combining the city's Roman history with the natural beauty of its coastline. The Roman Amphitheater and the inviting beaches make Durrës a perfect destination for anyone seeking to enjoy both Albania's rich history and its coastal charm.

Shkodër: The City of Legends and the Rozafa Castle

A day trip to Shkodër, often referred to as the "City of Legends," offers visitors a deep dive into Albania's rich history and culture. Located in the northern part of the country, Shkodër is one of Albania's oldest cities and is known for its lively atmosphere and the remarkable Rozafa Castle. Perched high on a hill overlooking the meeting point of three rivers, the castle offers both a stunning view and a fascinating glimpse into Albania's past.

The Rozafa Castle is steeped in legend. According to local folklore, the castle's walls were collapsing during construction until a woman was sacrificed and entombed within the walls to ensure its stability. This myth is a central part of Shkodër's identity, adding a layer of mystique to the already impressive fortress. Exploring the castle, visitors can walk along its ancient walls, visit the ruins of its interior structures, and take in the breathtaking views of Lake Shkodra and the surrounding landscape.

Beyond the castle, Shkodër itself is a lively city, known for its rich cultural scene and artistic heritage. Visitors can explore the city's lively streets, visit local museums, and discover the unique blend of history and modern life that defines this northern city.

A day trip to Shkodër and the Rozafa Castle provides a perfect mix of legend, history, and scenic beauty. It's an ideal destination for those looking to explore Albania's northern regions while immersing themselves in the country's rich storytelling traditions and historic landmarks.

A Weekend in Korçë: Culture and Art in Southern Albania

A weekend in Korçë, a charming city in southern Albania, offers a rich experience of culture, art, and history. Known for its lively cultural scene, Korçë is often referred to as the intellectual heart of Albania, with its longstanding tradition of music, art, and education. Visitors can explore the city's National Museum of Medieval Art, which houses a vast collection of religious icons and artifacts, offering a glimpse into the country's artistic heritage. This museum is a must visit for those interested in Albanian and Balkan art, showcasing centuries of creativity and craftsmanship.

Korçë's cobbled streets and well-preserved Ottomanera architecture provide a pretty setting for a leisurely stroll. The city is home to the famous Korçë Bazaar, where visitors can experience local life and discover traditional crafts, foods, and souvenirs. The bazaar is a lively spot that reflects the city's historic role as a hub for trade and culture in the region.

For those looking to enjoy the city's cultural life, Korçë is known for its rich musical heritage, particularly the serenade tradition, which originated here. In the evenings, local restaurants and cafes often host live music, making it the perfect opportunity to immerse yourself in the soulful tunes while enjoying local cuisine.

A weekend in Korçë offers a perfect blend of culture, art, and history. Whether exploring the National Museum of Medieval Art, wandering through the lively Korçë Bazaar, or soaking in the city's musical traditions, Korçë provides a memorable and enriching experience for visitors seeking to explore southern Albania.

Crafting the best itinerary for yourself

Crafting the best itinerary for your trip to Albania can feel like an exciting part of the adventure. With so many incredible destinations, cultural landmarks, and natural wonders to explore, having a clear plan in place will help you make the most of your visit. While this book provides all the information you need to discover the best places in Albania, it's up to you to design an itinerary that suits your personal preferences, pace, and style of travel.

To assist with that, we've included a 14page printable itinerary planner, which you can access by scanning the QR code on the following page. The planner is intentionally left blank, giving you complete freedom to fill it in with your own plans, preferences, and must-see locations. Whether you're looking for adventure, relaxation, or cultural experiences, this planner will serve as your guide to shaping each day according to what excites you most.

The beauty of a blank itinerary is that you can tailor it completely to your liking. If you're more interested in historical sights, you might fill in a few days with visits to Gjirokastër and Berat, where you can wander through the cobbled streets of these ancient cities and explore their stunning castles. For those who prefer beaches and scenic coastlines, you could dedicate multiple days to the Albanian Riviera, where you can relax in beautiful spots like Dhërmi and Ksamil or try out water sports such as kayaking and snorkeling.

The planner allows you to block out time for specific activities, such as a day trip to Rozafa Castle in Shkodër or a visit to Butrint National Park, giving you a clear structure to follow while still leaving room for spontaneous exploration. You can even plan your meals, noting down the best local spots where you'd like to try traditional dishes like Fërgesë or enjoy a glass of Albanian wine.

Since the planner is flexible, you can adjust it as your trip progresses. If you decide to spend more time hiking in the Albanian Alps or exploring the hidden beaches near Himara, you can easily reshuffle your plans. And if you come across a festival or cultural event, such as the Gjirokastër Folk Festival, you can add it to your schedule to make sure you don't miss out on any unique local experiences.

This planner is designed to help you create an itinerary that fits you perfectly. Whether you're spending a few days or a few weeks in Albania, this tool gives you the freedom to organize your travel according to your interests, while also allowing space for unexpected discoveries. With a little planning and flexibility, you can look forward to a trip that's both well-organized and deeply enjoyable, filled with everything that makes Albania such a special place to visit.

HOW TO GET THE FREE PLANNER

To make your travel planning easier and more personalized, we've included a special 14page printable itinerary planner. This planner is designed to help you map out your trip to Albania, day by day, allowing you to organize everything from sightseeing and activities to meals and transportation. The planner is blank so that you can fill it in with all the things you want to do on your adventure.

SCAN THE QR CODE BELOW

To access the planner, simply follow these steps to scan the QR code:
1. **Open Your Camera:** Using your smartphone or tablet, open the camera app. Most modern devices automatically recognize QR codes through the camera.
2. **Scan the QR Code:** Point your camera at the QR code, making sure the entire code is within the frame. Hold your device steady for a few seconds until a notification or link appears on the screen.
3. **Tap the Link:** Once your device recognizes the code, a link will pop up. Simply tap the link, and you will be directed to the page where you can download and print the itinerary planner.
4. **Download and Print:** Once on the page, download the planner to your device. You can either save it for later use or print it out immediately to start filling in your itinerary.

CONCLUSION

This book has been designed to give you not only a deep Knowing of the country's rich history, lively culture, and stunning landscapes, but also practical tips and advice to make the most of your experience. Albania is a land full of hidden treasures—whether you're wandering through ancient cities, relaxing on the pristine beaches of the Riviera, or hiking through its rugged mountains, you're bound to discover something unforgettable.

By using the information in this guide, and with the help of the 14page printable itinerary planner, you now have everything you need to create a trip that reflects your personal interests and travel style. Albania offers a unique blend of experiences, from its cultural festivals and historical landmarks to its natural wonders and friendly local hospitality. This book has provided the details, but your journey will be truly defined by the moments you create, the places you explore, and the memories you bring home.

Remember to take your time, stay curious, and enjoy every step of your adventure. Whether this is your first time in Albania or you're returning to rediscover it, the experiences awaiting you are rich, diverse, and rewarding.

Thank you for choosing this guide as your travel companion. May your trip to Albania be as inspiring and adventurous as you've dreamed it to be.

Printed in Great Britain
by Amazon